C000183442

JAPHY WILSON is Lecturer in International Political Economy at the University of Manchester. He has published in the fields of political economy, human geography, and development studies. He is co-editor with Erik Swyngedouw of *The Post-Political and Its Discontents: Spaces of Depoliticization, Spectres of Radical Politics* (Edinburgh University Press, 2014).

COUNTERBLASTS

COUNTERBLASTS is a series of short, polemical titles that aims to revive a tradition inaugurated by Puritan and Leveller pamphleteers in the seventeenth century, when, in the words of one of their number, Gerard Winstanley, the old world was 'running up like parchment in the fire'. From 1640 to 1663, a leading bookseller and publisher, George Thomason, recorded that his collection alone contained over twenty thousand pamphlets. Such polemics reappeared both before and during the French, Russian, Chinese and Cuban revolutions of the last century.

In a period where politicians, media barons and their ideological hirelings rarely challenge the basis of existing society, it is time to revive the tradition. Verso's Counterblasts will challenge the apologists of Empire and Capital.

Jeffrey Sachs:
The Strange Case of
Dr Shock and Mr Aid

Japhy Wilson

V E R S O
London • New York

First published by Verso 2014
© Japhy Wilson 2014

All rights reserved

1 3 5 7 9 10 8 6 4 2

Verso
UK: 6 Meard Street, London W1F 0EG
US: 20 Jay Street, Suite 1010, Brooklyn, NY 11201
www.versobooks.com

Verso is the imprint of New Left Books

ISBN-13: 978-1-78168-329-3 (PBK)
eISBN-13: 978-1-78168-330-9 (US)
eISBN-13: 978-1-78168-660-7 (UK)

British Library Cataloguing in Publication Data
A catalogue record for this book is available from the British Library

Library of Congress Cataloging-in-Publication Data
Wilson, Japhy.
 Jeffrey Sachs : the strange case of Dr. Shock and Mr.
Aid / Japhy Wilson.
    pages cm
  ISBN 978-1-78168-329-3 (pbk.) – ISBN 978-1-
78168-330-9 (e-book)
1. Sachs, Jeffrey. 2. Economists–United States–
Biography. 3. Neoliberalism–Developing countries.
4. Economic development–Philosophy. 5. Economic
development–Developing countries. 6. Developing
countries–Economic conditions. 7. Millennium
Villages Project. 8. Poverty–Developing countries.
9. Development economics. I. Title.
 HB119.S24W55 2014
 330.092–dc23
 [B]
                              2013043817

Typeset in Minion Pro by MJ & N Gavan, Truro, Cornwall
Printed in the US by Maple Press

The doom and burthen of our life is bound forever on man's shoulders, and when the attempt is made to cast it off, it but returns upon us with more unfamiliar and more awful pressure.

Robert Louis Stevenson, *Strange Case of Dr Jekyll and Mr Hyde*

CONTENTS

INTRODUCTION: THE SACHS CONUNDRUM

The fifteenth of October 2011 was a global Day of Rage. In 950 cities around the world, people took to the streets to protest against rising inequality, endless austerity, and the unbridled power of investment banks and multinational corporations. This was the legacy of three decades of economic reforms dominated by the 'neoliberal' principles of privatization, deregulation, and the dismantling of the welfare state. These reforms were supposed to deliver society from the dead hand of the state, in the name of individual freedom. First implemented by Augusto Pinochet in Chile in the 1970s, and driven forward by Margaret Thatcher and Ronald Reagan in the 1980s, the free market revolution had swept across the entire planet. Its vanguard promised rapid economic growth and the opportunity for everyone to improve their personal circumstances through hard work and private initiative. As long as there was free competition in all dimensions of economic life, the 'invisible hand of the market' would ensure the best of all possible outcomes. Yet, in contrast to this utopian vision, the outcome had been persistent poverty, economic oligarchy, and a whirlwind of financial crises that had spiralled around the world before finally entering the heartlands of global capitalism with the financial crash of 2008 and the ensuing 'Great Recession'. Neoliberalism was in crisis, and the people were on the streets demanding radical change.

The epicentre of these protests was Occupy Wall Street in Zuccotti Park, at the heart of New York's financial district. At some point around midday, a clean-cut middle-aged man arrived in the park, and began to address the crowd. He started by criticizing the *Wall Street Journal* for its dismissal of the Occupy movement, before attacking hedge fund managers, businessmen, and a series of banks and corporations. The crowd amplified him with the 'people's mic', chanting each sentence in response, waving their hands in agreement, and spontaneously bursting into applause. As they cheered him on, the man became increasingly agitated, gesticulating violently, his voice shaking with emotion:

> This is a democracy! We are the 99 per cent! We have the votes! You [the corporations and the hedge funds] may have the money, but we have the votes ... And across America they're hearing this message. And around the world today they're hearing this message. This is the beginning of change long overdue! Ronald Reagan put us on a path of disaster thirty years ago. He said 'Cut the taxes', 'Squeeze the poor', 'Throw people out of health', 'Don't educate the children'. And every president since then has followed the same path. Because the big money pays them! And they sup with the rich and the billionaires! And it's over now! We need a new direction for this country![1]

These words might seem unremarkable on a global Day of Rage. Similar things must have been shouted at many protest sites that day. Yet this man was not a typical grassroots agitator. This was Jeffrey Sachs – development guru and 'rock star economist'. Sachs has advised the governments of over 140 countries, and has been a tireless campaigner for the expansion of international aid in the name of 'the end of poverty'. He is special advisor to the secretary general of the United Nations, director of the UN's Sustainable Development Solutions Network, and has chaired prominent UN commissions on health, development, and happiness. He is director of the Earth Institute at Columbia University, with over 850 academic staff and an US$87 million annual research budget. His Millennium Villages Project is being rolled out across ten countries in sub-Saharan Africa, and is among the most high-profile development projects in the world. He is a friend of the stars, accompanying Bono, Madonna, and Angelina Jolie on high-profile journeys to Africa to publicize the plight of the continent. He has authored bestselling books on poverty alleviation, sustainable development, and the global economic crisis. He regularly provides his opinions on news channels such as CNN and the BBC, and makes frequent contributions to periodicals including the *Financial Times* and the *Guardian*. *Time* ranked him among the hundred most influential people in the world in 2004, and again in 2005, and the *New York Times* has described him as 'probably the most important economist in the world'.[2]

In short, Jeffrey Sachs is a man of considerable power and influence on the world stage. It was therefore rather surprising to find him making such a radical and impassioned speech at Occupy Wall Street. Surprising, you might say, but was it not all the more commendable for that? How uplifting, in these cynical times, to see a person of such status who is unafraid to take a principled stand. Perhaps ... yet something doesn't quite ring true. In the first place, Sachs's claim to represent the 99 per cent sounds rather strange, given that he earns over US$300,000 a year and lives in an US$8 million Manhattan townhouse.[3] And his demonization of bankers, businessmen, and politicians who 'sup with the rich and the billionaires' is also rather odd, considering his own close working relationships with billionaire financiers such as George Soros and Ray Chambers. His attack on corporate power is equally surprising, in light of his collaborations with multinational corporations such as GlaxoSmithKline, Merck, Monsanto, Nike, Novartis, and Pfizer. It also seems rather peculiar that Sachs should attack the *Wall Street Journal*, given that he has written for it in the past, using it as a platform for his triumphant celebration of the demise of communism.[4]

But all these inconsistencies pale into insignificance in the light of one glaring fact: this isn't just Jeffrey Sachs, development economist extraordinaire; this is *Jeffrey Sachs* – the notorious pioneer of economic 'shock therapy' in Latin America, in Eastern Europe and, most catastrophically, in Russia. Shock therapy was neoliberalism in its most ruthless form, based on the sudden implementation of a comprehensive set of free market reforms before resistance had time to organize, and imposing its greatest costs on the poorest and most disadvantaged sectors of society. Although he is now celebrated in many quarters for his promotion of international aid and the alleviation of poverty, Sachs is still loathed by the working classes of several countries for his merciless enforcement of shock therapy, and is known to social justice activists around the world as 'Dr Shock' – the malign embodiment of the worst excesses of the free market revolution.

In other words, Jeffrey Sachs played a central role in the construction of the very same neoliberal system that he is now so vocally opposing. The extent of this personal transformation is well illustrated by Sachs's advice to the government of Poland on its transition from central planning to a market economy, which began on 1 January 1990. Writing in a bankers' journal at the time, Sachs asserted the need for 'a radical break from the past' in which the government should 'move rapidly on several fronts'. His proposed reforms were a recipe for pure, unadulterated neoliberalism, including the immediate elimination of subsidies, price controls, tariffs, and quotas, and 'a massive and rapid privatization of ... enterprises under state control'.[5] Sachs emphasized that the reforms must be implemented quickly, to establish capitalist property relations in the face of inevitable resistance from those being dispossessed of their livelihoods:

> Even [President] Walesa's great political gifts will be challenged by the social pressures. It may be recalled that Ronald Reagan and Margaret Thatcher were both unpopular a year after the start of their [auster-ity] programmes ... In the face of these pressures the Government's medium-term strategy is clear: privatize the [state] enterprises as rapidly as possible to put real owners in control of the firms ... owners who care about the bottom line ... Real market behaviour inside the firm requires a real owner of the firm's capital.[6]

Here Sachs is explicitly promoting neoliberal reforms in the name of the capitalist class – the 'real owners', who 'care about the bottom line', and can be relied upon to engage in 'real market behaviour' (which is shorthand for wage reductions, downsizing, and cutthroat competi-tion). The level of incongruity between these words and his speech at Occupy Wall Street is bizarre, to say the least. How could Sachs now claim to speak for the 99 per cent when his advice to Poland was so clearly representative of the interests of the 1 per cent? And why was Sachs now attacking Reagan when he had previously celebrated Reagan and Thatcher as courageous free market reformers? In short, why was Jeffrey Sachs now railing against neoliberalism, given that he had been one of its chief architects and most prominent apologists? It is like seeing Thatcher fighting the police on a picket line, or hearing Reagan singing the 'Internationale'. *It just doesn't make sense.* This is the conundrum that this book explores.

On the face of it, this transformation might be unexpected, but is hardly paradoxical. Perhaps Sachs has just 'seen the light', realizing the errors of his previous approach, and altering his politics accordingly.

This, indeed, is the most commonly heard narrative about Jeffrey Sachs, which takes the form of a heart-warming story in which the dastardly Dr Shock has been miraculously transformed into the magnanimous Mr Aid. Sachs now regularly appears in the media as a spokesman for the liberal left against neoconservative political commentators and orthodox neoliberal economists, and even such prominent critics of neoliberalism as David Harvey and Naomi Klein have suggested that Sachs can no longer be considered a neoliberal.[7] In my research for this book, I was repeatedly confronted by similar responses from progressive policymakers, left-leaning academics, and informed members of the general public, which ran more or less as follows: 'Sachs is a reformed character. He may have made some mistakes in the past, but he has learned from them, and now he is a powerful advocate for development in Africa, and a passionate opponent of free market economics, for which he should be celebrated.'

But things are not so simple. Far from having learned from his mistakes, Sachs denies having ever made any. When confronted with the social consequences of shock therapy, he attributes them to the inadequate implementation of his recommendations, rather than accepting responsibility or acknowledging fault. Sachs also denies that any personal transformation has occurred. He does not claim to have had the change of heart that others attribute to him, but insists that he *never was a neoliberal*. Sachs now argues that his role in shock therapy has been misunderstood, claiming that he has always been a critic of free markets, and that his career has been consistently focused on aid, debt relief, and human development.[8]

I agree with Sachs that there has been no fundamental break in his political project over the course of his career. My argument, however, is not that Sachs has never been a neoliberal, but rather that *he has always been a neoliberal, and continues to be*. Instead of Sachs abandoning a static neoliberal 'shock doctrine', as other accounts suggest, this book argues that neoliberalism has morphed in tandem with Sachs's own transformation. As we will see, Sachs's policy trajectory has evolved from the austere brutality of shock therapy to the comprehensive social engineering of the Millennium Villages Project, which painstakingly attempts to produce the same market society that he had previously sought to shock into existence. In the same way, the notoriously destructive Structural Adjustment Programmes of the IMF and the World Bank have been superseded by the more complex and nuanced project of 'globalization with a human face', which remains faithful to neoliberal fundamentals. Thatcherism and Reaganomics were likewise replaced long ago by the Third Way of the Blair and Clinton era, which retained a commitment to market economics within a more complex set of social interventions. There is therefore a sense in which the story of Jeffrey Sachs is the story of neoliberalism itself.

Sachs's prominent role in the history of neoliberalism is due in part to the strength of his personality. Sachs is a charismatic figure who writes and speaks in powerful moralizing language, and who generates strong reactions in the people around him. For many, he is an inspirational leader. Volunteers in his Millennium Villages wear T-shirts reading 'Sachs is my homeboy', observers describe the 'devotional' atmosphere at his public lectures, and he has been introduced to the congregation of Washington Cathedral as the 'prophet of economic possibilities for the poor'.[9] Yet his colleagues in the development community have spoken of his 'abrasive' personality, his tendency to fly off the handle, and his refusal to listen to alternative points of view. Indeed, the head of a prominent development institute described Sachs to me as 'the most reviled person in international development', while other interviewees have referred to his 'megalomania' and 'enormous ego'. One development practitioner who has worked closely with Sachs was even forced to invent an entirely new word, struggling to express herself before at last defining Sachs's ego as 'over-dimensional'.[10]

People who have met Sachs have been astonished by his drive and determination, as well as his arrogance and ruthlessness. Doug Henwood interviewed Sachs in 2002, and describes him as 'a very unpleasant fellow, cocky, vain, and free of doubt'.[11] But, under closer inspection, Sachs's conduct betrays an insecurity and vulnerability that such accounts neglect. Despite his apparent self-assuredness and inflexibility, Sachs is constantly altering his position, without ever admitting that he has done so. His denial of his neoliberal past is just one instance of this tendency, which can be traced back to the single most significant event in Sachs's life and work: the failure of shock therapy in Russia.

Jeffrey Sachs made his name through his shock therapy experiments in Bolivia and Poland, which led to his appointment in 1991 as economic advisor to the Russian president, Boris Yeltsin. From 1991 to 1994, Sachs played a key role in the planning and implementation of Russia's shock therapy programme, which reproduced his prescriptions for Poland. But in contrast to the 'success' of his previous experiments, the sudden and dramatic dismantling of the Russian state under shock therapy resulted in a catastrophic economic collapse that has been described as the most severe recession in modern world history. A definitive study of the period concluded that '[t]he years since the launching of shock therapy have led to devastating consequences for the Russian economy and society in terms of their productive capacities, human capital, health, demographic indicators, culture and education, as well as in terms of people's mutual trust and the nation's psychological self-confidence.'[12] Sachs's response to this disaster has always been to deny all responsibility, and to place the blame squarely on the shoulders of others. But he has been unable to forget it. In the words of a profile of Sachs in the *Boston Globe*, published in 2001, 'Sachs entered [Russia] as a star and left with his lustre badly tarnished. The place still haunts him like a ghost.'[13]

The catastrophe of shock therapy in Russia, Sachs's refusal to accept responsibility for it, and the unflattering accounts of his subsequent behaviour, together indicate that his transformation from Dr Shock into Mr Aid might be more complex than the standard account suggests. Far from being a man who has learned from his mistakes, Sachs is perhaps better understood as 'a man who is not prepared to confront his past, a man who evades crucial questions concerning it – in short, a man whose basic feature is a refusal to work through the traumatic past.'[14] Russia was the defining moment in the career of Jeffrey Sachs. His subsequent transformation can be interpreted as a series of inadvertent responses to this event, which have served to shield him from its traumatic content, while preserving his commitment to the neoliberal project within his new humanitarian persona. To quote G.K. Chesterton's analysis of *Dr Jekyll and Mr Hyde*, in the case of Dr Shock and Mr Aid, 'The real stab of the story is not in the discovery that the one man is two men; but in the discovery that the two men are one man.'[15]

THE NEOLIBERAL FANTASY AND THE REAL OF CAPITAL

Before going any further, it is important to clarify the understanding of neoliberal ideology that informs this book.[16] Neoliberalism is often criticized as a utopian project, which violently imposes an abstract market model upon a complex social order. While this may be an accurate representation of neoliberalism *in practice*, it does not grasp the distinctive structure of neoliberal *ideology*. This is better captured by Slavoj Žižek's critique of ideology, which draws on the work of the psychoanalyst Jacques Lacan. In its deepest and most powerful form, Žižek argues, ideology operates not as an appearance projected onto reality, but as a 'social fantasy' structuring reality against what Lacan called the Real.[17] The Real is an ominous presence that is excluded from everyday experience, but that imposes itself on reality in disturbing and inescapable ways. It is most directly encountered in moments of trauma and psychotic breakdown, in which reality disintegrates, and the Real confronts the subject as a terrifying and incomprehensible force.[18]

Neoliberalism can be understood as a social fantasy that is structured against the Real of Capital. Neoliberal ideology is based on Adam Smith's vision of a natural and harmonious market society, in which the self-interested activities of individual entrepreneurs are mediated by the invisible hand of the market to ensure the optimal allocation of resources. As a system of norms, individuals, and institutions (such as private property, entrepreneurs, and markets), capitalism is incorporated into neoliberal ideology. But the Real of Capital is excluded from this symbolic order. The source of profit in exploitation is concealed by the understanding of economic value as an expression of subjective preferences, rather than a measure of labour time. The antagonistic relationship between capital and labour is obscured by the conceptualization of workers as entrepreneurs selling their own 'human capital' on the market. The inherent tendency for capitalism to generate vast economic crises is papered over by the assumption that efficient markets operate under conditions of 'perfectly competitive equilibrium'. And capital's relentless transcendence of collective social control is represented as the benign operation of the invisible hand of the market.

In contrast to the imagined futures of other transformative political projects, neoliberalism conceptualizes the market not as an institution to be constructed, but as the natural order of society to be liberated from the tyranny of the state. For the neoliberal, market society is something to be revealed, not produced. This is evident in the following passage from Jeffrey Sachs's early writings on shock therapy:

Some have claimed that any attempt to develop an economic blueprint for Eastern Europe's future development betrays the same mistake as Lenin's: the false, and dangerous, presumption that human society can be arranged, rather than simply allowed to evolve. I think that this is wrong, a mistaken analogy to the recklessness and hubris of earlier revolutions ... The current revolutions under way in Eastern Europe are not utopian, nor do they seek to impose a new social experiment, as was the case in Lenin's revolution. Today's revolutions are relentlessly pragmatic in character. This makes all the difference.[19]

For Sachs, then, shock therapy is to be distinguished from communism and other such 'utopian' ideologies precisely because it constitutes the 'pragmatic' recognition of market society as an expression of human nature, as opposed to the 'reckless' construction of an imagined communist future. Yet this seemingly laissez-faire attitude conceals a hidden dogmatism. Neoliberalism *is* a utopian project, which *does* attempt to impose a 'new social experiment', and its denial of this fact makes it more resilient than other failed utopias. For neoliberals like Sachs, market economics is not a mere policy framework to be utilized or discarded at will, but a natural structuring principle of social reality. The failure of the neoliberal project is thus experienced as an inexplicable violation of reality, in the form of financial crashes, credit crunches, economic depressions, and so on. Rather than responding to such traumatic events by discarding their economic model, neoliberals attempt to hold their sense of reality together by explaining their failures in terms that leave their fantasy intact. Hence the seemingly irrational resilience of neoliberal ideology in the face of all failures, up to and including the global economic crisis of 2008–09, from which neoliberalism has once again emerged as the dominant social fantasy of Western capitalism.

Understood in this way, the evolution of the neoliberal project appears not as the revelation of a pre-existing reality, nor as the unfolding of a master-plan, but as a series of failed attempts to prevent the traumatic Real of Capital from disturbing the fantasy of a harmonious market society. This is important not only conceptually, but also politically. By understanding neoliberalism as a desperate form of crisis-management, we can strip it of its seemingly all-encompassing power. And by demonstrating the continuity of neoliberalism within the supposedly progressive projects and discourses that Sachs now espouses, we can attempt to jam the gears of its relentless ideological shape-shifting.

In what follows, I develop this understanding of neoliberal ideology through an exploration of the life and times of Jeffrey Sachs. Chapter 1 details the rise of Dr Shock, from Sachs's early life to his shock therapy experiments in Bolivia and Poland. Chapter 2 focuses on the catastrophe of shock therapy in Russia, which ruptured Sachs's neoliberal fantasy, confronting him with the Real of Capital. Chapter 3 explores Sachs's transformation from Dr Shock into Mr Aid, whereby 'Africa' has come to function as a repository for all the contradictions of capitalism. Chapter 4 assesses the conceptual limitations of the Millennium Villages Project, in which Sachs has attempted to reconstruct his neoliberal fantasy through the radical transformation of rural African societies. Chapter 5 reports on my visit to the Millennium Villages Project in Uganda in 2013, where I discovered a reality far removed from Sachs's celebratory promotion of the project. Chapter 6 documents Sachs's responses to the ecological crisis and the Great Recession, and seeks to make sense of his bizarre appearance at Occupy Wall Street. In conclusion, I diagnose Sachs as a neurotic neoliberal, and ask whether communism is his greatest fear or his most repressed desire.

The argument that I present in this book is based chiefly on Sachs's own voluminous writings, in the context of the historical events he has participated in. Sachs's standard response to critical engagement is to dismiss it as the idle chatter of 'armchair critics', who have no understanding of the realities of development on the ground.[20] To an extent, I am happy to accept this charge. Simply reading what Sachs has written is enough to demonstrate the glaring inconsistencies and disturbing continuities that mark his transition from Dr Shock to Mr Aid. But I am not just an armchair critic. In the course of my research I have interviewed numerous people who have worked with Sachs, who have clashed with him, and who have expertise in the countless areas in which he operates. I have also spent some time living in Ruhiira, Uganda, which is part of Sachs's Millennium Villages Project. Among the many things I discovered there was that Sachs has very little understanding of the reality of his own projects on the ground. Perhaps by attacking armchair critics, Sachs hopes to discredit those who have gone to the trouble of reading him thoroughly. But he should be careful what he wishes for, as the critique is only strengthened once the armchair is abandoned.

1 THE RISE OF DR SHOCK

Jeffrey Sachs was born in Detroit, Michigan, in 1954. Detroit at that time was the centre of the American automobile industry, and a hotbed of working-class radicalism. Sachs's father, Theodore Sachs, was a key figure in the class politics of the city – a prominent labour lawyer and a staunch defender of unionization and workers' rights, who fought several cases in the Supreme Court.[1] Jeffrey was also engaged in leftist politics in his teenage years, marching against the Vietnam War on Moratorium Day, and attending a rally addressed by the legendary United Farm Workers leader Cesar Chavez.[2] According to Sachs, the turning point in his life came in his high school sophomore year, when he went on a family holiday to Russia, and met an East German student who told him 'about the wonders of socialism'.[3] They stayed in touch, and following his high school graduation two years later Sachs flew to East Germany to visit his friend. In interviews, Sachs has repeatedly returned to this experience of actually existing socialism as a key moment in his intellectual development, in which he was confronted with fundamental questions about the nature of capitalist society that he found himself unable to answer:

> My exposure for a week to socialist society was a big eye-opener. I was absolutely befuddled by the experience … I was besieged with questions from young East Germans. Why do you have unemployment in the US when we do not? Why do you have poor people and inequality in the US? I could not challenge or give satisfactory answers to these questions … I did not even know … what the appropriate framework was to think about these kinds of questions.[4]

Sachs recalls that his initial response to this unsettling experience was to purchase a book by Karl Marx, which he 'took home and tried to make sense of.'[5] On his return to the United States, however, Sachs enrolled at Harvard to read economics, and Marx was quickly abandoned. The assigned pre-reading was Joseph Schumpeter's *Capitalism, Socialism and Democracy*,[6] an influential anti-Marxist tract, which celebrates the 'creative destruction' wrought by entrepreneurial capitalism. Sachs entered Harvard in 1972, and was placed under the charge of Abraham Bergson, the pre-eminent authority on the Soviet economy in the field of mainstream economics. Bergson conceived of his life's work as a confirmation of Friedrich Hayek's proto-neoliberal critique of communism as 'the road to serfdom', according to which economic planning necessarily leads to totalitarianism and mass impoverishment.[7] In weekly meetings, Bergson introduced Sachs to the canon of neoclassical economics. In Sachs's words, 'I read extensively; we discussed; and I learned about a way of seeing the world.'[8]

Within a year of his arrival at Harvard, the troubling ambiguity of Sachs's early experience of socialism had been emphatically resolved. He had been fully immersed in the symbolic universe of neoclassical economics, and, to quote a *Fortune* magazine profile of him two decades later, 'He had an answer for his East German friend: Socialism was dead.'[9] Sachs excelled in economics, and rose rapidly through the ranks at Harvard. He graduated in 1976 with the third-highest grade among 1,650 students, completed his Masters in 1978, and received his PhD in 1980. Economics at Harvard underwent a dramatic transformation during this period. Over the previous three decades, Keynesianism had been the dominant economic doctrine of the capitalist world. Harvard and MIT had placed Cambridge, Massachusetts at the heart of this intellectual orthodoxy, while the radical free market theories of Hayek and Milton Friedman at the University of Chicago were largely ignored. In the early 1970s, however, the Long Boom of the post-war era degenerated into global 'stagflation' – high inflation, high unemployment, and low productivity growth. Meanwhile, the centre of intellectual gravity began to shift towards the neoliberalism of the Chicago School, which seemed to offer a compelling account of the collapse of the Keynesian compromise, based on a critique of the market distortions resulting from state interventionism and the power of organized labour. Hayek received the Nobel Prize in Economics in

1974, followed by Friedman in 1976, symbolizing the rapid elevation of neoliberalism from relative obscurity to hegemonic status.[10]

This transition was also occurring within Harvard and MIT, led by a vanguard of new professors and PhD students, many of whom would become key figures in the neoliberal revolution. Stanley Fischer moved from Chicago in 1973 to become professor of economics at MIT, and went on to serve as managing director of the IMF from 1994 to 2001.[11] Alejandro Foxley was also teaching at MIT in the 1970s, and was later appointed finance minister in Chile, where he continued the neoliberal reforms initiated under Pinochet. The PhD students in this group included David Lipton, Larry Summers, Pedro Aspe, Domingo Cavallo, and Jeffrey Sachs. Lipton went on to work for the IMF, and collaborated with Sachs on the shock therapy programmes in Poland and Russia. Summers would serve as chief economist of the World Bank from 1991 to 1993, and as US secretary of the treasury during the Clinton administration, when he unleashed the financial deregulation that led to the Great Recession. Aspe was Mexico's secretary of finance from 1988 to 1994, masterminding a massive privatization programme and the North American Free Trade Agreement (NAFTA). And Cavallo served as Argentina's minister of the economy between 1991 and 1996, overseeing the free market reforms that led to Argentina's crisis and default in 2001.[12]

For a talented young economist like Sachs, intent on making sense of the world, the intellectual atmosphere in Cambridge must have been intoxicating. A theoretical revolution was taking place that was inspiring dramatic political transformations around the world. These transformations began with Pinochet's coup in 1973, and the implementation of radical free market reforms in Chile under the guidance of Milton Friedman and the 'Chicago Boys', which Sachs's PhD group followed with avid interest.[13] Margaret Thatcher was elected in 1979, and Ronald Reagan came to office in 1980. Sachs received his PhD in the same year, and immediately joined the Harvard economics faculty, where he continued to excel. 'As a young faculty member', Sachs recalls, 'I lectured widely to high acclaim, published broadly, and was on a rapid academic climb to tenure, which I received in 1983 when I was twenty-eight.'[14]

Sachs's early academic work was focused on the stagflation of the 1970s, and on the policy responses that it demanded. He published extensively in leading economics journals, and contributed numerous working papers to the National Bureau of Economic Research (NBER), a think tank funded by Fortune 500 companies, which specialized in polemical attacks on Keynesianism, social democracy, and the welfare state.[15] Sachs's work from this period challenged the expansion of state expenditure and the power of organized labour, which he repeatedly identified as the primary culprit in the economic crisis. The fundamental problem, Sachs argued, was that the increase in union membership during the post-war period had driven up the price of real wages, causing them to rise 'faster than productivity, so that the distribution of income shifted towards labour, while the rate of return on capital was substantially reduced'.[16] The solution was to return capital to profitability by forcing reductions in real wages. Short of direct confrontation with the unions, this objective could be achieved either through currency devaluations or through the disciplinary power of large-scale and prolonged unemployment.[17] Sachs criticized Keynesians for repeatedly intervening in economic recessions to avoid extensive job losses, which had removed the fear of long-term unemployment from the labour force, making it more difficult for employers to convince workers to accept wage reductions.[18]

In a paper published in 1983, for example, Sachs argued that Thatcher was to be commended for her unwavering commitment to austerity and high unemployment, as she had succeeded in convincing workers and employers that there would be no swift economic recovery. This had forced workers to take pay-cuts, while pushing employers into firing workers they might otherwise have kept on:

> An economic downturn perceived as permanent should raise productivity, as least-efficient firms and workers are booted out of the productivity data … Until recent years, economic downturns were thought to be transient affairs, giving strong incentive to firms to hoard labour during the cyclical trough. Prime Minister Thatcher's main accomplishment in this regard seems to have been to convince firms that high unemployment and slow growth will be present for the long haul.[19]

Sachs's early work was thus devoted to returning capital to profitability through a variety of mechanisms, including the austerity and high unemployment deemed necessary to break the power of organized labour. This strategy has been central to the class politics of neoliberalism. Since the 1970s, the maintenance of capitalist profits in conditions of low economic growth has been achieved through the dismantling of the welfare state, the stagnation of real wages, and the weakening of labour unions.[20] This strategy lies at the heart of the spiralling inequality that has characterized global capitalism since the early 1980s, and that Sachs himself would condemn at Occupy Wall Street three decades later. By providing the economic justification for this class strategy, Sachs had already played a significant role in the history of neoliberalism. Somehow, in the space of a decade, the son of a tireless defender of workers' rights had gone from reading Marx and marching with Cesar Chavez to fixating on organized labour as the enemy to be defeated in order to increase the profit margins of the capitalist class. This was already a peculiar and unfortunate state of affairs. But things were about to get much worse.

THE INVENTION OF SHOCK THERAPY

In 1985, at just thirty years of age, Jeffrey Sachs was established as a leading macroeconomist of the new free market orthodoxy. Then, suddenly, in his words, 'my life changed'.[21] Sachs was invited to attend a presentation at Harvard by a delegation from the Bolivian government concerning the hyper-inflation that was afflicting their country at the time. He disagreed with the delegation's analysis, and recalls 'walking to the blackboard with great confidence [and saying] "Here's how it works"'.[22] On the basis of his explanation, Sachs was invited to La Paz to advise the government on their economic reform programme. He accepted the invitation, arriving in Bolivia on 9 July 1985.

The doctrine that came to be known as shock therapy was forged through Sachs's experience in Bolivia, but was only formalized in his later work on the post-communist transition. Before addressing the specificities of the Bolivian case, it is important to clarify the economic and political logic of shock therapy. According to Sachs, his advice to the Bolivians was based on Milton Friedman's work on hyperinflation.[23] For Friedman, hyperinflation was less a crisis to be solved than an opportunity to be utilized, as a state of emergency in which radical free market reforms could be rapidly implemented. By justifying the massive reduction of state expenditures in terms of reducing the need to print money, a right-wing ideological doctrine could be presented as a pragmatic response to economic necessity. In 1975, Friedman and the 'Chicago Boys' used hyperinflation in Chile in precisely this way, as a means of legitimating an unprecedented neoliberal programme of privatization, trade liberalization, tax reform, deregulation of foreign investment, and fiscal and monetary austerity.[24]

During his shock therapy period, Sachs praised Friedman for his 'very clear message', claiming that 'his faith in markets, his constant insistence on proper monetary management – is far more accurate than fuzzy structuralist or pseudo-Keynesian arguments one hears a lot in the developing world'.[25] Friedman famously argued: 'Only a crisis – actual or perceived – produces real change. When the crisis occurs, the actions that are taken depend on the ideas that are lying around.'[26] Sachs's own argument for shock therapy was identical:

> When is real politics the main push, and when do ideas really count? Most of the time in normal periods it's the vested interests, it's the special interests, it's the normal politics that plays the role. But when things come apart, when societies are in crisis, when new choices have to be made, when the old structures no longer have legitimacy or no longer have the power, that's when ideas can play a tremendous role.[27]

Shock therapy was therefore both an economic and a political strategy. In economic terms it entailed the sudden and comprehensive implementation of a set of reforms designed to shock an economy out of crisis and into stability, through a rapid transition from state planning to free markets. The recipe was the same set of free market principles set out by Friedman in Chile – privatization, liberalization, and austerity.[28] In his prescription for Eastern Europe's transition from communism to capitalism, Sachs set out these core principles with clinical precision:

> *Economic liberalization*: freeing of most prices; open trade policy (low tariffs, elimination of quotas, ending licensing of trading firms); and a legal basis for private property ...
> *Macroeconomic stabilization*: sharp cuts in subsidies; devaluation of the exchange rate and subsequent currency convertibility; positive real interest rates; and restriction on domestic credit expansion.
> *Privatization*: conversion of state enterprises into corporate form, followed by transfer of ownership of state enterprises to the private sector.[29]

This economic shock implied the dismantling of national industry and social protection, and the reduction of the role of the state to that of protecting private property and maintaining public order. As Sachs explained in the context of shock therapy in Russia, 'What radical laissez-faire policies entail, in circumstances of extreme crisis, is shucking off the secondary burdens of government so that government can focus on its core functions.'[30] Just as important as this economic shock, however, was the political shock that accompanied it. In Sachs's own words, shock therapy 'requires the use of radical laissez-faire policies for a reason that is rarely recognised: it is a political strategy as well as an economic strategy'.[31] In his advice to Russia, Sachs acknowledged that the dispossession and impoverishment inflicted by free market reforms would be politically explosive, arguing that the success of the reforms depended on their sudden and unexpected implementation, which would lock them into place before resistance could mobilize:

> The reform team must make its reforms an accomplished fact. A key human attribute is attachment to the status quo ... If reformers want free prices, they should not ... talk about it – they should do it, because everyone will be against freeing prices until it has been done, until it is an established fact. But once done, there is no going back.[32]

Critics of shock therapy have compared this political strategy to Bolshevism, suggesting that both were 'ruthless attempts to implement one or another set of prescriptions deduced from abstract theories ... via a revolution from above'.[33] Beyond their obviously divergent political objectives, however, there is a further crucial difference between these two projects. As I explained in the Introduction, whereas Marxism–Leninism consciously projects a utopian vision onto social reality, neoliberalism seeks to reveal the market as a pre-existing social order. Sachs has emphasized this distinction in his own retrospective justifications of the logic of shock therapy:

> Shock therapy has been attacked by many intellectuals as being yet another 'constructivist' system of social engineering, trying to replace one dogma with another. This is mistaken ... Whereas Lenin had also advocated a kind of 'shock therapy' in 1902 in his fateful and disastrous *What Is to Be Done?*, his version of shock therapy was to create a new

world that had never existed ... Shock therapy was relentlessly down to earth by contrast ... [34]

And:

Like the old discussion of how you make a sculpture of an elephant ... You just cut away everything that doesn't look like an elephant.[35]

According to Sachs, shock therapy thus differs from Bolshevism in that it is premised not on the creation of a new world, but on the removal of everything that does not correspond to the pre-existing reality of a market society. It thus appears as non-ideological – as 'relentlessly down to earth', in contrast to utopian ideologies such as Marxism–Leninism. Yet, as Žižek has observed, 'it is precisely the neutralization of some features into a spontaneously accepted background that marks out ideology at its purest'.[36] Sachs's understanding of shock therapy as non-ideological and anti-utopian thus constituted a deeper and more powerful form of ideology. This generated dangerously unconscious 'illusions about the ease with which social engineering experiments could be carried out on entire nations'.[37] The first of these nations was Bolivia.

THE AVENGING ANGEL OF ECONOMICS

By the time Sachs arrived in Bolivia, the state was in the midst of the debt crisis that had gripped the Third World since Mexico's default in 1982, driven by high levels of sovereign debt, rising interest rates, and falling commodities prices. The government had resorted to printing money to meet its obligations, and inflation was running at an annualized rate of 60,000 per cent.[38] The political situation in the country was one of 'class stalemate', in which the peasantry and the miners' unions were highly mobilized in opposition to austerity, while the business elite was equally organized in its push for liberalization.[39] Sachs recalls: 'It was an extraordinary and terrifying thing to see. One felt ... on the streets at that time ... that anything could happen.'[40] Expressing a fear of communist revolution that would haunt him throughout his career, Sachs notes that it was unclear 'whether mass demonstrations would overthrow ... the existing political system ... Obviously it was society at the edge of the precipice.'[41]

Abstracting from these political realities, Sachs identified the source of hyperinflation in the low fixed price of oil in the country, which was preventing the state from collecting adequate tax revenues and thus forcing it to print money to cover its costs. He therefore advised the Bolivian government to impose a tenfold increase in the price of oil, combined with a package of drastic austerity measures.[42] Together, these reforms would close the budget deficit, removing the need for the government to print money and thus bringing inflation under control. Sachs provided this advice to the Nationalist Democratic Action party (ADN), the right-wing party of the former dictator Hugo Banzer, who was running for office at the time. When Banzer lost the election, Sachs's plan was passed on to the victorious Revolutionary Nationalist Movement (MNR), a centrist party led by Victor Paz Estenssoro. The MNR then incorporated Sachs's plan into the notorious Decree 21060, which constituted a comprehensive strategy for the rapid neoliberalization of the Bolivian state. Decree 21060 implemented the oil-price increase recommended by Sachs, combined with further price deregulation, trade liberalization, macroeconomic stabilization, the elimination of food subsidies, the privatization of state businesses including the mining sector, and the reduction of the public-sector wage bill through redundancies and a wage freeze.[43] The Decree was drawn up by the presidential team behind closed doors, and enacted without public consultation on 29 August 1985.[44]

Decree 21060 epitomized the economic and political logic of shock therapy, combining the economic shock of wholesale neoliberalization with the political shock of its sudden imposition upon an unsuspecting public. In Sachs's verdict at the time, the Decree was 'remarkably wide ranging, even radical', entailing 'nothing less than a call to dismantle the system of state capitalism that had prevailed over the years'.[45] Hyperinflation was indeed brought under control, but the cost of such savage price increases and government cutbacks fell heavily on the working classes. This led to mass mobilizations across the country, which were met with what Naomi Klein has described as 'quasi-fascist measures'. Tanks were put on the streets, a curfew was imposed, marches and political assemblies were banned, and 200 union leaders were detained in remote jails in the Amazon.[46]

Prices surged again towards the end of the year, at which point growing social unrest led the government to agree to a 50 per cent increase in wages to keep pace with inflation.[47] With the reform process faltering, Sachs was called back to Bolivia by Paz Estenssoro, and was influential in convincing the government to maintain its shock therapy programme in the face of powerful resistance. Members of the Bolivian government describe Sachs as being 'blunt'[48] and 'abrasive'[49] in his message. Gonzalo 'Goni' Sanchez de Lozada was finance minister at the time, and worked closely with Sachs on the reforms. He recalls: 'Jeff kept telling us "Now look, if you don't cut this expenditure, and if you listen to the sirens of being popular, you guys are going to go right down the drain."'[50] The government cancelled the proposed wage increase and continued its neoliberal reforms, and Sachs became known to Bolivian politicians as 'the avenging angel of economics'.[51]

Shock therapy in Bolivia succeeded in stripping back the state and creating a free market economy, but the social consequences were severe. Two years into the programme, the official unemployment rate had risen from 20 per cent to 30 per cent, real wages had declined by 40 per cent, and poverty and inequality had increased significantly.[52] State companies were sold off, and the state mining sector was decimated: 20,000 miners lost their jobs during the first year of reforms. Bolivia's nascent industrial sector was also destroyed, with 35,000 private-sector manufacturing jobs being eliminated between 1985 and 1990.[53] Following trade liberalization and the abolition of subsidies, Bolivia's peasant farmers were unable to compete with cheap food imports, and agricultural production fell by 17 per cent between 1985 and 1988. The loss of livelihoods in mining and agriculture resulted in a dramatic increase in the production of coca and cocaine, a rapid acceleration of urbanization, and the explosive growth of the precarious informal economy, which by 1988 had expanded to include almost 70 per cent of the working population.[54] In the words of one journalist, 'To the average Bolivian, the reforms have brought unemployment, displacement, and misery. Much of the blame locally is laid at Sachs' door.'[55]

But the voices of the poor and powerless could not be heard from the commanding heights of global economic policymaking, where Sachs was now welcomed as an economic miracle-worker. Bolivia's pioneering approach to reform provided inspiration for the IMF's infamous Structural Adjustment Programmes,[56] and Sachs was invited to advise the governments of several Latin American countries, including Argentina, Brazil, Peru, and Venezuela.[57] By the late 1980s, the market revolution was all but complete, and neoliberalism had become the economic orthodoxy of the capitalist world. Only communism remained undefeated. This was Sachs's next challenge.

CROSSING A CHASM IN ONE LEAP

The role that Jeffrey Sachs played in the transition from communism to capitalism in Eastern Europe and the former Soviet Union remains his most enduring legacy, and it was here that his shock therapy approach was planned and implemented in the most ruthless and calculating way. The nature and significance of Sachs's role is captured in the following assessment by an expert on the region:

> The influence of Harvard economist Jeffrey Sachs in setting the basic terms of the theoretical debate on the nature of the post-communist economic transformation has been both far-reaching and profound ... Sachs does not hesitate to claim universal superiority for the big-bang approach to post-communist reform. Indeed, [he] quite self-consciously adopts the posture of a neoliberal missionary.[58]

This missionary role began in 1989, when the financial speculator George Soros provided funding for Sachs to take on an advisory role in Poland's economic reforms, accompanied by his Harvard PhD colleague David Lipton, who was now working at the IMF. When Solidarity won Poland's election in June 1989, Sachs and Lipton were charged with writing the first ever plan for a transition from central planning to a market economy. The plan was accepted by Solidarity, and provided the basis for Poland's shock therapy programme, which was launched on 1 January 1990.[59]

Solidarity's long struggle against the communist regime had not been fought in the name of the free market, but in pursuit of an alternative form of socialism based on worker self-management. In recognition of this inconvenient political reality, Sachs framed his plan in a disingenuous 'pro-worker' discourse, which was immediately discarded once Solidarity's approval had been obtained.[60] From this point onwards, the plan was formulated and implemented by a technocratic vanguard isolated from democratic pressures.[61] Significantly, it was first presented, in September 1989, not to the Polish public but to the IMF.[62] The true nature and scope of the plan was then set out in an article in the *Economist*, which Sachs entitled 'What Is to Be Done?' The reference to Lenin was mocking, of course, but Sachs's own plan was no less dogmatic and authoritarian than the Bolshevik agenda. Sachs insisted that 'the eastern countries must reject any lingering ideas about a ... chimerical "market socialism" based on public ownership or worker self-management, and go straight for a western-style market economy'.[63] He dismissed any attempt at the gradualist sequencing of market reforms over time, asserting that 'You don't try to cross a chasm in two jumps.' 'Poland's goal', he claimed, 'is to establish the economic, legal, and institutional basis for a private sector market economy in just one year.'[64] The strictly neoliberal formula of this 'shock programme' was then laid out with abrupt clarity:

> There should be four simultaneous parts to a programme of rapid market transformation. First, let prices find market-clearing levels, in part based on free trade with the West. Second, set the private sector free by removing bureaucratic restrictions. Third, bring the state sector under control, by privatization and by imposing tougher disciplines on such state firms as remain. Fourth, maintain overall macroeconomic stability through restrictive credit and balanced budgets.[65]

Free trade, deregulation, privatization, and austerity: these were the four pillars of the neoliberal project, and they were being implemented all at once with total disregard for the structures of the pre-existing communist system. Sachs understood this system in purely negative terms – not as a complex set of institutions, ideas, and practices to be modified and transformed over time, but as the irrational, inefficient, and corrupt antithesis of the market economy, which needed to be completely destroyed.[66] Rather than engage in the purposeful construction of the new system, the priority was to release 'the power of natural market forces',[67] which would spontaneously generate the institutional structures of 'normal capitalism'.[68] Once the distortions of the command economy were dismantled, Sachs assumed that this 'normal' order would emerge of its own accord, so long as 'market forces are allowed to guide the transformation'.[69] The radical free-market ideology underpinning this project has been summarized by one critic as follows:

> If the state withdraws from the economy, markets and market activity will lead to capitalist development through voluntary exchanges in the pursuit of profit. In this world, there are only two types of economies – state dominated and the more 'natural' market economy ... With the collapse of communism, neoliberals advocated moving to the 'market' on all fronts, and as quickly as possible ... the emphasis was on

destroying old communist institutions, and relying on the spontaneous generation of new institutions produced by market forces.[70]

Shock therapy in Poland was therefore premised on the neoliberal understanding of the market as a spontaneous order, rather than a set of institutions to be constructed over time. Yet Sachs was fully aware of the social consequences of this supposedly natural process. As he argued at the time, the freeing of prices 'will raise overall prices in January by 45–50%. At the same time wages are to be sharply controlled in the state sector, so that the devaluation and cuts in subsidies [do] not get dissipated in wage rises. All this will reduce real wages sharply ... That is a brave step.'[71] In this context, Sachs anticipated that '[t]he hardest part of the transformation ... will not be the economics at all, but the politics.'[72] Sachs therefore advised Poland's government to capitalize on the Communist Party's evisceration of civil society by fully implementing its reform programme before an organized democratic opposition could emerge:

> So far, the reform effort has been guided by technical solutions rather than partisan politics. But this has not been a period of normal politics. Organized political parties and lobbying groups barely existed when the post-Communist government took office ... since the Communists had virtually destroyed all organized groups in society. It is inevitable, however, that 'normal politics' will once again dominate the policy process, and the scope for decisive policy actions will be greatly circumscribed.[73]

Sachs's strategy here is overtly anti-democratic, despite his repeated claims to be acting in the name of democracy. Yet from Sachs's point of view, there simply was no contradiction here: 'The revolutionaries of Eastern Europe ... were not utopians or would-be inventors of a new social system. They simply demanded that Poland and its neighbours should become "normal" again.'[74]

For Sachs, the most crucial and pressing factor in this return to 'normal market life'[75] was the 'massive and rapid privatization' of Poland's state-dominated economy,[76] which would shatter the command economy and lead to the spontaneous 'birth and development of millions of new businesses'.[77] The scale of the privatization that Sachs envisaged was historically unprecedented. As Sachs himself pointed out at the time, 'Mrs Margaret Thatcher, the world's leading privatiser, has overseen the transfer of a handful of state enterprises in a decade. Poland has more than 2,500 enterprises that should be candidates for privatization.'[78] The rationale for this vast privatization programme was again both economic and political. Its economic logic was based on the neoliberal assumption that state enterprises are necessarily less efficient and competitive than their private counterparts.[79] In political terms, rapid privatization was identified as the surest means of locking in the broader reform programme. As Sachs argued in a presentation to the World Bank in 1991:

> The need to accelerate privatization in Eastern Europe is the paramount economic policy issue facing the region. If there is no breakthrough in the privatization of large enterprises in the near future the entire process could be stalled for political and social reasons for years to come … the operating guideposts of the World Bank should be that privatization is urgent – and politically vulnerable.[80]

For Sachs, the greatest threat to the continued implementation of shock therapy in Poland was posed by the worker self-management councils of the existing state enterprises – the social base of the Solidarity movement that had overthrown the Communist regime, under whose banner shock therapy was now being implemented. The central political objective of privatization was to prevent these councils from strengthening their control of their own workplaces. Sachs set out his anti-worker position most clearly in an influential paper co-authored with David Lipton in 1990, entitled 'Privatization in Eastern Europe: The Case of Poland'. In the paper, Sachs acknowledged the awkward fact that, owing to the 'Marxist ideology'[81] of the pre-existing Communist state, the workers were the formal holders of the ownership rights of the state enterprises.[82] This significantly complicated the privatization process, as 'privatization requires a disenfranchisement of the workers' council'.[83] Such a disenfranchisement was necessary, however, due to the inefficiencies and irrationalities that worker-ownership allegedly introduced into the enterprise. Returning to his old theme of rising real wages as the key cause of economic crisis, Sachs blamed the workers' councils for wage and price inflation, before triumphantly announcing: 'Wage controls have been put in place to prevent enterprises from appropriating their own profits.'[84]

This sounds like an odd statement for a neoliberal to make, but Sachs is in fact expressing the cold logic of capitalist exploitation – of preventing workers from appropriating the full value of their labour:

> We can expect that unless the claimants of the residual income are quickly defined through the privatization process, management and workers will, through indirect means, find ways to enrich themselves. Some of the profits might be enjoyed through a reduced work effort, or through low-return investments, like new factory cafeterias, for example, that benefit the incumbents of the firm.[85]

Instead of the workers benefiting from the fruits of their own labour through short working days and pleasant working spaces, the property rights and 'residual income' of the enterprise should be reallocated to a hypothetical capitalist class, which Sachs refers to as 'the real owners', even though they do not yet exist:

> The shift to a Western European ownership structure will require that enterprise governance be removed from the workers' councils and managers and be placed squarely with … the owners of the enterprise. In essence, privatization requires first that ownership rights, now vested in … the workers' councils, be eliminated so that the property rights to an enterprise can be transferred to the real owners.[86]

Sachs acknowledges that the privatization process will be politically difficult, but warns that these difficulties will only increase in the future, as workers witness rising levels of unemployment in other 'transition' economies in Eastern Europe, and realize 'that their job tenure will be undercut by the privatization of their firm'.[87] For this reason, he concludes, 'it would be preferable … for all enterprises regardless of their financial position to be corporatized and quickly put into private hands'.[88]

According to David Ellermen, a dissident ex–World Bank economist who also worked as an advisor in Eastern Europe during the transition, 'Sachs had no real economic principles behind his privatization plans, other than breaking the workers' councils', and dismissed defenders of the workers' councils as 'self-management imbeciles'.[89] In notes from the time, Ellerman comments on a conversation with Bulent Gultekin, an employee of the Polish Ministry of Ownership

Changes, and emphasizes the irony of Solidarity's legitimation of Sachs's agenda:

> The workers first challenged the communist government in the glory days of Solidarity at the beginning of the 1980s. After being suppressed by the Polish military and after Solidarity was outlawed, the workers worked through the enterprise self-management councils to gain power ... This is the hard-won power that Sachs and the right-wingers in the government are trying to destroy ... Gultekin clearly pointed out that Sachs confided in him that his real purpose was to take the power of the workers at the enterprise level away from the workers and return it to the government (now anti-communist).[90]

If the worker was the target of shock therapy in Poland, then the weapon was brutally effective. By 1993 industrial production had declined by 30 per cent. Unemployment, which had been almost nonexistent under Communism, had reached 25 per cent in some areas, and poverty and inequality had increased dramatically.[91] Sachs blamed these outcomes on the distortions and inefficiencies of the Communist regime.[92] Indeed, deindustrialization and unemployment were not only disregarded by Sachs, but were openly celebrated. Sachs was impressed by the speed with which inefficient state enterprises were being 'suddenly thrust into competition with newly available imports',[93] driving them out of business, and redirecting resources from heavy industry to the services sector, where 'new private traders [had] sprung up by the tens of thousands'.[94] Responding to concerns over soaring unemployment, Sachs insisted that 'Western observers should not over dramatise lay-offs and bankruptcies. *Poland, like the rest of Eastern Europe, now has too little unemployment, not too much*.'[95] Echoing his earlier celebration of high unemployment in Thatcher's Britain, Sachs now praised unemployment for exerting the same disciplinary pressures on Poland's workforce:

> The rising risk of unemployment has greatly affected the behaviour of workers. Poland's over-full employment has long meant that workers could find new jobs easily, while businesses had difficulty finding workers, combating absenteeism and motivating a strong work effort. Now, with employees worried about potential job losses, sick leave has dropped sharply ... wage pressures have abated, and strike activity is negligible.[96]

As in Bolivia, the social consequences of shock therapy in Poland were studiously ignored in the corridors of global power, where Sachs's latest experiment was celebrated once again as a resounding success. Leading periodicals around the world ran glowing portraits of Sachs as an economic miracle-worker. The *New York Times* called him 'the Indiana Jones of economics',[97] and *Euromoney* marvelled at his 'Sachs appeal'.[98] With the support of his newly established consultancy firm, Sachs and Associates, Sachs travelled the length and breadth of the post-communist world, advising governments from Slovenia to Mongolia on their own transitions. When confronted with the accusation that his consultancy was prescribing a one-size-fits-all shock therapy package to individual countries without concern for their particular circumstances, Sachs responded dismissively: 'I've worked in a large number of countries and in every one of these policy-makers start out saying "we're unique", and they go on to explain their perception of uniqueness in a way that is exactly the same that the finance minister in another country just explained the uniqueness of his country.'[99]

This attitude again suggests an understanding of market society as the natural structure of social reality, independent of historical or geographical context, rather than as a social order that must be constructed in specific ways in specific situations. It also resonates with anecdotes concerning the arrogance and aggressiveness with which Sachs conducted his consultations at this time. David Ellerman, for example, notes that 'several people ... described a "pitbull" or "bulldog" style of argumentation', and claims that an American journalist and members of government in Poland and Slovenia had independently 'described phone calls with Sachs screaming and cursing at them'. By this time, in Ellerman's assessment, 'Sachs was intoxicated with his globe-trotting and highly visible role'.[100]

This intoxication can only have increased in November 1991, when Sachs was invited to serve as economic advisor to the Kremlin in the management of Russia's economic reforms.[101] This was surely destined to be the culmination of Sachs's already illustrious career, as well as the completion of a personal odyssey that had begun over twenty years previously on his 'life-changing' holidays to Russia and East Germany. These unsettling experiences had inspired his study of economics at Harvard, where he had been caught up in the seductive rush of neoliberalism's ascent to intellectual and political hegemony.

The neoliberal fantasy had come to structure his sense of reality, resolving his youthful doubts concerning capitalism, and identifying communism as the enemy to be vanquished. This fantasy had become profoundly intertwined with Sachs's identity, providing the bedrock on which he constructed a high-flying academic career at Harvard, and serving as the basis for his shock therapy experiments in Latin America and Eastern Europe. All of this seemed to confirm the natural order of a market society, while simultaneously reinforcing his identity as a capitalist revolutionary. Now, at the height of his powers, and at an unprecedented moment in the historical march of global capitalism, Sachs was presented with the opportunity to return to Russia, the place where his journey had begun, and where his initial doubts concerning the possible superiority of communism had first been sown. As economic advisor to the Russian president, Sachs now had the extraordinary opportunity to bury these doubts once and for all, through the triumphant repetition of his failsafe shock therapy method, which would destroy communism forever and allow the spontaneous order of a market society to emerge from the ruins of the communist order. As Sachs himself recalls, 'Communism was falling, and I was pinching myself, because I was in the centre of this, absolutely the epicentre of it.'[102]

At that moment, disaster struck.

2 RUSSIA

Jeffrey Sachs arrived in Russia at a time of intense political turmoil. The failed putsch against Gorbachev's leadership of the Soviet Union in August 1991 had strengthened Yeltsin's position as president of Russia, and he had assembled a group of economic advisors intent on ensuring that Russia's transition to capitalism would follow radical free market lines. Inspired by Poland's shock therapy experiment, this group invited Sachs and David Lipton to participate in a team of Western economists assisting their planning of the reforms. Sachs and Lipton arrived in November 1991, and spent several days in a dacha outside Moscow drawing up the plan.[1] Anders Aslund – another Western advisor and a close colleague of Sachs – recalls one of the Russian reformers assuring him that 'there would not be any talk of social democracy but of real liberalism. He made it clear that they wanted to pursue a so-called big bang reform of the Polish type. I told [him] that Sachs, Lipton, and I would be happy to work with them.'[2]

Within the team of advisors, it was Sachs who took the lead, becoming, in his own words, 'the main drafter and spokesman of the group'.[3] Aslund recalls that Jeffrey Sachs was 'our intellectual leader' and 'the grand strategist', and claims that their key contribution to Russia's reforms was based on the fact that 'Jeffrey Sachs in particular possessed great knowledge of economic theory. We could thus contribute to a fuller conceptualization of the reforms.'[4] Bolstered by such power and adulation, Sachs's self-belief continued to scale new heights. A former Soviet official recalls Sachs visiting the deputy prime minister at the time, Yegor Gaidar, himself an arch-neoliberal and the man responsible for pushing through the reforms:

It was in Gaidar's ante-room and there were a number of officials waiting quietly, papers under their arms to see Gaidar. There was Sachs slumped in a chair, feet on the table and talking loudly. Gaidar's assistant walked over and said 'Excuse me Mr Sachs, would you please take your feet off my table?' So Sachs takes his feet off, the assistant turns around, and there he is tying up his shoes with his foot back on the table.[5]

This trivial incident is indicative of the dangerous hubris with which Sachs was afflicted by this time. Gorbachev and many other politicians and academics were calling for a gradual transition, warning that shock therapy in Russia would lead to catastrophe.[6] But Sachs dismissed these concerns, insisting that radical reform was necessary to cut away 'the deep economic cancer of seven decades of communism'.[7] This point of view was set out in an article in the *New York Times*, entitled 'Dr Jeffrey Sachs, Shock Therapist', which described Sachs as 'a boyish-looking ... Harvard professor who is now probably the most important economist in the world':[8]

Sachs's special insight was that the logic [of shock therapy] could apply to economies with no collective memory of free markets or history of even-handed rules of contract law and property rights. In fact, he is confident that revolution is a natural means of economic change. 'If you look at how reform has occurred, it has been through the rapid adaptation of foreign models', he concludes, 'not a slow evolution of modern institutions.'[9]

This disregard for the specificities of Russia was evident in the proposed reform programme, which prescribed a virtually identical set of policies to those applied in Poland, Bolivia, and elsewhere. The economic basis of the plan was set out in a 1992 paper by Sachs and Lipton entitled 'Prospects for Russia's Economic Reforms'. It included fiscal austerity, trade liberalization, 'rapid privatization', the immediate removal of price controls, and 'the construction of a legal system for private property and market-based activity'.[10] A temporary unemployment compensation scheme would be required to prevent social unrest, and de-industrialization was to be actively encouraged.[11]

Beyond this, there was very little substance to the plan. In Sachs's opinion, the communist system had no positive features, nothing that could be salvaged or modified, but was simply an aberration that had 'destroyed every vestige of society for normal human life', and that must be destroyed in turn.[12] This crude assessment overlooked the high levels of education and healthcare that had been achieved in the Soviet Union, as well as the complex socio-cultural system that had evolved around the planned economy.[13]

For Sachs, this complex social fabric was a mere illusion to be shattered in order to reveal the entrepreneurial nature of humanity. As he was drawing up his plans for shock therapy in Russia, Sachs celebrated the outcome of his experiments in Poland and elsewhere, claiming that '[i]n all of the countries, new entrepreneurs [were] coming to the fore, with a flair that dispels old notions that socialism has created a "Homo sovieticus" in which the market spirit has been vanquished'.[14]

Sachs also misrepresented the political struggles of the time, which he cast as a battle between 'reformers' and 'reactionaries', and between 'democracy' and 'communism'. In fact, by the time Yeltsin came to power the real political debate was not between capitalism and communism, but between shock therapy and gradualism, and it was the shock therapists, rather than the gradualists, who constituted the anti-democratic side of the struggle. As in Poland, the original reform movement in Russia was driven more by a demand for democratic participation than for entrepreneurial capitalism. Yeltsin's change team worked to stifle this democratic impulse, by seizing power as 'democratic reformers' and labelling the opposition as 'reactionaries' and 'communists'.[15] In November 1991 Yeltsin consolidated his political control by convincing the Russian parliament to grant him the right to govern by decree for one year.[16] In December of the same year, Sachs recalls being in the meeting in the Kremlin at which Yeltsin announced the dissolution of the Soviet Union.[17] Russia was now an independent sovereign state. The perfect conditions for radical reform had thus fallen into place: unlimited executive power over a new state in conditions of crisis and popular disorientation. As one analyst has noted, 'to the extent that any policy-making environment is appropriate for implementing shock therapy, Russia ... was ideal'.[18]

CAPITALISM UNLEASHED

Russia's shock therapy programme was launched on 2 January 1992. Prices on almost all producer goods and consumer items were liberalized on the first day, resulting in an immediate 250 per cent increase, and leading to desperate calls from parliament to cancel the reforms from the outset.[19] Trade was totally liberalized in a single day, on 29 January, allowing anyone to sell anything at any time with no permit. Faced with widespread layoffs, rapidly declining real wages and spiralling inflation, many Russians were reduced to selling their personal possessions on the streets. The mass privatization of state enterprises was announced in August of the same year. Due to the vast scale of the state sector, and the absence of a national capitalist class, privatization was implemented through the distribution to managers, workers, and the general public of vouchers that could be sold or exchanged for shares.[20] In 1992 alone, almost 47,000 state companies were privatized, constituting 'easily the largest, most rapid transformation of ownership in world history.'[21]

Sachs and his fellow reformers thus 'unleashed "capitalism from above" via a full dose of shock therapy.'[22] The social consequences were immediate and extreme. In 1992 alone, GDP fell by 14.5 per cent, industrial production fell by 19 per cent, and inflation averaged 1,354 per cent – cutting real incomes by 46 per cent,[23] and effectively destroying the savings of most ordinary Russians.[24] Rather than creating a vibrant shareholder society, as Sachs had anticipated, mass privatization was leading to the rapid concentration of wealth in the hands of enterprise managers and a new investor class, who were buying up the shares of impoverished Russians for next-to-nothing.[25] Lacking markets for their products under conditions of economic depression and hyperinflation, the new owners of the enterprises resorted to asset-stripping – selling off plant and machinery, and shifting monetary assets overseas. The fiscal crisis of the Russian state was also deepening sharply, as the state was deprived of the revenues from its newly privatized enterprises, which Sachs had erroneously assumed to be uniformly corrupt, inefficient, and loss-making.[26] Furthermore, the dissolution of the state enterprises was not only leading to rapidly rising unemployment, but was also contributing to a profound social crisis, as the welfare services and sense of community and identity that they had fostered were lost along with the jobs they had provided. Russia, in short, was coming apart at the seams. Incredibly, in the midst of this unravelling crisis, Sachs presented a paper to a Washington think tank in which he celebrated the success of shock therapy and represented Russia as a flourishing market society:

At the start of 1992, less than six months after the fall of communism ... Russia embarked with remarkable dispatch on a program of radical economic reforms. The economic reforms ... have created an enormous opening for ... market-based economic activity. Within a short period of eight months, almost all centralized operations of the command economy ceased; meanwhile, new commercial structures are developing rapidly. Spontaneous market activity is evident, not only in the kiosk boom of Moscow, but also in growing market-based trade within Russia and between Russia and the rest of the world. The benefits of sustained economic reforms are likely to be very great – much greater than is commonly supposed. The old command system was so inefficient and destructive of the quality of economic life that enormous scope exists for increases in average living standards within a few years.[27]

The 'kiosk boom' that Sachs celebrates here was not an expression of entrepreneurial zeal, but a scene of desperation that came to symbolize the social consequences of shock therapy – 'a kind of distressed merchandise bazaar' in which 'people whose incomes and savings had been wiped out ... were now grimly accepting the humiliation of taking to the streets to sell some family heirloom for a pittance'.[28] For Sachs, however, this tragic situation not only appeared as an exhilarating manifestation of spontaneous market activity, but also offered a novel break from his high-powered jet-setting lifestyle, and a chance to pick up some bargains. A *New York Times* portrait of Sachs from this period includes the following description of Sachs enjoying the 'kiosk boom':

It is almost time for Sachs to board a Swissair jet for Zurich (business class). There he will connect for the 6,000-mile flight for Sao Paolo, where he has been invited to spend a few days proselytizing shock therapy ... But before leaving, he squeezes in an hour for cruising the Arbat, a once-quaint shopping street that has become a flea market. Tourists can buy everything here, from trash art to Red Army colonels' caps to a pensioner's family jewels. And the raw bargaining brings a rare glimpse of the material side of Sachs. 'My wife hates it when I shop for bargains' he confides – his gain, she reasons, must come at the expense of sellers who live on far less.[29]

The idle pleasures of Sachs's bargain-hunting, and the fame and fortune of his globe-trotting role, were both underpinned by the social catastrophe of his own policy prescriptions. In contrast to Sachs's celebration of this state of affairs, however, the alarm over the economic and social consequences of shock therapy was palpable on the Russian streets, in the Russian parliament, and even among the global neoliberal policy elite who had previously held Sachs in such esteem. Stanley Fischer – Sachs's mentor and colleague since the 1970s, and now the managing director of the IMF – responded angrily to the blithe optimism of the paper Sachs had delivered in Washington. Fischer criticized 'the paper's implication that whatever happens after markets are freed represents an improvement on the status-quo ante',[30] and asserted that 'price-liberalization in itself is not necessarily a good idea; recent experience in Eastern Europe shows that it invariably results in higher prices, inducing a severe recession'.[31] At the same event, Edmund S. Phelps – a future Nobel laureate and another trailblazing neoclassical economist – drew a comparison between Sachs and Dr Frankenstein that was to prove remarkably prescient:

> Recall the story of the creature artificially constructed by Dr Frankenstein. A brute of a man, he was strong in a number of resources and full of drive; yet he suffered from a flaw in design. His creator did not include an appropriate kind of brain, so he lacked the suitable control mechanisms. The parallel danger in Russia is that the government, in its design of a market economy, is drawing up a defective system that lacks corporate control [and] mechanisms for monetary and fiscal control ... On this subject, Jeffrey Sachs ... has for some time given the impression that well-functioning markets plus competition of private firms – together with an end to soft budgets through fiscal policy and hyperinflationary monetary policy – would be sufficient. A number of economists agree with that view. But in the view of many of us ... it is terribly risky to fail to set up, early on, some control mechanisms ... If these mechanisms do not arise or they are not built in, I am afraid Frankenstein's monster may prove to be an applicable cautionary tale.[32]

Fatefully, Sachs chose to ignore this warning about the dangerous excesses of his shock therapy programme. Instead, he became increasingly assertive in his conviction that shock therapy had not advanced far or fast enough. In December 1992, Gaidar was forced out of office by immense popular opposition to the pain of the reforms. But Sachs stayed on as Yeltsin's advisor, and was rumoured to be personally editing his decrees.[33] Sachs also played an increasingly prominent public role in defending shock therapy, attacking Western governments for failing to support the reforms, and arguing that they had 'no guts, no concept of strategy, and they act, quite frankly, as if they can't tell the difference between a reformer and a Communist'.[34]

This belligerent tone was particularly evident in Sachs's keynote speech to an international conference of neoliberal policymakers in early 1993. The event was organized by John Williamson, the codifier of the 'Washington Consensus' – the set of neoliberal policy prescriptions that had now become standard practice across the world, and that reproduced the formula of shock therapy. As the pioneer of this new paradigm, Sachs was billed as the conference's star attraction. But far from the motivational pep talk that his audience were hoping for, Sachs's speech was aggressive and confrontational, and tinged with a sense of rising desperation. Sachs began by warning his audience: 'We are close to missing a historical opportunity in Russia'.[35] Describing himself as a 'free market ideologue',[36] Sachs implored his fellow neoliberals to recognize that 'the market cannot do it by itself',[37] arguing that increased international aid to the Russian government was a vital ingredient in driving the reform process forward in the face of growing opposition. Addressing public unease in Russia concerning the rapid enrichment of a small group of managers and investors, Sachs defended 'profiteers [as] the active and constructive element in capitalist society',[38] and condemned 'society's antipathy to those who make profits in ... turbulent market conditions'.[39] Celebrating the ruthlessness of free market capitalism, he argued that Russia was 'undergoing the Schumpeterian "creative destruction" of old, moribund industrial sectors'.[40] Despite its brutal social consequences, this process was 'desirable, as it frees resources for other sectors of the economy'.[41] Sachs then asked: 'What does one do in these circumstances?'[42] before answering his own question emphatically. In contrast to the suggestions of 'many or most economists' that the reforms are 'too hard, too dangerous, too costly, too destructive', Sachs insisted that 'flexibility or willingness to compromise' was 'an unforgivable failing', and recommended a 'Machiavellian' approach to driving the reforms forward:[43]

If you are the reform team, I think it is absolutely clear. You lead; you press forward ... The reformers are the people that know what to do – the ones with the energy, ideas, and the capacity to operate, and they are in charge of the key ministries. There is little point in asking where the power 'really' lies. Most likely it lies nowhere in particular; it is there for the taking. And if the reformers act coherently and aggressively, they have the chance to carry these reforms through.[44]

By the end of 1993, the level of aggression required to take power and drive through the reforms had become clear. In September, under pressure from the US government and the IMF to continue with free-market reforms, Yeltsin brought Gaidar back into his government as deputy prime minister responsible for the economy. Gaidar immediately accelerated the shock therapy programme, implementing measures including the abolition of price controls on basic items such as bread. A few days after Gaidar's re-appointment, Poland's elections delivered a strong victory to the former Communist Party in a powerful rejection of Sachs's shock therapy programme there. This emboldened the Russian parliament in its opposition to Gaidar's renewed shock therapy offensive, which contributed to Yeltsin's decision to illegally dissolve parliament on 21 September. Escalating tensions between the Kremlin and parliament eventually concluded on 4 October, when Yeltsin launched a tank assault on the parliament building that finally crushed the opposition. For the next three months Yeltsin's regime operated as an unlimited dictatorship, and used its now unchallenged powers to force through further neoliberal reforms.[45]

The authoritarianism of these actions made a mockery of the Yeltsin administration's pretentions to 'democracy'. Yet Sachs celebrated Yeltsin's actions in precisely these terms, arguing that 'Yeltsin's showdown with the parliament is likely to be viewed in retrospect as the last stand of communism in Russia, and the beginning of open democratic competition.'[46] Noting that voucher prices for newly privatized companies had jumped following the bombardment of parliament, Sachs concluded that this was 'presumably a reflection of the public confidence in the long-term success of the reforms.'[47] Up to this point, the reforms had been 'only incoherently and fitfully put into practice. Now there is a chance to do something.'[48] Unfortunately for Sachs, however, he had misjudged the popular support for shock therapy in Russia, just as he had in Poland. The parliamentary elections in December

1993 demolished Gaidar's party, forcing him out of power once again, and dramatically strengthening the power of the opposition.[49] The new prime minister, Viktor Chernomyrdin, announced that 'the era of market romanticism [was] over',[50] and even the incoming US deputy secretary of state, Strobe Talbott, publically acknowledged that the lesson for Russia might be 'less shock and more therapy'.[51]

By the end of 1993, Russia was mired in political chaos and social disintegration, and its economy was plummeting ever further into a seemingly bottomless abyss. Faced with the onslaught of this accelerating catastrophe, and weakened by the loss of internal and international support for his shock therapy programme, Sachs finally decided to resign. He announced his resignation in January 1994, along with his faithful colleague Anders Aslund, stating that the 'aims and policies' of the new prime minister implied 'the end of fundamental reform'.[52] In response, Chernomyrdin made clear that he had no need for Sachs's services, declaring that the 'mechanical transfer of Western economic methods to Russian soil has done more harm than good'.[53] Sachs's shock therapy experiment in Russia was over, and it had been an unmitigated disaster. His last journey to Russia was in 1995, as the crisis continued to deepen. Since then, he has never returned.[54]

THE TRAUMA OF SHOCK THERAPY

The economic crisis induced by shock therapy in Russia has been described as 'the longest and deepest recession in recorded human history'.[55] From 1991 to 1998, Russia's GDP declined by 43.3 per cent.[56] Industrial production fell by 56 per cent between 1991 and 1996, and capital investment in the Russian economy fell by 78 per cent between 1991 and 1995.[57] By 1998 more than 80 per cent of Russian firms had gone bankrupt, and approximately 70,000 factories had closed, resulting in a massive increase in unemployment.[58] Agricultural production also collapsed. In 1994, total food production was estimated to be about half of the 1986–1990 average,[59] while the breakup of collective farms led to widespread dispossession and the dissolution of the social structures of subsistence.[60] A New York Times article notes that 'Living standards dropped by half in Russia during the three years that Professor Sachs advised President Boris Yeltsin.'[61] The number of people living in poverty increased from 2 million in 1989 to 74 million in 1997.[62] In Naomi Klein's words, 'In the absence of major famine, plague or battle, never have so many lost so much in so short a time.'[63] This loss was not only pecuniary. The fiscal crisis of the state in the context of mass privatization led to the collapse of Russia's previously world-class public health and education systems. Suicides doubled and deaths from alcohol abuse tripled,[64] and the population as a whole lost almost five years of life expectancy between 1991 and 1994 – unprecedented for a modern industrial economy not at war.[65] A major statistical study published in the medical journal *The Lancet* has attributed this dramatic increase in mortality to the explosion of unemployment and destitution resulting from mass privatization. The study concludes with the pointed understatement that 'Although this period was predicted by the shock therapists, who viewed it merely as a time of so-called resource reallocation, it had considerable human costs.'[66] In his analysis of shock therapy in Russia, Michael Burawoy is more forthright: 'Adopting the neoliberal view that there are only two alternatives – failed communism and successful capitalism – Russia's reformers attempted to leap from one to the other, and plunged the economy into the abyss of involution.'[67]

For Jeffrey Sachs, the catastrophic failure of shock therapy in Russia was an utterly unexpected event, which radically violated his understanding of the world. Sachs had been convinced that there was a natural, market-based essence to all societies, and that the removal of the distortions of economic planning would reveal this harmonious social order. Russia was the Real of Capital blasting through this brittle fantasy. As Phelps had warned Sachs in 1992, the decision to privatize and liberalize without first establishing the necessary institutional structures led to Frankenstein's monster going on the rampage. Caught in the midst of this maelstrom, Sachs was suddenly confronted, not with the calm waters of perfectly competitive equilibrium, but with capitalism as a 'monstrous formation whose very "normal" state is permanent dislocation.'[68] Rather than flourishing from the mutually beneficial activities of millions of newly liberated entrepreneurs, 'the market' was being consolidated through the dispossession of the majority of the population and the repression of dissent, revealing the violence inherent in the creation of capitalist property relations.[69] What was emerging was not a vibrant commercial society, but a brutal class system of vertiginous inequality, in which the notorious oligarchs and their cronies were utilizing the power of the state to appropriate natural resources and asset-strip public companies.[70] This accumulation of vast wealth through the seizure of the collective property of the Russian population presented Sachs with an extraordinarily clear demonstration of the antagonistic class relationship that lies at the heart of capitalism.

Russia thus revealed the exploitation, dispossession, and destruction that neoliberalism produces yet disavows. But despite this shatteringly direct encounter with the Real of Capital, Sachs was unable to make sense of the experience, or to draw any lessons from it. This is unsurprising, as the Real is precisely that which the subject is unable to symbolize, and is thus experienced, not as a revelation of a hidden reality, but as the disintegration of 'reality' itself.[71]

In subsequent writings and interviews, Sachs has recalled his experience of the crisis in Russia in terms that convey this traumatic loss of reality, describing it as 'chaos',[72] 'harrowing',[73] a 'whirlwind',[74] and a 'dark panorama'.[75] He has spoken of 'the disarray that comes … a dynamic that things get further and further out of control'.[76] He recalls feeling as if he was 'shouting in the middle of a hurricane',[77] and has described the experience as 'Very painful, and not so easy to reconstitute in the end'.[78] As the crisis was spinning out of control, Sachs began his keynote speech at the 1993 conference on the Washington Consensus by announcing that 'I have entitled my talk "Life in the Economic Emergency Room", or even more aptly, the shock-trauma unit'.[79]

At one particularly peculiar moment in the speech, Sachs compared himself to a party apparatchik in Solzhenitsyn's *Cancer Ward*. He described the character lying in the ward, waiting for news concerning Stalin, the absence of which confirmed Stalin's demise. Sachs suggested that the Western media's lack of attention to Yeltsin made him feel a similar sense of betrayal and loss. Speaking of the apparatchik, Sachs said, 'He knows that a political earthquake has occurred; his political life is finished'.[80] In drawing this strange comparison between himself and the Stalinist, Sachs was clearly afraid that the 'political earthquake' of Russia would destroy his own career. He was right to be concerned. The appalling consequences of shock therapy in Russia not only shattered his neoliberal fantasy, but also destroyed his international reputation as a master of economic reform, transforming him into the embodiment of the worst excesses of free market fundamentalism. In the words of one Russian journalist, Sachs was now 'viewed by scores of millions of Russians … as an emissary either of Satan or the CIA'.[81]

Faced with the magnitude of this disaster, it is unsurprising that Sachs has failed to publically confront the full implications of shock therapy in Russia, and of his own role in its planning and execution. Several interviewers have commented on Sachs's discomfort when confronted on the topic, describing him 'bristling',[82] and 'his baritone voice jumping an octave'.[83] A *Boston Globe* portrait of Sachs from 2001 describes an everyday encounter:

> He arrives on Capitol Hill. Ninety minutes later, after seeing several members of Congress, Sachs heads for the World Bank. He walks into its sleek lobby … 'Hey, aren't you Jeff Sachs?' says a man who sidles up to him. Sachs smiles, and the two exchange pleasantries. It turns out they are both going to the same meeting … and they make small talk. As they head to the elevator, the man turns to Sachs: 'Been to Russia lately?'
>
> 'No,' says Sachs, pausing before pressing the elevator button, a smile frozen on his face. 'Not lately.'[84]

In his subsequent writings on shock therapy, Sachs refuses to accept any responsibility for the crisis in Russia, and even denies that he has ever been a neoliberal, casting himself as a champion of debt relief and a man unafraid to speak truth to power. As Žižek has observed, 'If something gets too traumatic … it shatters the coordinates of our reality, we have to fictionalise it.'[85] This should be borne in mind when considering Sachs's remarkable version of his own history.

THE NEOLIBERAL WHO WASN'T

Prior to his resignation from the Yeltsin administration, Jeffrey Sachs had been proud to emphasize the extensive implementation of shock therapy, and his own centrality to the process, announcing: 'Russia launched a massive programme of "economic shock therapy" at the start of 1992 … I have had the high honor of advising the Russian government on that program since its inception.' Since leaving Russia, however, Sachs has radically altered his story, insisting: 'I do not hold myself accountable [for the consequences of shock therapy in Russia], because the chosen strategy was not what I advised.'[86] Indeed, Sachs has even gone as far as to suggest that, '[d]espite all of the uproar in recent years about "shock therapy" in Russia, knowledgeable observers understand that it simply never occurred'.[87] Sachs supports this extraordinary claim by listing several components of the shock therapy programme that were not implemented to his satisfaction, concerning areas such as budgetary restraint and debt rescheduling:[88]

> 1992 proved to be a dreadful year for Russia's reforms and reformers. After the first moment of price liberalization, the other reforms never really got under way, or they got under way only in a truncated form. Many price controls remained in place. International trade was only partly opened. The currency was only partly convertible. And worst of all, monetary stabilization was not achieved.[89]

Sachs is right that the reform package was not implemented in full. But, as I have shown, by the end of 1992 the three principle elements of shock therapy – price liberalization, trade liberalization, and mass privatization – had already been extensively implemented, and Sachs had triumphantly celebrated their success. Indeed, by many estimates, Russia implemented shock therapy faster and more fully than any of the other post-communist economies.[90] As Peter Reddaway and Dmitri Glinski observe in their definitive account of Russia's transition to capitalism:

> It was inevitable that the abstract scheme of shock therapy would have to accommodate Russian political realities … Under the circumstances, Yeltsin's policies were the closest feasible approximation to Sachs's and the IMF's original intentions, and in this sense the present perverted form of Russian robber-baron 'capitalism' is the unavoidable product of the economic recipes purveyed by the shock therapists.[91]

Sachs accepts that mistakes were made in Russia, but places all the blame on the shoulders of others. In his narration of the crisis, Sachs returns again and again to the refusal of the United States and the IMF to provide the levels of aid and debt relief that he deemed necessary to underpin the reforms. This overlooks his close collaboration with both throughout the process, and the fact that his shock therapy programme was entirely consistent with their own ambitions for Russia's transition.[92] Reddaway and Glinski further suggest that Sachs was aware all along that aid was unlikely to arrive, yet pushed on with shock therapy regardless:

At a Washington meeting in January 1992, Sachs reportedly said, 'Shock therapy has a chance of success, but only if the West provides significant aid, especially for a ruble stabilization fund. Unfortunately, the West is unlikely to mobilize such aid.' Asked how he could, then, advocate a policy that was so dependent on Western aid, he replied testily: 'Whether or not the Russian government succeeds with this strategy, it is the only correct strategy.'[93]

Even if the aid had arrived, it is unlikely to have had a positive impact on the reforms, given the vast corruption and capital flight that characterized the shock therapy period.[94] Nevertheless, Sachs's version of his role in Russia's reforms gives great priority to his campaign for aid and debt relief, while downplaying the more obviously neoliberal elements of his involvement. In a Twitter exchange with a critic who had referred to him as a neoliberal, for example, Sachs responded: 'Neoliberal??? What a joke. I led the debt cancellation campaign. I fought the IMF and Treasury in Russia, and lost.'[95] Similarly, Sachs now claims: 'Many critics later accused me of peddling a ruthless form of free market ideology in Russia. That was not the case. My main activity for two years was an unsuccessful attempt to mobilize international assistance to help cushion the inevitable hardships that would accompany Russia's attempt to overcome the Soviet legacy.'[96] But if he was not 'peddling ruthless free market ideology', then why did he choose to describe himself as a 'free market ideologue' at the time? Why did he promote such rapid and extensive free market reforms when so many people around him – even neoliberals like Fischer and Phelps – were warning him of the dangers of doing so? And why, if his main concern was to 'cushion hardships', did he respond to such warnings by celebrating 'creative destruction' and mocking 'Western calls for allegedly more "humane" policies'?[97]

Rather than explaining such glaring inconsistencies, Sachs simply erases them from his account of events. This is most evident in the case of mass privatization, which was the most radical and catastrophic of the shock therapy reforms in Russia. At the time, of course, Sachs had been a fervent advocate of rapid mass privatization. Towards the end of 1993, for example, he reviewed the privatization process, noting that the reform team 'have much to be pleased about. In just two years, privatization has gone from being an abstract idea of a few radical reformers to an operational fact for tens of thousands of enterprises and millions of workers – and this after seventy-five years of the brutal repression of private property.[98] Yet in his subsequent accounts of his involvement in Russia, Sachs ignores mass privatization completely, passes over it quickly, or criticizes it as the antithesis of his own recommendations at the time. In a 2012 essay, for example, Sachs attacks the Russian government for its management of the privatization process:

> The Government's privatization strategy was to move radically and quickly, so that there would be no reversal in political power and no reversion to a communist regime. The idea was to push the assets out into private hands as quickly as possible, even if corruption and unfairness ensued. This was not my approach, and I disagreed with it.[99]

Compare this to the following account of his role in Russia's privatization programme, which he provided in 1993:

> As early advisors on the privatization process, [we] argued strongly for speed above perfection in the distribution of shares. For the general success of the reforms, which were extremely precarious from the start, it was important to 'make facts', by establishing widespread private property rights. If that meant heavy insider representation, that was a cost that should be accepted.[100]

Comparing the two statements, it is difficult to avoid the conclusion that the government's privatization strategy that Sachs now claims to have disagreed with was precisely the strategy that he was advocating at the time – namely, to establish capitalist property relations as quickly as possible in order to make the reforms irreversible, without worrying about the institutional organization or distributional consequences of the privatization process itself. This should not surprise us, given that Sachs's advice to Poland was consistently animated by the same determination to 'make facts' through rapid privatization.

This brings us to the issue of Sachs's own comparison of his respective roles in Poland and Russia. While denying all responsibility for the crisis in Russia, Sachs is always quick to congratulate himself for the alleged success of shock therapy in Poland.[101] Whereas in Russia, according to Sachs, shock therapy simply did not happen, in Poland he claims that his programme was much more fully implemented. Given Poland's relatively positive economic performance since the

early 1990s, Sachs concludes that 'the most radically reforming countries have indeed gone the furthest in restoring stability and laying the
foundations for rising living standards'.[102] This assessment overlooks
the punishing social costs of the deep recession that shock therapy initially induced in Poland, and paints a very selective picture of Poland's
post-transition economy, which has been incorporated into globalized
circuits of capital on a decidedly dependent basis, and is held together
by strong currents of xenophobia and right-wing populism.[103] It also
completely misrepresents the implementation of shock therapy in
Poland relative to Russia. In Russia, the key elements of shock therapy
were rapidly implemented and broadly adhered to. In Poland, by contrast, popular resistance quickly forced the government onto a more
gradualist path, and shock therapy was abandoned entirely following
the re-election of the renamed Communist Party in 1993. Numerous
experts on the post-communist transition in Eastern Europe and the
former Soviet Union have therefore concluded the precise opposite of
Sachs's analysis: Poland's relative success is due to the fact that it *did
not* implement shock therapy as fully as Russia did.[104]

Crucially, although the reform team in Poland drew up a mass
privatization programme along the lines set out by Sachs, the implementation of this programme was prevented by widespread strike
action organized by the workers' councils that Sachs had been so
determined to 'disenfranchise'.[105] Sachs now denies ever having been
a strong advocate of privatization in Poland, claiming that, for him,
'privatization was the area of greatest uncertainty'.[106] Yet, as we have
seen, mass privatization was Sachs's absolute priority at the time. In
September 1991 Sachs warned that 'opportunistic behaviour by political parties as well as resistance by entrenched interests could begin
to tighten the noose around the privatization process'.[107] Sachs was
proved right, and mass privatization was indeed blocked, thus potentially avoiding a Russian-scale catastrophe.[108]

The erasure of privatization from his biography has been crucial to
Sachs's transformation from Dr Shock into Mr Aid. This was particu-
larly evident during his failed 2012 campaign for the presidency of the
World Bank (see Chapter 6). During the campaign, Sachs promoted
himself as the progressive alternative to the neoliberal old guard at the
Bank, but was repeatedly confronted by his own record as a neolib-
eral shock therapist. After enduring several weeks of sustained abuse,
Sachs finally snapped, posting an uncharacteristically forthright essay

on his website entitled 'What I Did in Russia'. The essay includes many of his standard defences concerning Russia, Bolivia, and Poland. It concludes, however, with a broader discussion of shock therapy. Sachs distinguishes between shock therapy as 'the rapid end of price controls in order to re-establish supply–demand equilibrium'[109] under conditions of economic crisis, and shock therapy as 'the dismantling of all government intervention in the economy in order to establish a "free market" economy', noting: 'This second variant of shock therapy is also sometimes called "neoliberalism"'.[110] Sachs claims: 'I have occasionally been an advocate of the first kind of shock therapy (notably in Bolivia, Poland, Russia, and some other post-communist countries).' Switching to bold type for the only time in the essay, he then insists: '*I have never been an advocate of shock therapy in its second, neoliberal context*'.[111]

Sachs attempts to back up this astonishing claim by setting out 'the essence of shock therapy as I practiced it, not as critics have interpreted my advice after the fact'. His list includes five components: 'an end to most price controls'; currency convertibility; 'an end of the budget deficit'; aid and debt relief; and the 'bolstering of the social safety net'.[112] Amazingly, there is *no mention of privatization*, despite the fact that, as we have seen, Sachs considered privatization to be the core of the reform process, and promoted it with evangelical zeal in Russia, Poland, and elsewhere.[113] Instead, Sachs places emphasis on safety nets, aid, and debt relief, which he claims were 'designed to end shortages ... and provide social protection'.[114]

Now, it is true that these elements were present in Sachs's shock therapy programmes. Indeed, Sachs can claim some success in this regard. In Bolivia he contributed to the establishment of an Emergency Social Fund and helped to convince the IMF to cancel debt repayments, and in Poland he helped to organize debt cancellation and a currency-stabilization fund.[115] However, the political significance of these policies lies less in the policies themselves than in the context of their implementation. Social safety nets and debt relief are entirely consistent with 'neoliberalism' – so long as safety nets are designed to gain legitimacy for neoliberal reforms, and debt relief is made conditional on the implementation of those reforms.[116] For Sachs, this is precisely how these policies were conceived. In the case of social safety nets, Sachs clearly saw them as a means of co-opting resistance to shock therapy, arguing that '[o]ne response to the political challenges to the reforms is to strengthen the social safety net ... so that "losers" in the reform do not feel the sense of panic that can accompany necessary change'.[117] In arguing for debt relief, he repeatedly insisted on making such assistance conditional upon structural reforms.[118] Debt relief in Poland, for example, was not based on humanitarian grounds, but was conceived by Sachs as a disciplinary strategy to ensure the full implementation of shock therapy in general, and privatization in particular:

> The debt relief should ... be phased in over time, perhaps over three years, in order to provide the incentive for Poland to stay the course on reform. Each new tranche of relief would be made contingent on Poland's progress on reforms ... *the most important conditions for debt reduction should be progress on privatization* and maintenance of macroeconomic discipline.[119]

Tellingly, the example that Sachs identifies in his early work as a model for successful debt relief is the international support provided to the Suharto dictatorship in Indonesia in the 1960s, following its military coup against the previous president, Sukarno, the left-leaning founder of the Non-Aligned Movement. Sachs recounts that, in 1966, '[a]fter a civil war, a new military regime under President Suharto began to bring economic order to the country', and was promptly granted three years of debt relief from the government's official creditors.[120] The 'civil war' that Sachs casually mentions was an anti-communist pogrom – one of the worst atrocities of the twentieth century, which is estimated to have involved as many as 1 million deaths.[121] Following the coup, the World Bank provided soft loans, and a group of American economists restructured the Indonesian economy along proto-neoliberal lines.[122] In Sachs's words, 'All of the right things happened in Indonesia: a hyperinflation was ended, a trade liberalization occurred, and economic growth and creditworthiness were restored. And the financial basis of the success was a generous and concessionary treatment of Indonesia's debt.'[123]

This example not only illustrates the distinctly non-humanitarian political functionality of debt relief for Sachs, but also provides further evidence of his tacit support for authoritarian rule and his prioritization of economic principles over democratic concerns. Sachs likes to emphasize his democratic credentials, repeatedly pointing out that his shock therapy experiments in Bolivia, Poland, and Russia were all conducted under democratically elected regimes. Yet while this is true in a formal sense, I have shown that in each of these cases shock therapy was implemented in an authoritarian style by a narrow technocratic elite isolated from democratic pressures. Indeed, in both Poland and Russia, Sachs and the respective reform teams acted in the name of democratic movements in order to impose reforms that were antithetical to the spirit of the movements themselves. Sachs also supported Yeltsin's violent dissolution of parliament, and failed to condemn the 'quasi-fascist' tactics that accompanied shock therapy in Bolivia.

These authoritarian tendencies can be explained, if not excused, by Sachs's understanding of market society as a natural order. From this perspective, the free market appears as the necessary foundation of democratic politics. As Sachs himself has argued, 'the first goal for reformers ... is to get across the message that democracy and capitalism are inextricable.'[124] Just as Milton Friedman collaborated with Pinochet, so Sachs could justify authoritarian strategies in the name of a market society, to the extent that this society was understood as the precondition for democracy itself. But Sachs has become extremely sensitive to comparisons with Friedman. In 'What I Did in Russia', for example, Sachs angrily challenges the persistence of such comparisons: 'There is a long-standing narrative that says that I was out to help impose the "Washington Consensus", a Milton Friedman–style free market economy. This is patently false. Yet it is repeated. It should stop being repeated.'[125]

Forgive me, but just to repeat: Jeffrey Sachs was out to help impose the Washington Consensus, a Milton Friedman–style free market economy. Indeed, it would be difficult to formulate a more concise description of a man who once described himself as a 'free market ideologue' at a conference organized by the founder of the Washington Consensus, and who has expressed his admiration of Milton Friedman in the following exultant tones: 'Milton Friedman had so much right, it's fabulous ... I think Milton Friedman has gotten, and deserves, fabulous credit for continuing to hammer home the incredible power and efficiency of markets in places where they belong, which is most of the places of economic exchange.'[126]

If this isn't enough to demonstrate his affinity with Friedman, free markets, and the Washington Consensus, we need only remind ourselves of the stubborn historical fact that Sachs has expended immense time and effort, and taken extraordinary risks with millions of human lives, in order to restructure entire economies in accordance with Washington Consensus principles derived from the free market theories of Milton Friedman.[127] In Bolivia, Poland, Russia, and elsewhere, Sachs's overriding objective was the removal of the institutional structures of the socialist or developmental state, in order to uncover the supposedly natural order of a market society, based on 'the Chicago mentality that spontaneously organizing social and market forces will somehow automatically fill the vacuums created by retrenched state institutions and disorganized collective spaces'.[128] So, just to be absolutely clear about this, the 'Milton Friedman–style free market economy' that Sachs now disavows is precisely what he sought to impose through shock therapy.

By taking issue with Sachs's account of his role in shock therapy, I do not mean to imply that he is being deliberately dishonest about his own past. Rather, I am suggesting that he is simply unable to confront the catastrophic failure of shock therapy in Russia. It is through such acts of repression that 'subjects maintain themselves, however precariously, in reality: namely, at the cost of *not seeing* something'.[129] Sachs now denies all responsibility for the crisis, distancing himself from shock therapy, rejecting any association with neoliberalism, the Washington Consensus, and Milton Friedman, and erasing privatization from his account of his own past. But that which is repressed is not escaped, and the Real of Capital that Sachs unleashed in Russia has pursued him into the present. Like Doctor Frankenstein, Sachs's entire subsequent career can be understood as a series of increasingly desperate and ultimately futile attempts to escape this monster of his own creation.[130]

3 THE MAGNIFICENT MR AID

Following his resignation from the Yeltsin administration in January 1994, it would have been perfectly understandable if Jeffrey Sachs had abandoned his economic theories, changed his career, or even adopted a different identity. After all, he had just played a significant role in one of the greatest economic catastrophes of modern history. As we shall see, there is a sense in which Sachs did eventually do all these things, dramatically amending his theoretical approach, shifting his specialism from macroeconomics to development, and transforming himself from Dr Shock into Mr Aid. Initially, however, he attempted to reaffirm his neoliberal fantasy and carry on as normal, publishing a series of articles celebrating the end of the Cold War and the triumph of global capitalism. A 'capitalist revolution' had heralded the consolidation of 'a global capitalist world system, with profound benefits for both the rich and the poor countries'.[1] 'Never before', Sachs happily declared, 'has the world had the opportunity to adopt an international system ... in which ... all have the chance to benefit from an open, market-based global economy'.[2] We had finally arrived at the best of all possible worlds, and Jeffrey Sachs could not overemphasize how delighted he was to be there. It was as if the ongoing crisis in Russia had never happened. Everything was *fine*.

Sachs's writings from this time presented an account of capitalism from which all traces of contradiction had been meticulously erased. In various articles, Sachs quoted the famous passage from *The Communist Manifesto* that acknowledges the capacity of 'the bourgeoisie [to] compel all nations, on pain of extinction, to adopt the bourgeois mode of production'.[3] Sachs congratulated Marx and Engels for having 'surmised, correctly, that capitalism would eventually spread to the entire world, based on the superiority of its economic productivity.'[4] Lest this sarcasm be taken as a serious compliment, however, he hastily dismissed the labour theory of value, according to which capitalist profits originate in exploitation. According to Sachs, 'Marx's most deadly legacy, indeed, was the interpretation that gaps in income between rich and poor are caused by exploitation rather than differences in productivity. This Marxist attack on wealth as ill-gotten exploitation fuelled most anti-capitalist ideologies of the twentieth century.'[5]

Having disposed of the Marxist theory of exploitation, Sachs attacked Keynesian crisis theory, arguing that the Great Depression was a 'one-time fluke of grotesque proportions,'[6] rather than crisis being 'an intrinsic feature of industrial capitalism.'[7] Keynes's misdiagnosis of capitalism had led him to 'lose faith in free trade,'[8] and to mistakenly believe that 'capitalism was inherently unstable and needed the steadying rudder of the state.'[9] Adopting a stringently neoliberal line, Sachs argued that the application of Keynesian theory had led to 'debilitating' experiments with import-substitution industrialization, and 'even darker' mistakes concerning 'the relative merits of socialism versus capitalist market organization.'[10] According to Sachs, these misguided experiments had failed to grasp that 'open trade leads to convergent rates of growth', and that the opening of markets would therefore lead to an equalization of wealth between rich and poor nations.[11]

There was something desperate in Sachs's determination to present an image of capitalism from which all contradictions had been erased – no exploitation, no economic crises, even the promise of a future equality of nations. It was as if his euphoric celebrations of the triumph of global capitalism were driven not only by a desire to justify a political project, but by a deeper need to repress the reality of capitalism that had confronted him in Russia. Meanwhile, however, events were taking a dramatic turn for the worse, both in Russia and in the global economy as a whole. In 1995 and 1996, Yeltsin's notoriously corrupt loans-for-shares scheme consolidated capitalist class relations in Russia by facilitating the transfer of Russia's natural resources from the state to the now dominant 'oligarchs'. In 1997, Andrei Shleifer, who had worked closely with Sachs on Russia's shock therapy package, was discovered by the US government to have been making personal investments in newly privatized Russian assets while simultaneously advising the Yeltsin administration on its privatization programme. His deputy, Jonathan Hay, was also involved in the scam. Both Shleifer and Hay were Sachs's colleagues in the Harvard economics department at this time, and, as director of the Harvard Institute for International Development, Sachs was technically their boss. After a seven-year investigation, Shleifer and Hay were fined for self-dealing. Harvard was found to be in breach of its USAID contract, and was forced to pay a settlement of US$26.5 million – the largest in the university's history.[12] No connection was ever established between Sachs and these activities, and he never accepted any responsibility for the actions of his staff. But the incident once again confronted Sachs with the catastrophe of shock therapy in Russia and the sordid realities of capitalist profiteering. In 1999, in the midst of the scandal, Sachs resigned from the Institute.[13]

Meanwhile, instead of the harmonious convergence of the wealth of nations that Sachs had predicted, it was becoming increasingly clear that the brave new world of global capitalism was one of intensified inequality, growing social unrest, and extreme financial volatility. The poverty and dispossession resulting from neoliberal reforms had motivated protests and riots across the so-called 'developing' world, and social movements were organizing against the Structural Adjustment Programmes of the World Bank and the IMF. Furthermore, a whirlwind of financial crises was sweeping around the world, including Mexico in 1995, East Asia in 1997, and Brazil and Russia in 1998. As in Russia, but now on a global scale, Sachs was once again confronted with the uncomfortable fact that 'the real world of capitalist development does not conform to the harmonious social relations predicted by neoclassical thought'.[14] His determined exclusion of the Real of Capital from his symbolic universe was no longer working. A new approach was required.

FROM SHOCK THERAPY TO CLINICAL ECONOMICS

During the shock therapy era, Sachs cast himself as a doctor in the 'economic emergency room',[15] and justified his extreme actions and their brutal social consequences by arguing that 'when a guy comes into the emergency room and his heart's stopped, you just rip open the sternum and you don't worry about the scars that you leave'.[16] Since his abandonment of Russia, Sachs has maintained this medical fantasy, but has transformed his imaginary role from surgeon to clinician. His economic writings have sought to represent the internal contradictions of capitalism as external pathologies of bad geography, poor technology, and debilitating disease. Appropriately enough, Sachs has come to conceptualize this approach as 'clinical economics'.[17] Sachs describes how multiple 'economic pathologies ... outside the traditional ken of economic practice'[18] can contribute to the crisis of a healthy economic system, provoking 'a downward spiral of catastrophe'.[19] As with shock therapy, clinical economics thus conceptualizes capitalism not as a social order to be constructed, but as a natural body to be restored to health. The changes and continuities between shock therapy and clinical economics have underpinned Sachs's transformation from Dr Shock into Mr Aid, and have been central to his reincorporation into elite networks of neoliberal policymaking.[20]

In the mid 1990s, Sachs began to develop a theory of economic geography, through which he sought to explain the persistence of international inequality by appealing to geographical and climatic factors. Uneven development, Sachs argued, is primarily due to relative distance from navigable coastlines, and to whether a given country has a tropical or temperate climate.[21] This argument absolved neoliberalism of responsibility for intensified inequalities, and allowed Sachs to explain away the negative social consequences of his shock therapy experiments by appeal to geographical factors. In arguing that landlocked countries are condemned to poverty, for example, Sachs repeatedly cited the examples of Bolivia and Mongolia, both of which had seen dramatic increases in poverty and inequality following the implementation of his shock therapy programmes.[22] The same theory also gave Sachs an angle from which to respond to uncomfortable comparisons between the failure of shock therapy in Russia and the relative success of China's gradualist transition. Sachs now argued that China's success was due not to the superiority of its gradualist approach, but to the fact that 'China had a large navigable coastline that supported its export-led growth, whereas the Soviet Union ... did not have the benefit of large coastlines and the resulting low-cost access to international trade'.[23] The ideological utility of this argument has been noted by the geographer David Harvey:

The thesis that lack of access to navigable water was the problem for Russia is convenient, since Sachs played a very important role in administering the market-based 'shock therapy' to the former Soviet

Union that had such disastrous economic and social consequences in the early 1990s. (We could conclude from this that the main advantage in China's case was that Sachs had no influence over policy there.)[24]

In the late 1990s, Sachs began to combine this geographical theory of inequality with a historical account of economic development that draws heavily on Walt Rostow's *Stages of Growth*, which was published in 1960 with the telling subtitle *A Non-Communist Manifesto*.[25] Rostow denied that the wealth of Western nations was based on the exploitation of the Third World, and insisted that all nations were destined to follow the West in a smooth assent to modernity, as long as they followed its instructions on free markets and the rejection of socialism. Sachs reframes Rostow's stages of growth as a 'ladder of development',[26] which is to be ascended through a combination of neoliberal economic policy and technological advance. He claims that 'the world's poorest live the way that virtually all of humanity lived before the onset of the scientific and industrial revolutions of the nineteenth century'.[27] To develop, they must proceed 'through four basic stages, each stage representing a higher level of income and development than the preceding one. The progression is from a subsistence economy, to a commercial economy, to an emerging market economy, to a technology-based economy'.[28] To reach the first rung of the development ladder, 'subsistence economies' must shift into export-oriented cash-crop production, and adopt GM technologies to increase productivity.[29] To reach the next rung, 'commercial economies' should encourage foreign direct investment and technology transfer by establishing 'labour-intensive assembly operations in export-processing zones'.[30] And so on.

Sachs promises that, by following this path, all countries will eventually arrive at 'a technology-based economy [and] a sophisticated information-based society'.[31] Yet this narrative of linear progress driven by free markets and technological modernization overlooks numerous complications. Sachs fails to consider the devastating impact of free trade and cash-crop production on food security and peasant livelihoods. He dismisses the social and environmental dangers associated with genetically modified crops. And he ignores the appalling levels of exploitation characteristic of export processing zones, including low wages, long working hours, dangerous working conditions, the banning of trade unions, and the sexual harassment of workers. The understanding of development as a temporal scale of ascending stages of civilization also abstracts from the causal relationship between the enrichment of the global North and the impoverishment of the global South, representing capitalist development as a natural and inevitable process, and reproducing colonial representations of non-Western societies as primitive and inferior.

Despite the theoretical weakness of Sachs's economic work from this period, it had the ideological appeal of explaining poverty and inequality in terms of geographical and technological factors, thereby absolving neoliberalism of any causal role in these problems. On this basis, Sachs was welcomed back into the neoliberal policy elite, from which he had been expelled following the failure of shock therapy in Russia. In 1998 Sachs was invited to participate in the Annual World Bank Conference on Development Economics, which was held in the midst of a profound crisis of the neoliberal project. In his opening address, the chief economist of the Bank, Joseph Stiglitz, warned that the East Asian financial crisis and other events had led to 'increasing doubts over the Washington Consensus, or the "neoliberal model of development"'.[32] World Bank president James Wolfensohn was also concerned by this threat to the free market, suggesting that the Washington Consensus needed to be 'expanded and broadened ... beyond macroeconomic concerns' to include issues such as education, health, and geography.[33] The conference was a key moment in the formation of what became known as the 'Post-Washington Consensus'. In this new paradigm, the Washington Consensus of standard neoliberal reforms was not abandoned, but was extended and deepened, evolving from the free market fundamentalism of shock therapy towards an increasingly comprehensive form of social engineering:

> The neoliberal 'alternative' did not amount to a full service blueprint for a new political–economic order. The initial applications of shock therapy, it may be fair to say, had been meticulously planned, but when the patient refused to respond spontaneously to subsequent market stimuli, further rounds of treatment would be required ... Thus, in a progressively deeper and ever-more contradictory sense, neoliberalism gradually morphed into a dynamic form of government practice.[34]

Sachs was in the right place at the right time, and from this point onwards he came to play a key role in the formulation, implementation, and legitimation of the Post-Washington Consensus. In this regard, his work on the economics of health has been particularly influential. It is unsurprising that health should trouble Sachs. After all, the erosion of public health provision has been one of the most socially destructive legacies of neoliberalism in the 'developing' world. More specifically, Sachs's own shock therapy experiments were in many cases followed by serious declines in health indicators, particularly among the poorest sectors of society. In Bolivia, for example, cases of malnutrition and tuberculosis increased following the implementation of shock therapy.[35] In Mongolia, shock therapy included deep cuts to the public health budget, which have been blamed for a marked increase in maternal mortality.[36] And the Russian population lost nearly five years of life expectancy during the period that Sachs was operating there.[37] The uncomfortable truth was that 'the social protections afforded by the old socialist [regimes] provided households and individuals far more health, economic, and social security than are now afforded under the new capitalist system',[38] and Sachs himself had played a key role in engineering this transition.

Rather than confronting this truth, Sachs has disavowed it by reversing the causal relation between poverty and disease. Instead of identifying poverty as the primary cause of ill health, as is clearly indicated by the health consequences of his own shock therapy experiments, Sachs has reconceptualized ill health as the primary cause of poverty. According to Sachs, it is not free market reforms that have had a negative impact on health, but ill health that prevents markets from functioning, by lowering levels of worker productivity and human capital, discouraging foreign direct investment, and limiting economic growth.[39] Sachs calculates, for example, that 'on a "disabled day"', a worker in Côte d'Ivoire can be expected to be over 10 per cent less productive, and a worker in Ghana can be expected to be 11.7 per cent less productive than if he or she were in good health.'[40] He even reduces the death of a child to these economistic terms, arguing that 'under conditions of high child mortality, each child who dies before the fifth birthday represents an average loss of 1,300–1,800 hours of parental work time … In order to ensure three children who survive to age five … parents would have to "waste" 800–3,000 hours on children who would not survive.'[41] Such children are not only a waste of their parents' labour time, according to Sachs, but also of their financial resources:

Childhood diseases like malaria prevent a large proportion of birth cohorts from maturing to economically productive age ... Therefore, it is possible that where childhood mortality rates are very high, countries may become caught in a demographic trap, with high fertility rates leading to a greater demand for household and community resources, large proportions of which are 'wasted' on children who do not survive to economically productive age.[42]

This description of children as 'birth cohorts' whose lives are valued in terms of their 'economic productivity' reflects the neoliberal reduction of human beings to abstract factors of production. In contrast to his shock therapy period, when Sachs viewed 'the worker' as a potentially disruptive political agent, the figure of the worker is now dissolved into a passive bundle of human capital to be upgraded in the name of increased productivity. Sachs has become fixated on diseases like Aids and malaria, which he sees not only as threats to worker productivity but also as the primary causes of poverty itself. Overlooking the close association of free market reforms with the collapse of public health systems and the increase in poverty, Sachs claims that it is Aids that is 'accomplishing a sweeping undoing of past human development advances'.[43] Similarly, Sachs argues that the 'impact of malaria on economic growth rates through the mechanism of depressing the rate of human capital accumulation could be considerable,'[44] and claims that the evidence points to 'a causation from malaria to poverty, and not vice-versa'.[45] Yet, as Sachs himself admits, malaria has been successfully eradicated in wealthier countries such as Italy, Greece, Spain and the United States,[46] which suggests that it is precisely the poverty of sub-Saharan Africa that explains the continued prevalence of malaria there. Furthermore, if the value of health is to be judged strictly in terms of its economic impact, then it follows that limited resources should be focused on improving the health of those who will deliver the highest economic return, to the exclusion of other, less economically productive sectors of the population. This, in fact, is precisely Sachs's position: 'The economic evidence ... suggests that high priority targets should include port cities, potential tourist destinations, mining operations and high-value-added agricultural settings. Even when disease incidence is lower in such settings than in other places, the economic benefits of disease control in these locations (through increased tourism, trade and investment) could be enormous.'[47]

Here Sachs provides another stark example of the one-dimensional logic of neoliberalism, according to which investments in health should be concentrated on those places that promise the greatest 'economic benefits', *even if more people are suffering and dying elsewhere.* The improvement of health services is a good thing, of course, regardless of its motivations and limitations. The problem is that Sachs's economistic understanding of human health functions to cancel out more progressive and egalitarian alternatives. In 2000, Sachs was appointed as chair of the World Health Organization's Commission on Macroeconomics and Health. In marked contrast to the WHO's previous conceptualization of health as a universal human right, the Commission's report was built around Sachs's reduction of health to a factor in labour productivity, and set out a policy framework that was entirely consistent with neoliberal fundamentals. 'Public spending should be better targeted to the poor', with private health provision encouraged in most other cases.[48] Governments and international institutions should encourage the pharmaceutical industry to supply low-income countries with essential medicines at 'the lowest viable commercial price',[49] but must 'ensure that increased access for the poor does not undermine the stimulus to future innovation that derives from the system of intellectual property rights'.[50] The report even justified improved healthcare for the poor on the basis of its benefits for the rich, arguing that it would result in 'spillovers to wealthier members of society',[51] presumably in the form of the added profits to be extracted from an increasingly productive workforce. Nowhere, needless to say, was there any recognition of the impressive levels of healthcare achieved with very limited resources in Cuba, Kerala, or other places in which human wellbeing is not subordinated to capital accumulation.[52]

Under Sachs's guidance, the Commission on Macroeconomics and Health functioned to integrate health into neoliberal development policy, by reconceptualizing it not as an end in itself, or as one of the foremost goals of development, but as a factor of human capital to be mobilized in the service of improved productivity. The Commission's report was influential in changing the nature of the debate in this regard, and played a key role in the evolution of the Post-Washington Consensus. Sachs recalls that the report 'was launched with the kind of pizzazz that it deserved, with ... the CEO of Merck and Bono as enthusiastic supporters'.[53] The report was thus a major step in Sachs's public rehabilitation, and the warm words and back-slapping from rock stars and CEOs must have helped him to forget his association with the health disasters of shock therapy.

FROM DR SHOCK TO MR AID

The Commission on Macroeconomics and Health called for a dramatic expansion of overseas development assistance to finance its recommendations, and Sachs's name began to be associated with the promotion of international aid. Specifically, the report demanded increased aid for sub-Saharan Africa, as the region of the world in which malaria, HIV/Aids and tuberculosis were most prevalent. More than any other factor, it is Sachs's work on Africa that has facilitated his personal transformation from Dr Shock into Mr Aid. Sachs first visited sub-Saharan Africa in 1995, just one year after his abandonment of Russia. 'I felt an increasing urgency to understand the development challenges in the world's most distressed region', he recalls. 'What I found was a crisis much more severe than I had expected ... Beyond anything I had experienced or could imagine, disease and death became the constant motif of my visits to Africa.'[54] Since then, Africa has changed his life, allowing Sachs to distance himself from the failure of shock therapy in Russia, and to reinvent himself as the saviour of the continent.

When Sachs speaks about 'Africa', he almost always means sub-Saharan Africa. His use of the term is therefore geographically inaccurate at best. More problematic, however, are Sachs's persistently negative representations of the continent. Sachs depicts Africa as a 'horrific catastrophe',[55] 'collapsing from social and economic disorder',[56] and plagued by 'the omnipresence of disease and death'.[57] Africa is described as the land of 'the voiceless dying',[58] a 'place of unrelieved crisis',[59] in which 'people have nothing and are not even successful enough to stay alive'.[60] Sub-Saharan Africa is of course confronted with very serious socio-economic problems. But it is also as vibrant, thriving and diverse as any other space of human sociality. Sachs's representation of the continent as a void of negativity defined by deprivation and disease is uncomfortably reminiscent of colonial discourses about the 'heart of darkness', in which Africa was constructed as a space of barbarism and lack, against which the West defined its own 'enlightenment' and justified the supposedly 'civilizing mission' of colonialism.

For Sachs, however, 'Africa' seems to function less as a description of an empirical reality than as a cipher standing for something else. Writing in 1994, only months after leaving Russia, Sachs contrasted Russia's prospects to those of Africa, arguing: 'If its reforms are given a chance, Russia will prove not merely viable economically, but highly promising. The same cannot be said of ... Africa, where misrule, disease, and civil strife have left hundreds of millions untouched by the forces of global economic integration.'[61] As Russia's crisis deepened, and international resistance to neoliberalism increased, Sachs became fixated on the African continent, which came to embody all the problems that he refused to see elsewhere. In contrast to the supposedly harmonious convergence of the rest of the global economy, 'Africa' was framed as the space of exception, the developmental failures of which were due not to its subordinate incorporation into global capitalism, but to its *exclusion* from globalization. According to Sachs, this exclusion was due to Africa's unique 'triple whammy' of economic pathologies discussed in the previous section: poor geography, backward technology, and a high disease burden.[62]

This representation was profoundly misleading. Sub-Saharan Africa had in fact been at the forefront of neoliberal reforms from the mid 1980s onwards, and its reformers had even taken inspiration from Sachs's own shock therapy approach.[63] The crisis that Sachs confronted on his arrival in the continent was largely a consequence of these reforms – including privatization, trade liberalization, macroeconomic austerity, and the removal of subsidies and price controls.[64] In the words of one expert on African development:

> From the early 1980s, Africa was subjected to a pervasive and concentrated project of economic liberalisation ... During the 1980s, average incomes in sub-Saharan Africa had fallen by about 20 percent, leaving the average African poorer than she was in 1970 ... Between 1981 and 2001, the number of poor people (people below the international poverty line) doubled, reaching 313 million.[65]

The economic crisis in sub-Saharan Africa was thus due not to its exclusion from globalization, as Sachs has suggested, but to the specifically neoliberal manner in which the region had been forcibly integrated into the global economy.

By representing Africa as an abject space beyond the reach of globalization, Sachs was able to justify a solution to African poverty based on the very same policies that had contributed to the crisis. In his early work on Africa, Sachs praised 'structural adjustment, which rightly focused on markets [and] has produced some real gains',[66] and argued for the continuation of an orthodox neoliberal agenda including 'openness to trade, domestic market liberalization, private rather than state ownership [and] protection of private property rights'.[67] Sachs also demanded additional measures, such as the scrapping of 'food and housing subsidies for urban workers',[68] 'flexibility in hiring and dismissing workers, [and] low (or zero) taxation on multinational income'.[69] He even insisted: 'My concern is not that there are too many sweatshops [in Africa], but that there are too few.'[70]

Sachs's early policy advice for Africa was therefore entirely consistent with his shock therapy prescriptions for other parts of the world. His focus on the continent intensified towards the end of the millennium, and was particularly influenced by his involvement in the Jubilee 2000 drop-the-debt campaign and his engagement with the so-called anti-globalization movement. Jubilee 2000 sought to cancel the national debt of several African nations. For Sachs, the campaign had obvious resonances with his unsuccessful demands for aid and debt relief for Russia, and he became an enthusiastic participant. Sachs likes to emphasize his involvement in Jubilee 2000 as evidence of his 'progressive' credentials, and nostalgically recalls 'working closely with Bono' in its promotion to the Clinton administration.[71] Like his advocacy of debt relief in the shock therapy era, however, Sachs's endorsement of Jubilee 2000 remained consistent with neoliberal fundamentals. Debt forgiveness was not to be unconditional, but was to be conducted under the auspices of the IMF's Heavily Indebted Poor Countries (HIPC) Initiative, which made debt-forgiveness conditional on the consolidation of neoliberal reforms.[72]

Sachs enjoyed the high-level celebrity-driven lobbying of Jubilee 2000, but his confrontation with the anti-globalization movement was much less pleasurable. In 1999 Sachs was participating in a conference on global health in Seattle, which Bill Gates had organized to coincide with the ministerial conference of the World Trade Organization.[73] Suddenly, this orderly world of billionaire philanthropy and elite policymaking was overturned by massive street protests involving unions, NGOs, and activist groups, demanding an end to the global neoliberal agenda of free trade, privatization, and corporate power. The demonstrators clashed with riot police in the streets, attacked the headquarters of multinational corporations, and succeeded in shutting the WTO conference down. This event was profoundly troubling for Sachs. He recalls walking through the streets of Seattle, and encountering 'lots of different grievances … as well as hooligans'. He found the scene 'disturbing', and realized that 'you would not see these demonstrations if all were right with the world'.[74] His instinct, however, was not to question globalization, but to mock the politics of the protesters, and to emphasize his ideological alignment with the agenda of corporate capital:

> As I crossed Seattle's downtown streets filled with protesters of every variety – antiwar, antitrade, and especially anticorporate – I whispered to my walking companion, Bill Gates, Sr, the father of Microsoft founder Bill Gates, Jr, and president of the Gates Foundation, that it was probably just as well that he was not recognized by the crowds! The profound irony, of course, is that the Gates Foundation is the world's leading foundation for promoting public health in poor countries, yet to the anti-globalization movement, multinational companies are part of the problem, not the solution.[75]

There are actually two 'profound ironies' in this little vignette, but Sachs misses both of them. In the first place, the irony in the relationship between corporate wealth and philanthropy is not the anti-globalization movement's failure to acknowledge the charitable acts of the Gates Foundation, but rather the notion that the vast profits of multinational capital are the solution to the poverty on which they are premised. An even greater irony, however, is that Sachs thought Bill Gates' father was in danger on the streets of Seattle, whereas if anyone should have feared being identified by the anti-globalization movement, it was Jeffrey Sachs himself.

Despite his reputation as the architect of shock therapy and a key agent of neoliberal globalization, Sachs chose to respond to the anti-globalization movement by posing as the representative of the movement's true concerns, which he sought to reframe in terms of the salvation of Africa. This audacious strategy was most clearly and comprehensively expressed in 2005, in his bestselling anti-poverty manifesto, *The End of Poverty*, which remains his most influential work. In the book, Sachs presents his solution to extreme poverty as a radical challenge to structural adjustment, the Washington Consensus, and the economic, political, and moral failings of the contemporary world order. Yet, despite being framed in these terms, *The End of Poverty* does not endorse the anti-globalization movement's critique of free market capitalism. On the contrary, Sachs rejects what he describes as its 'knee-jerk antipathy to capitalism', arguing that the movement 'is too pessimistic about the possibility of capitalism with a human face'.[76] According to Sachs, the anti-globalization movement should stop attacking free trade and multinational corporations, and should mobilize 'its vast commitment and moral force into a pro-globalization movement on behalf of a globalization that addresses the needs of the poorest of the poor'.[77]

In fact, Sachs's prescriptions in *The End of Poverty* seem designed to legitimize the system of global free market capitalism that the anti-globalization movement was opposing. Despite calling his book *The End of Poverty*, Sachs insists that his objective is 'to end extreme poverty, not to end all poverty, and still less to equalize world incomes or to close the gap between the rich and the poor'.[78] His concern with poverty-alleviation is therefore restricted to 'the poorest of the poor', by which he means the 1 billion poorest members of the global population – those living on less than US$1 a day. Despite the planetary dispersion of this 'bottom billion', Sachs effectively reduces it to 'Africa', arguing that 'Africa is as hungry as can be because you have hundreds of millions of impoverished people who are too poor to be part of any market'.[79] 'Extreme poverty', Sachs claims, 'is not caused by exploitation ... It is caused by factors such as isolation, drought, disease, poor infrastructure, and bad governance'.[80] Africa's uniquely disadvantageous conditions in these regards 'create the worst poverty trap in the world', from which Africa is unable to reach the bottom rung of 'the ladder of development'.[81]

On the basis of this analysis, Sachs proposes a new 'Marshall Plan', based on an 'African Green Revolution', which will reproduce the alleged successes of the Green Revolutions in Mexico and India, in which large-scale capital-intensive agriculture replaced traditional subsistence farming. Agricultural production will be massively increased, transport infrastructure will be improved, and the continued implementation of 'traditional market reforms' will guarantee access to export markets.[82] All of this will be funded by conditional debt relief and a massive time-bound infusion of international aid, after which 'Africa [will] lift itself up by its bootstraps',[83] and will begin to ascend the ladder of development unaided.

Sachs claims that, if his agenda is followed, extreme poverty can be ended by 2025. There are several reasons for treating this claim with the greatest scepticism. First, Sachs's approach maintains an unquestioning faith in market mechanisms and denies the exploitative nature of free market capitalism, despite the increases in poverty and inequality resulting from his previous experiments with market-based reforms. Second, his definition of 'extreme poverty' implies that wage labourers earning anything over US$1 a day are not 'extremely poor', while stigmatizing subsistence-based societies by defining well-being in purely monetary terms. Third, his endorsement of international aid is conditional upon the adoption of free market reforms, including trade liberalization and export-led development, and overlooks the well-established role of aid in stabilizing corrupt and authoritarian regimes.[84] Fourth, his unqualified affirmation of the Green Revolution ignores its destruction of subsistence livelihoods, its intensification of inequalities, its depletion of soils, its creation of debt-dependency, and its failure to end rural poverty in either Mexico or India.[85] Fifth, his conceptualization of 'Africa' as a poverty trap languishing beneath the ladder of development reproduces colonial representations of the continent, stripping Africans of political agency and suggesting that Africa's salvation depends on the charity of the West.

In short, *The End of Poverty* replaces the universalizing and potentially revolutionary politics of the anti-globalization movement with a reactionary ethic of charity and salvation, which both presupposes and affirms the existing distribution of global wealth and power. Sachs summarizes the political implications of this approach in unambiguous terms: 'What a deal the poor world is offering the rich world. The poorest of the poor are saying "We buy into your system. You can keep your wealth. We don't call for a revolution. We just want a little help to stay alive" … That is all the poor are asking for in the world.'[86]

As these words make clear, the political function of Sachs's anti-poverty agenda is not to challenge the global status quo but to reinforce it by depoliticizing inequality and reducing development to the administration of survival. Indeed, in contrast to his post-Russia eulogies to the triumph of global capitalism, the word 'capitalism' is suddenly all but erased from Sachs's lexicon, and appears only twice in the 368 pages of *The End of Poverty*. Capitalism thus disappears as a potential object of critique, becoming the quasi-natural horizon within which any attempt at poverty-alleviation must unquestionably take place. The end of poverty ceases to be the terrain of political struggle, and is reduced to an ethical injunction in which 'our generation' is called upon to 'heal the world'.[87]

This discourse was well received by the key institutions of global capitalism, which were seeking to re-legitimize neoliberalism in the context of the anti-globalization movement. In 2002, the United Nations secretary general, Kofi Annan, appointed Sachs as his special advisor on the Millennium Development Goals and as chair of the Millennium Project, a 250-strong taskforce charged with producing a global strategy for fulfilling the Goals by their deadline of 2015. In the same year, Sachs was lured from Harvard to head the Earth Institute at Columbia University, with over 850 academic staff, an annual budget of US$87 million, and a focus on sustainable development solutions.[88] Sachs was also embraced by financial speculators and transnational corporations, whose wealth and privilege had been called into question by the anti-globalization movement. In setting out his anti-poverty agenda, Sachs has consistently defended the interests of the global capitalist elite, denying that 'the rich have gotten rich because the poor have gotten poor',[89] and insisting that 'the overriding job of business is to make money for the owners, but that in no way precludes an active role for business in solving nonmarket problems'.[90] In a remarkable inversion of the relationship between poverty and wealth, Sachs even claims that it is the dramatic increase in inequality under neoliberalism that has made the end of poverty possible: 'The rich world today is so vastly rich. An effort to end extreme poverty that would have seemed out of reach even a generation or two ago is now well within reach because the costs are now a small fraction of the vastly expanded income of the rich world'.[91]

This argument provided the capitalist class with a moral platform from which to present themselves as the solution to the very same problems that the anti-globalization movement had been blaming them for. As if in recognition of this service, Sachs was invited to form close working relationships with some of the world's wealthiest capitalists, including Bill Gates and George Soros, as well as corporations such as Merck, Monsanto, and Novartis. Sachs became particularly involved with pharmaceutical corporations, and worked closely with them in his campaign to provide anti-retroviral drugs to those who could not afford them. This is one Sachs's favourite stories to tell about himself, and he especially likes to emphasize his role in the establishment of the Global Fund for Aids, Malaria, and Tuberculosis, which was launched in 2001.[92] The Global Fund, however, is a distinctly neoliberal institution, which limits its development solutions to those consistent with corporate power. It is the world's largest public–private partnership, involving major pharmaceutical corporations, philanthropists like Bill Gates, Bono's Product Red foundation, and multilateral institutions including the World Bank. Though it has had considerable success in the provision of anti-retroviral drugs and other medicines, the Global Fund has been criticized for its narrow focus on specific diseases, its exclusion of 'developing' country governments from its decision-making processes, and its reinforcement of the intellectual property regime of multinational capital.[93] Throughout his work on HIV/Aids, Sachs has argued in favour of the intellectual property rights of multinational corporations in the provision of anti-retroviral drugs, despite the devastating consequences that this has had for thousands of the world's poorest people. As one prominent Aids activist has observed, 'The more [Sachs] hangs out with the Merck guys, the more he's focused on helping Merck. It's bizarre. It's simply not in the poor's interest to have the high levels of intellectual property. He should be horsewhipped for saying that.'[94]

As in the days of shock therapy, however, such critical voices were difficult for Sachs to hear now that he had been welcomed back into the corridors of global power. If anything, his star had now risen even higher than in those heady times. Sachs was invited to meet with Pope John Paul II and other religious and political leaders, who were eager to seek his counsel in his capacity as the self-appointed spokesman of the poor. He became close friends with Bono, and made high-profile journeys to sub-Saharan Africa with Hollywood celebrities such as Madonna and Angelina Jolie. *The End of Poverty* became a bestseller, and Sachs became something of a celebrity himself, lecturing and advising governments around the world, and setting out his solution to extreme poverty in newspapers and glossy magazines.[95] *Time* listed Sachs among its '100 most influential people in the world' in 2004 and again in 2005, and a portrait in *Vanity Fair* introduced him as follows: 'Jeffrey Sachs – visionary economist, savior of Bolivia, Poland, and other struggling nations, advisor to the UN and movie stars – won't settle for less than the global eradication of extreme poverty.[96] Russia was all but forgotten. His metamorphosis, it seemed, was complete.

THE SECOND COMING

In his performance of Mr Aid, Sachs abandons the dry economics and ruthless neoliberal strategizing of Dr Shock, and adopts a distinctly evangelical tone. He frames his development project as nothing less than a 'simple plan to save the world',[97] and *The End of Poverty* concludes with the following exhortation to his readers: 'Let the future say of our generation that we sent forth mighty currents of hope, and that we worked together to heal the world.'[98] This cloying sentimentality is mixed with bursts of moral outrage. Sachs warns us: 'We are leaving people to die by the millions … I am seeing them dying, many more than I want to see, and I expected to see in my life.'[99] In demanding billions of dollars of aid to fund his development solutions, Sachs condemns 'the incredible capacity of the so-called international community to stare human disaster in the face and not flinch from ignoring it',[100] and accuses the US government of 'turning a cold and steely eye away from the millions dying of hunger and disease.'[101]

Such emotive language has led Sachs to be depicted as an 'economic proselytizer'[102] and a 'dispenser of moral medicine'.[103] It is notable that his own 'second coming' occurred around the turn of the millennium, and was framed by the biblical references of 'Jubilee' 2000 and the 'Millennium' Development Goals. Sachs frequently refers to God in his writings on development, and his public appearances have become increasingly messianic. In 2005, for example, he gave a lecture in Washington Cathedral in which he was introduced to the congregation as the 'prophet of economic possibilities for the poor'.[104] Sachs's public performances, however, are more televangelist than old-testament prophet. According to a fellow development economist, 'He's one of the most charismatic, persuasive people in the world. I've seen people bend over crying at his speeches … He knows how to move people, and that's a beautiful thing.'[105]

If we momentarily forget his role in shock therapy, his continued affirmation of inequality and market-led development, and his consistent support for multinational capital, we might be tempted to excuse Sachs for such emotional manipulation in the name of 'the end of poverty'. But as we have seen, Sachs's development agenda is much less progressive than it might at first appear. His emotive representations of extreme poverty in Africa are also problematic in themselves, to the extent that they indulge in explicit depictions of starvation and death. Such representations have been criticized as 'poverty porn',[106] in which the audience does not empathize with the sufferers but derives a disavowed thrill from its imagined proximity to their raw, unmediated suffering. The voyeuristic power of poverty porn is evident in the first chapter of *The End of Poverty*, which Sachs introduces with a prolonged description of the supposedly apocalyptic horrors of everyday life in Malawi, which is presented as if it were representative of 'Africa' as a whole. Sachs paints a nightmarish scene in which nameless Africans mutely succumb to poverty, disease, and death, including the following description of a visit to a local hospital:

> In truth it is not a medical ward at all. It is a place where Malawians come to die of AIDS … In most cases, two people are lying head to toe, toe to head – strangers sharing a death bed. Alongside or underneath the bed there is somebody on the ground, sometimes literally on the ground or on a piece of cardboard, dying beneath the bed. The room is full of moans. This is a dying chamber … Family members sit by the bed, swabbing dried lips and watching their loved ones die … The world has seen fit to look away as hundreds of impoverished Malawians die this day as a result of their poverty.[107]

In criticizing Sachs's language here, I am not questioning the severity of the suffering he describes, or the need for urgent action to address it. Rather, it is the ideological function of such depictions of Africa that is problematic. As Žižek has argued, such representations remove all political agency from the people they describe, depicting them as anonymous victims, and constructing a phantasmatic image of Africa as 'Hell on Earth, as a place so utterly desolate that no political activity, only charity and compassion, can alleviate the suffering'.[108] By introducing *The End of Poverty* in this way, Sachs immediately elides his project with the saving of human lives. This enables him to dismiss anyone who questions his vision of development on the grounds that they are not just wrong but morally abhorrent. In a lecture at a development institute in 2006, for example, Sachs was challenged over the cultural politics of anti-malarial bed-nets, which is a real problem when it comes to ensuring that free bed-nets are not misused or sold by their recipients. Rather than engaging with this criticism, however, Sachs angrily retorted: 'Children are dying, for God's sake.'[109] In another lecture in 2011, Sachs was confronted with serious questions concerning the capacity of his top-down development agenda to achieve lasting and meaningful results on the ground. In response, Sachs simply stated: 'These things were not things said in good faith. These were things said ... through immoral ignorance, because ... issues of life and death carry a moral burden to know what you're talking about.'[110] While Sachs's use of moral language may be rhetorically powerful, it is therefore disingenuous, to the extent that it is deployed to silence rational debate, and to demand unquestioned support for a highly problematic and contested vision of 'development'.

Sachs likes to combine his graphic accounts of poverty and death in Africa with eulogies to the saving powers of 'transformative billionaire philanthropy'.[111] He tells us 'not to blame the rich for the poverty of the poor.'[112] Instead, we are encouraged to join him in marvelling at their luxurious lifestyles and their vast accumulated wealth:

> There are now around 950 billionaires in the world, with an estimated combined wealth of $3.5 trillion. That's an amazing $900 billion in just one year. Even after all the yachts, mansions, and luxury living that money can buy have been funded many times over, these billionaires will still have nearly $3.5 trillion to change the world ... All in all, it's not a bad job for men and women who have already transcended the daily economic struggle faced by the rest of humanity![113]

Note the smoothness with which Sachs shifts from apocalyptic melodrama to motivational cheerleading when praising the representatives of global capital. Rather than suggesting that the abject poverty of the world's 'bottom billion' might be causally related to such obscene concentrations of wealth, Sachs feels compelled to point out '[h]ow fitting [it is] that the world's richest people would share a small percentage of their vast incomes to help save millions of people each year from death in the world's poorest countries.'[114] He hurries to assure the wealthy readers of *Forbes* magazine that the beneficiaries of their charity in Africa would 'be delighted to meet you ... with a hearty smile, a handshake, and a food offering.'[115] Reporting on a charity gala attended by the chief executive of Novartis and the president of News Corporation, an article in the *New York Times* describes Sachs giving 'a rousing, almost euphoric speech, insisting that the end of poverty and disease in Africa was within our grasp.'[116] Once again, the problem here is less with the sentiments being expressed than with the fact that they function to legitimize the vast disparities of poverty and wealth that have been produced by free market economics on a global scale, and that neither Sachs nor his wealthy audience have any intention of challenging.[117]

HEART OF DARKNESS

By performing the role of 'development guru', Sachs has transformed his symbolic identity from 'Russia's destroyer' into 'saviour of Africa'. A *New York Times* profile of Sachs from 2004 describes attending a lecture on Africa, in which Sachs appeared '[l]ike a preacher rapt by his own evangelical zeal'.[118] The article then turns to the possible relationship between this emotive performance and Sachs's experience in Russia:

> Whenever I asked Sachs about Russia, he bristled, the only times in months I saw him lose his composure or stray off message. When it first came up, we were standing outside his four-story town house off Central Park West … There was a clap of thunder. Then raindrops. Sachs's words seemed to race ahead of him. 'You try to do your best and do what you can do, but you couldn't imagine all of the blame that came afterward', he said. 'Say that malaria aid didn't work. It would be like being blamed for malaria for the next ten years. Am I going to be blamed for AIDS too?' The rain started coming down harder … He paused for a moment and his voice lowered, cracking slightly. 'Frankly, the Russia thing was a very painful period.' Instead of wallowing in the pain, however, Sachs has set out to redeem himself. It's as if having failed at the second-greatest challenge of modern history – the transition from communism to capitalism – he is intent on solving the first: the persistence of global poverty.[119]

The narrative of redemption provides an appealing explanation for Sachs's transformation from Dr Shock into Mr Aid. Yet it overlooks the extent to which Sachs remains committed to neoliberal fundamentals, including free market economics, economic inequality, and the unbridled power of corporate capital. An alternative explanation lies in Sachs's repression of the Real of Capital. Rather than seeking redemption for his failure in Russia, Sachs has simply refused to confront it. As I have argued, the apocalyptic imagery with which Africa is relentlessly portrayed by Sachs, and his abrupt shift of attention from Russia to Africa, together suggest that the disturbing symptoms of the former may have been displaced onto the latter. By locating Africa in a 'poverty trap' beneath the 'ladder of development', Sachs can place these symptoms outside the bounds of the capitalist system, diminishing their traumatic content, and framing capitalism itself as their solution. In the process, Sachs has been able to redefine himself not as a man to be blamed for poverty and suffering, but as the man with the solution to these problems. Crucially, he has done so without confronting his own past, and without altering the fundamental structures of his neoliberal fantasy.[120]

The publication of *The End of Poverty* in 2005 helped to establish Africa as an ideological priority not only for Jeffrey Sachs, but for the neoliberal project as a whole. The year 2005 was declared the international 'Year of Africa'. *The End of Poverty* was accompanied by Tony Blair's Commission for Africa report, which reproduced Sachs's strategy, and the G8 summit in Gleneagles, which became the focus of intense campaigning for increased aid to Africa. Sachs's Millennium Project also published its report, with Sachs himself playing the leading role in its promotion. The remit of the Project was to produce a strategy for the fulfilment of the Millennium Development Goals on a global scale by their 2015 deadline. The report reproduced Sachs's development agenda in *The End of Poverty*, combining an orthodox neoliberal agenda of trade liberalization, export-led development, and private sector–led growth, with the Post-Washington Consensus embellishments of upgraded human capital and economic infrastructure. If raised to an adequate level, these factors would generate 'take off', and African economies would begin to scale the ladder of development.[121] This would require an immediate doubling of overseas development assistance from US\$65 billion in 2005 to US\$135 billion in 2006, rising to US\$195 billion by 2015.[122] The success of such an unprecedented increase in international aid, needless to say, was contingent on every last cent being exclusively devoted to Sachs's own project.

Incredibly, the G8 summit at Gleneagles seemed destined to provide Sachs with the opportunity to realize this dream. In the run-up to the summit, the Make Poverty History campaign pressured the G8 to end extreme poverty in Africa through increases in international aid in line with Sachs's prescriptions. At Gleneagles, world leaders responded by pledging to double international aid – an unprecedented gesture, which potentially provided Sachs with the astronomical sums required to implement his plan.[123] Surveying this scene, Sachs must have felt contented with a job well done. He had mobilized extraordinary economic resources and political will around his vision of development, and had participated in a successful process of mass co-optation, in which the anti-globalization movement's rage against global capitalism had been sublimated into Make Poverty History's polite request for 'capitalism with a human face'. In place of the spontaneous anarchism of the Battle of Seattle, the G8 summit was accompanied by an orderly demonstration, attended by politicians and members of the public alike, in which everyone was dressed in white as if to celebrate their collective depoliticization. Around the world, a series of 'Live 8' concerts was organized by Bob Geldof to raise awareness of African suffering. The shows combined sensuous pleasure and horrified fascination, interspersing performances by famous white rock stars with footage of starving black Africans. At one point between songs, the audience was asked to stand in silence and click their fingers every three seconds, in time with the death rate of African children, before getting back to enjoying the music. This symbolic replacement of the political struggle for social justice with the complacent enjoyment of salvation could be said to mark the final evisceration of the so-called 'anti-globalization movement'. Needless to say, Sachs loved it, celebrating Live 8 for building 'trust, understanding, and a common global ethic'.[124]

Thanks to 'Africa', popular faith in capitalism had been restored, along with Sachs's personal reputation as an economic superhero. Writing in the *Sunday Times* on the eve of the G8 summit, Sachs allowed himself to dream of a future in which Africa had been fully integrated into global capitalism. In the article, entitled 'How Africa Lit Up the World', Sachs imagines that the year is 2025, and Africa has rapidly scaled the ladder of development, thanks to the 2005 G8 summit agreeing to fund the Millennium Project's recommendations. Suddenly the world is gripped by a deadly virus. Millions are dying. 'And then, at the darkest moment, salvation arrived … from Africa.'[125] Rwanda's science facilities are now among the most advanced in the world, and have come up with a vaccine, leading to worldwide celebrations:

The Rwandan President ... praised her country's scientists, declaring: 'From the heart of darkness has come light' ... Songs of thanks ... reverberated through the churches, mosques, temples, and city plazas of the world. The most popular of these was the classic 'One', written decades earlier by U2's Bono: 'We're one but we're not the same, We get to carry each other, carry each other ...' Yes, the world was one interconnected whole.[126]

So, let's get this straight. Africa has been rescued from poverty, and the whole world has been saved from certain death, thanks to everyone doing exactly what Jeffrey Sachs told them to do. Not only that, but all the contradictions of global capitalism have been smoothed out into 'one interconnected whole', and the entire population of the planet has gathered in religious buildings in order to sing U2 'songs of thanks' to *someone*, presumably Sachs himself. This fantasy of a contradiction-free capitalism guaranteed by his own omnipotence might appear to be the deluded indulgence of a man who has completely lost himself in the enjoyment of an imagined identity. Yet, as we have seen, it might be better understood as a defence strategy against his repressed knowledge of the Real of Capital, and of his own impotence in the face of its blind destructive power. As for his staggeringly offensive description of Africa as 'the heart of darkness', we can perhaps excuse Sachs by recalling that 'Africa' is not a geographical place for him so much as a symbolic repository for all the symptoms of the Real of Capital that confronted him in Russia. In this sense, the heart of darkness is not Africa's, but his own.

4 DEVELOPMENT DREAMLAND

From his abandonment of Russia in 1994 to the 'Year of Africa' in 2005, Jeffrey Sachs had avoided direct involvement in project planning and implementation, restricting his role to economic theory and policy advice. Now Russia was all but forgotten, and Sachs was ready to get back to work. The scale of the Millennium Project was truly global, dwarfing the already vast ambitions of his shock therapy experiments. Yet, despite the promises of increased aid that had been made at the G8 summit in Gleneagles, the resources to fund the Millennium Project were not immediately forthcoming. Indeed, as Sachs was eventually forced to admit, the majority of the promised aid never arrived at all.[1] Rather than confronting the possibility that his scheme was condemned to failure from the outset by its colossally unrealistic expectations, Sachs embarked on an ambitious 'proof of concept', devoted to demonstrating the efficacy of his solution to extreme poverty. In 2006 Sachs launched the Millennium Villages Project (MVP), with the support of the Earth Institute, the United Nations Development Programme, and Millennium Promise – a philanthropic foundation that he cofounded in 2005 with the billionaire Wall Street venture capitalist Ray Chambers. The MVP applies the Millennium Project's recommendations in eighty pre-existing villages, organized into fourteen 'clusters', which are distributed across ten countries in sub-Saharan Africa. The aim is to achieve the Millennium Development Goals within the Villages by 2015.[2]

Since its launch, the MVP has become the most high-profile development project in the world, and has acquired the support of a growing array of celebrities, philanthropists, and multinational corporations.

Sachs is effectively micromanaging the lives of 500,000 Africans in the name of proving his solution to extreme poverty. His reputation is staked on the success of the project, as are the reputations of the powerful organizations and individuals who have endorsed his plan. There is therefore intense pressure for the MVP to produce positive results. Its conceptual limitations, however, make such success unlikely, and have led to serious questions being raised concerning its viability. Furthermore, my own research on the MVP in Uganda suggests that it is failing to end extreme poverty there, and indicates widespread discontent among its staff on the ground.

A PARADOXICAL UTOPIA

Like shock therapy, the Millennium Villages Project sets out a strict blueprint, based on a comprehensive, integrated set of reforms, which are assumed to be applicable to all countries regardless of local context or political institutions. Sachs is careful, however, to locate his Millennium Villages only in countries with established records of 'good governance', which is World Bank-speak for countries that have undergone structural adjustment programmes and continue to do the bidding of the International Financial Institutions.[3] Indeed, the Millennium Project specifies that selected countries should have received 'favourable reviews' from the World Bank and the IMF.[4] The countries involved in the MVP are Ethiopia, Ghana, Kenya, Malawi, Mali, Nigeria, Rwanda, Senegal, Tanzania, and Uganda. It is no coincidence that all of these countries were regarded as good pupils of the World Bank and the IMF at the time the Project was launched.

In contrast to the economic minimalism of shock therapy, the MVP includes countless interventions in agriculture, environment, health, nutrition, energy, roads, communications, education, microfinance, and business training.[5] The Project conceptually reduces everyday life to five forms of capital, which it lists as human, social, natural, physical, and financial.[6] The aim is to upgrade these forms of capital to the point at which the 'villagers' can 'get their foot on the ladder of development'.[7] Every year, US$120 is being invested in each villager for a period of ten years, after which subsidies are to be replaced by credit.[8] The first phase of the Project, from 2006 to 2011, was aimed at raising inhabitants' five forms of capital to the requisite levels. The second phase, from 2011 to 2015, is focused primarily on 'business development', including a broad array of initiatives devoted to nurturing the 'entrepreneurial spirit', through business training, micro-credit loans, the promotion of co-operatives, and partnerships with multinational agri-businesses.[9] The central objective is to transform the 'villagers' 'from sub-subsistence farmers to small-scale entrepreneurs', and to fully integrate them into the market economy.[10]

There is something profoundly paradoxical about this project, which is symptomatic of the neoliberal project as a whole. The fundamental tenet of neoliberal ideology is that the market is the natural order of society, which will spontaneously emerge once all institutional impediments have been removed. This was the fantasy that underpinned Sachs's shock therapy experiments, which assumed that the removal of the state from the sphere of economic activity would be sufficient to guarantee the emergence of a market society. Following the catastrophic failure of that experiment in Russia, Sachs was forced to incorporate a growing list of non-market variables, such as geography, technology, and health, in order to explain away the pathologies of global capitalism, and to provide the grounds for markets to work effectively – modern transport infrastructure, a healthy workforce, and so on. The tendency, therefore, was for the neoliberal project to become ever more interventionist, and to increasingly reproduce the very forms of social engineering that it was rhetorically opposed to. The Millennium Villages constitute the absurd endpoint of this process, in which Sachs is finally forced to directly manage every single aspect of everyday life at the village level, in order to produce the supposedly natural and spontaneous order of a market society.

The MVP has been criticized within the mainstream development community as 'a utopian folly and an international publicity stunt'.[11] In the words of former World Bank economist William Easterly, 'It seems like a development Disneyland where planners go to enact their fantasies.'[12] What, then, is the nature of the fantasy that Sachs is enacting here? The basic premise of the MVP is that, '[i]f every village has a road, access to transport, a clinic ... and other essential inputs, *the villagers in very poor countries will show the same determination and entrepreneurial zeal of people all over the world*.'[13] Here we can see the outline of the acquisitive individual of neoliberal fantasy. More specifically, the MVP can be seen as an attempt to recreate Adam Smith's account of the origins of capitalism. According to Smith, capitalism originated through private smallholding farmers accumulating capital by dint of their own frugality, and putting it to work in the process of further accumulation, leading to the division of labour and the growth of trade, and resulting in the peaceful emergence of a commercial society of small-scale entrepreneurs.[14] This history, of course, is a fabrication, which Marx scathingly described as 'the paradise lost of the bourgeoisie, where people did not confront one another as capitalists, wage-labourers, land owners, tenant farmers, usurers, and so on, but simply as persons who produced commodities and exchanged them'.[15] This fairytale, Marx argued, had functioned to obscure the violence of primitive accumulation – the forced separation of the peasantry from the land through which capitalism was actually established.[16]

This is precisely the fairytale that Sachs is staging in the Millennium Villages. Through generating a surplus and acquiring capital, each farmer escapes the 'sub-subsistence' of peasant life, and enters the 'market economy' as a 'small-scale entrepreneur', leading the village as a whole to 'escape the poverty trap'.[17] By taking charge of the inhabitants' everyday lives, and raising them to the point that their innate 'entrepreneurial zeal' can spontaneously generate a harmonious market society, Sachs appears to be re-enacting Smith's mythical prehistory of capitalism. This is further indicated by Sachs's own explanation of the vision underlying the Project:

> Almost all of Africa is the private sector. Farmers, that's the private sector … But private sector doesn't mean you just leave them alone … they can't get started because they're so impoverished. So we should help a private sector–led development by helping these farmers use inputs, boost their productivity … Bring in microfinance and let them rip. And that's basically the model.[18]

The MVP can be interpreted as the final step in the reconstitution of Sachs's neoliberal fantasy. In place of the uncontrollable market dynamics, widespread dispossession, spiralling social catastrophe, and brutal class relations that characterized the creation of capitalism in Russia, the Millennium Villages present a fairytale of the peaceful and harmonious emergence of capitalist social relations within the socially undifferentiated fantasy space of the 'African village'. As in Smith's fairytale, the Millennium Villages magically combine entrepreneurial self-interest with community spirit, based on a patronizing representation of the deserving poor. Sachs tells us that 'the poor … are ready to act, both individually and collectively. They are already hard working, prepared to struggle to stay afloat and get ahead ... They are also ready to govern themselves responsibly, ensuring that any help that they receive is used for the benefit of the group rather than pocketed by powerful individuals.'[19] Indeed, when describing his experience of the Millennium Villages, Sachs seems oddly surprised by the capacity for African people to organize themselves in the most basic ways, despite what he appears to regard as their innate tendency towards violence, observing that '[t]he communities are quite well organised. It is a wonderful thing to learn ... these are not anarchic environments until the violence hits. These are communities. They have structure. They have committees.'[20]

When not praising African villagers for being just like other people, Sachs dehumanizes them as 'hungry, disease-ridden, and illiterate villagers struggling for survival',[21] and claims that they 'could be rescued ... with known, proven, reliable, and appropriate technologies'.[22] Despite claiming to be committed to the principles of 'community participation' and 'local ownership', the MVP is based on the premise that Sachs already knows 'the solution' to poverty. The power relations between 'expert' and 'villager' are evident in the visitors' brochure for a Millennium Village in Rwanda, in which 'Rule #1' is 'Please do not give anything to the villagers – no sweets, cookies, empty water bottles, pens or even money',[23] with the explanation: 'our desire is to encourage a culture of entrepreneurship and service provision rather than handouts'.[24] A Senegalese journalist visiting the Project responded to this as follows:

While I'm sure the rule is well-intentioned, it captures perfectly the revolting condescension that I feel from the Millennium Villages Project ... Celebrated professors at Columbia University cannot be excused through their ignorance. When highly educated people can objectify us with a 'Don't feed the animals' sign, the only explanation is blind arrogance ... The situation is entirely ludicrous – American professors spending tens of millions of dollars telling villagers how they should live their lives, so that American tourists can go and watch the new feature at the zoo in which the African natives are doing just as they are told by the American experts – with the careful warning to the tourists not to contaminate the zoo display by feeding the animals. This is how Sachs supports African entrepreneurship?[25]

BRAND AID BANTUSTANS

Unfortunately, the 'ludicrousness' of the Millennium Villages Project does not detract from its ideological appeal, and the Project has been widely celebrated as the greatest success story of contemporary international development. In the words of UN Secretary General Ban Ki-moon, on a visit to a Millennium Village in Malawi, 'This is a crucial time for African development. And this Millennium Village … is in many ways a model of how to do it.'[26] The MVP functions ideologically by presenting a fantasy image of capitalism without contradictions. There are no exploitative relationships among the 'villagers', or between them and the billionaire philanthropists funding their survival, and the pursuit of private profit by both 'entrepreneurial' villagers and their wealthy benefactors is rendered consistent with an unyielding concern for the public good. This is the story that the capitalist elite likes to tell about itself, and the Project has proved extremely appealing to a remarkable array of celebrities, billionaires, and multinational corporations.

Millennium Promise now has over 200 'partners', including the corporate foundations of Ericsson, Facebook, General Electric, GlaxoSmithKline, Goldman Sachs, KPMG, Merck, Monsanto, Motorola, MTV, Nestlé, Nike, Novartis, PepsiCo, Pfizer, Proctor & Gamble, Sony, Time Warner, Tommy Hilfiger, and Unilever.[27] For these corporations, the MVP offers a simple and heart-warming success story with which to demonstrate their ethical business practices while simultaneously opening new markets for their products – as Sachs explained in a public debate with Bill Gates at the World Economic Forum in 2010:

> What we're doing … in Millennium Villages throughout Africa, covering more than half a million people, we're finding that mobilized connectivity with Ericsson … the bed-nets that Sumitomo Chemical produce, the medicines that Novartis and others produce, mobilize the high-yield seeds that Monsanto [produce], the fertilizer of Yara and others, and what you have is a very low-cost package that is completely transformative of the lives of very poor people … *And you find out that what doesn't seem like a market when you started, whether it's mobile phones, or fertilizer purchases, or may other things, becomes a very dynamic centre for new business as well. So this is a business opportunity* and it's a matter of applying the knowledge in a systemic and system-

atic way … That's why I like the business community. It understands bottom lines. It understands timelines. It understands milestones. At least you people get things done. Government – I'm not so sure.[28]

The Millennium Villages Project, in other words, offers a smooth synthesis of profit and morality in the interests of both transnational capital and the world's poorest people, in contrast to the questionable motives and capacities of 'government'. This distinctly neoliberal confection has attracted philanthropists like George Soros, who has been among the biggest contributors to the Project, donating US$50 million in 2006, and a further US$47.4 million in 2011.[29] After funding Sachs's shock therapy experiments in Eastern Europe, Soros became notorious as a currency speculator, making an estimated US$1 billion from UK taxpayers on Black Wednesday in 1992 by betting against sterling, and allegedly triggering the East Asian financial crisis of 1997 by short-selling the Thai baht.[30] The Millennium Villages have provided a convenient means of restoring his reputation, and Sachs has been only too happy to assist him in doing so.

One of the most active of Sachs's corporate sponsors has been the Tommy Hilfiger Corporate Foundation, which donated US$2 million to the MVP in 2009[31] – a figure that should be viewed in the context of the market valuation of the company at over US$4.6 billion.[32] Tommy Hilfiger was nominated as the first Global Leader of Millennium Promise in 2010, and promptly returned the compliment, naming Jeffrey Sachs as his 'most admired living person' in an interview with the *Guardian*.[33] In April 2012, Tommy Hilfiger launched the Promise Collection, a fashion line fronted by the Hollywood actress Katie Holmes.[34] All proceeds from the collection were donated to the MVP in Uganda. The Tommy Hilfiger website featured upbeat slogans about the Project, alongside images of Katie Holmes smiling and clapping as the villagers performed various tasks for her. Consumers could choose which aspect of the Millennium Village they wished to contribute to, and purchase their product accordingly – the 'Congo swimshort' for agricultural development, for example, or the 'Paarl bikini' for environmental protection.

In the Promise Collection, a spectacle of white Western beauty and black African impoverishment was thus staged for the benefit of predominantly white Western consumers, who, despite having no knowledge of development issues, were granted the right to decide on the nature of the investments required to save African lives. The Promise Collection thereby typifies the trend in international development towards 'cause-related marketing', which has been critically labelled 'Brand Aid':

> Brand Aid ... provides an easy solution to current crises in international development – one that enables corporations to raise their Corporate Social Responsibility profile without substantially changing their normal business practices, while consumers engage in low-cost heroism without meaningfully increasing their awareness of global production–consumption relations ... In this form of Brand Aid, the problems and the people who experience them are branded and marketed to Western consumers just as effectively as the products that will 'save' them.[35]

Tommy Hilfiger's personal role as Global Leader of Millennium Promise has been extremely successful in enhancing the ethical reputation of the Tommy Hilfiger brand, helping to counter long-running negative publicity concerning his alleged racism,[36] as well as the company's exploitative manufacturing practices.[37] The launch of the Promise Collection was particularly well-timed in this regard, as two months earlier Hilfiger had been publicly humiliated at New York Fashion Week, where he was confronted by ABC News over a fire in a sweatshop factory in Bangladesh that produced Tommy Hilfiger products, in which twenty-nine people had died.[38] Sachs has participated in salvaging the brand's reputation through its inclusion in the Millennium Villages Project, and is also a big fan of sweatshops, particularly in Bangladesh. In *The End of Poverty*, Sachs chastises activists for challenging the labour standards of multinational corporations operating in Bangladesh. Sachs acknowledges the 'arduous hours, the lack of labour rights, and the harassment' suffered by workers in Bangladeshi garment factories, but insists that standards should not be raised, as this would render factories uncompetitive, and 'sweatshops are the first rung on the ladder out of extreme poverty'.[39] This attitude is yet another example of Sachs's enduring fixation upon the collectively organized worker as the primary obstacle to successful capitalist development. For both Hilfiger and Sachs, the disdain for workers' rights has thus become intertwined with the ethical injunction to 'save Africa'.

Other celebrities to have participated in the MVP include Bono, Matt Damon, Madonna, Brad Pitt, and Angelina Jolie. Madonna donated US$1.5 million to the Millennium Villages, and travelled to Malawi with Sachs, as part of her 'Raising Malawi' campaign, which included plans to teach Kabbalah spiritualism to Malawian orphans.[40] Angelina Jolie also accompanied Sachs on a visit to a Millennium Village in Kenya. Their journey was filmed by MTV, and screened in 2005 as a documentary entitled 'MTV Diary: Angelina Jolie and Dr Jeffrey Sachs in Africa'.[41] In the documentary, Jolie describes Sachs as 'the world's leading expert on extreme poverty'. Sachs leads Jolie on a carefully selected horror tour of the hungry, the sick and the dying in rural Kenya, before moving on to a thriving Millennium Village, in which we see Sachs and Jolie dancing with the locals, digging with makeshift hoes, and attempting to balance large buckets of water on their heads with 'hilarious' results. Having drawn its audience in with a synthesis of Hollywood sexiness and African suffering, MTV delivers the message that white Western men have the solution to black African problems, before returning its audience to their music videos with a clear conscience. As Jolie concludes, 'When you see the solution, it's ridiculous how simple it is.'

AN INCONVENIENT REALITY

If the Millennium Villages Project really were 'the solution', then we could all turn on MTV and let Jeffrey Sachs take care of the rest. 'Ridiculously simple', however, is an all-too-appropriate assessment. By appealing to the neoliberal fantasy of 'the market' as a natural social order, and projecting this onto a colonial fantasy of the homogenous, communal 'African village', Sachs manages to conceal the realities of capitalism from himself and his privileged associates. But the typical village in sub-Saharan Africa is not a homogenous mass of subsistence farmers longing to participate in the market. Instead, it is character- ized by an increasingly stark differentiation between a small class of capitalist farmers engaged in global markets and a growing population of wage labourers, who often retain small plots of land as an element of their survival strategies, and whose entry into the labour market has been motivated less by their 'entrepreneurial zeal' than by the decreased standards of living that have characterized their exposure to 'market forces'.[42]

By failing to recognize the reality of these power relations, the MVP threatens to reinforce them. Development experts have criticized the MVP for its similarity to the World Bank's ill-fated Integrated Rural Development Programmes, which were implemented in Africa and Southeast Asia in the 1970s. Research on the failure of these programmes provides cautionary tales for the MVP: village committees are likely to be dominated by powerful networks; inputs will be monopolized by these groups; and poverty will rapidly return to its previous levels once the Project ends, albeit in the context of intensified inequalities and a consolidated class structure.[43]

These predictions have been borne out by my own research on the MVP in Uganda (see Chapter 5). They are also supported by the findings of other researchers. Prior to my research in Uganda, I interviewed a development practitioner who had spent time in some of the Millennium Villages. Speaking on condition of anonymity, she was strongly critical of the Project, on the basis of its exacerbation of existing power structures, the improbability of its being scaled up beyond a few isolated village experiments, and the difficulty of its gains being sustained after the Project ends. She also made the following observation concerning the Project's misrepresentation of rural African reality:

> [According to the Millennium Villages Project,] an African village is a group of poor farmers who don't know how to run their lives. They don't have any power differences within themselves, they're all doing the same thing, they all have the same idea about what development should look like. Everyone has land and livestock. Everyone has the same rights to land, resources, and services. Everyone's nice to each other. This overlooks huge differences in terms of power, knowledge, access to information, social capital, access to networks. There is a complete lack of realising all these differences ... The idea behind [the Project] is that once people have stepped out of poverty ... then suddenly they become entrepreneurial, and whatever money they make will be reinvested in all these social investments. There's no link to reality. Those people who escape poverty will probably move to Nairobi and buy a Mercedes.[44]

The conceptual fallacies of the MVP thus condemn it to intensifying the very same contradictions of capitalist development that they function to conceal. We might be tempted to think that this is precisely

Sachs's intention, given that his early work praised the tendency for increased agricultural productivity to drive peasants from the land and into sweatshop labour in the cities – the process that Marx called primitive accumulation.[45] Yet Sachs now claims that increased yields of this kind will generate a harmonious commercial society of community-oriented 'small-scale entrepreneurs'. This shift is symptomatic of Sachs's broader transformation, from the tough political strategizing of Dr Shock, who was all too aware of the realities of power, to the insipid moralizing fantasies of Mr Aid, for whom power relations have completely ceased to exist. Rather than accusing Sachs of deliberately obscuring a strategy for primitive accumulation beneath an ideological cloak of village harmony, I would suggest that it is Sachs who cannot bear to confront the Real of Capital that he is in fact concealing from himself. Russia's transition to capitalism was marked by dispossession on a vast scale. The Millennium Villages provide Sachs with a fairytale of capitalist development in which the brutal foundation of capitalist social relations can be forgotten. This would help to explain why Sachs is so defensive of the Project, as indicated by the following extract from a 2007 interview in the *Financial Times*:

I bring the subject round to Russia again. 'I advised Russia for two years …' Sachs says defensively. 'It was an extremely frustrating period for me' … We move on to talk about the specific project Sachs is currently involved in, Millennium Villages, where his ideas on fertilisers, anti-malarial bed-nets and the like are tried on the ground. My less-than-ecstatic reaction to his reports of their success is clearly the same as that of many aid agencies. It instantly raises his hackles. I suggest there are many examples where success in pilots does not translate into something that can be replicated on a large scale, and that you don't necessarily need to try something to know that it won't work. 'I'm sorry,' he is almost shouting now. 'That, I disagree with completely. That's preposterous.'[46]

Sachs and others at the MVP are also very defensive of its reputation in their relationship to independent research. As we will see in the following chapters, close controls are placed on research conducted in the Villages, and Sachs has been accused of personally intimidating independent researchers who question the Project's claims to success. According to the development practitioner quoted above, 'At the top [of the Project], they have to prove that the model works. They don't really care what happens in the villages to the people. What they care about is that their model survives.'[47] If correct, this assessment suggests that the Millennium Villages Project is less about transforming reality than reconstructing a fantasy. If 'the model works', even in the supposedly abject space of 'Africa', then Sachs can claim that he was right all along, and that capitalism really is the harmonious social order of his fantasy, as opposed to the grotesque abomination that tore that fantasy apart in Russia.

But there is a problem: the model doesn't work.

5 THE VILLAGE THAT SACHS BUILT

In February 2013 I travelled to Ruhiira, Uganda, to judge the success of the Millennium Villages Project for myself. Ruhiira is a 'cluster' of eight Millennium Villages in the southwest of the country, which was launched in 2006. Despite being called 'villages', the cluster covers a total of 140 square kilometres of mountainous land, including numerous villages and farmsteads, with a population of approximately 50,000 people.[1] Sachs has identified Ruhiira as the 'flagship' of the MVP,[2] and, of all the Villages, it is Ruhiira that has received the greatest international attention. An award-winning *Vanity Fair* profile of Sachs is based around a trip to Ruhiira, and it is the focus of Tommy Hilfiger's Promise Collection. Multinational corporations involved in Ruhiira include General Electric, Procter & Gamble, Sony Ericsson, Sumitomo Chemical, and Monsanto, which has donated its patented seeds to the Project.[3] The UK chancellor of the exchequer, George Osborne, has visited Ruhiira, as have numerous political and corporate delegations from around the world.[4] All have been impressed by the achievements of the Project, leading to rapturous reports in the international press, with titles like 'Havens of Hope: The Ugandan Villages on Target to Meet the Millennium Development Goals'.[5] As the jewel in the crown of the MVP, around which many of its greatest claims to success are being made, Ruhiira seemed the ideal location to conduct an independent study. If this is the best of the Millennium Villages, then any problems in Ruhiira are likely to be magnified elsewhere.

Sachs's decision to locate a Millennium Village in Ruhiira may have been influenced by his relationship with Yoweri Museveni, the President of Uganda, whose powerbase is in the region. Museveni seized power in 1986, and has held on to it ever since. During the 1990s, his National Resistance Movement (NRM) abandoned its socialist principles and implemented a far-reaching programme of privatization and liberalization on the instruction of the IMF. In contrast to most other African economies undergoing neoliberal reforms during this period, Uganda's economy grew rapidly, and poverty declined (although this appears to have had less to do with the success of the reforms than with peasant farmers returning to their land and resuming cultivation after fifteen years of civil war). Museveni then pioneered the Post-Washington Consensus, combining free market principles with limited social measures such as universal primary education. The donor community was desperate for a success story of this kind, and flooded the country with funds, which have consistently provided over half of the government's budget since the late 1990s.[6]

For Sachs, Museveni's Uganda is proof of the transformative potential of international aid. Sachs has worked as an economic advisor for Museveni, and has consistently praised him over the years as a shining example of enlightened African leadership. Museveni has also offered support for Sachs, publically endorsing his campaign to become president of the World Bank (see Chapter 6).[7] The two have developed a close personal relationship, visiting Ugandan sweatshops together, and sitting in the presidential offices discussing the end of poverty.[8] After one such meeting in 2003, Sachs reported that 'President Museveni … was extremely engaged and interested in discussing … the progress that Uganda has made towards the Millennium Development Goals … We also talked about how the Earth Institute's expertise can be useful to Uganda in its efforts to meet the Goals.'[9]

But Museveni's record is not quite as unblemished as Sachs's praise might suggest. Poverty reduction has stagnated since the turn of the millennium, and inequality has grown dramatically.[10] The privatization and liberalization processes have been rife with insider dealing, and corruption has reached epidemic levels, leading Uganda to be identified by Transparency International as the most corrupt regime in East Africa in 2012.[11] Museveni's regime has been accused of deliberately prolonging the conflict with the Lord's Resistance Army in the north of the country, placing thousands of 'ghost soldiers' on the government payroll, and framing the conflict as part of the 'war on terror' in order to gain the military and financial backing of the United States.[12] In 2002, a UN Security Council Panel of Experts published a report on

Uganda's involvement in the civil war in the Democratic Republic of Congo, which it entered in 1997, and officially withdrew from in 2003. The report accused generals close to Museveni of using their military presence in eastern Congo to exploit the region's gold, timber, coltan, and diamonds, in alliance with Western business interests, while hundreds of thousands of Congolese were killed or displaced.[13]

Elections in Uganda have been rigged, presidential term limits have been abolished, and human rights organizations have accused the regime of systematic political repression. In March 2004, for example, Human Rights Watch published a report on Uganda, which offered the following assessment of the country:

> The use of torture as a tool of interrogation is foremost among an escalation in human rights violations by Ugandan security and military forces since 2001. In what most victims consider a state-sanctioned campaign of political suppression, official and ad hoc military, security and intelligence agencies of the Ugandan government have proliferated, practicing illegal and arbitrary detention and unlawful killing/extrajudicial executions ... These abuses are not acknowledged by the Ugandan government that instead fosters an enabling climate in which such human rights abuses persist and increase while perpetrators of torture, rather than being held accountable, act with impunity.[14]

Sachs is apparently unconcerned by such details. In May 2004, two months after the publication of this report, he wrote an article in the *Economist* celebrating Museveni and Ethiopia's Meles Zenawi – another authoritarian leader beloved by the donor community at the time:

> Effective leaders in Ethiopia and Uganda have taken two seemingly hopeless countries and set them on a path to development ... President Yoweri Museveni of Uganda has fashioned the fastest-growing economy is east Africa ... despite Uganda being landlocked and victimized by an insurgency in the north backed by Sudan's Islamist forces. Both Messrs Meles and Museveni have been staunch and unstinting supporters of America's anti-terrorism efforts ... On anybody's list – the World Bank, Freedom House, Transparency International – a growing and significant number of African countries has the quality of leadership and governance to achieve economic development and fight terrorism.[15]

In 2006, Sachs launched the Ruhiira cluster of Millennium Villages in southwest Uganda, with the Ugandan government as a full partner. Project documents identify Uganda as 'a fairly well governed country',[16] and exclude any analysis of its larger political and economic problems. Instead, Ruhiira is presented as a place of 'deforestation, environmental degradation ... high population density [and] land shortages.'[17] We are told that Ruhiira is poor, that malaria and HIV/ Aids are rife, and that it has one of the highest rates of tuberculosis in the region.[18] All this is true. But it tells us nothing of Ruhiira's politics, history, or class structure, all of which are crucial to understanding the causes of its poverty. We do not learn that the region was a focus of extreme violence during the Uganda–Tanzania war of 1978–79 and the subsequent civil war, which destroyed past development achievements and traumatized the population.[19] We do not learn about the impact of patronage and corruption on the political structure of the region, which is Museveni's birthplace and power-base.[20] And we do not learn about the intensification of inequalities within the region, as land ownership becomes increasingly concentrated and peasant farmers are pushed into the labour market.[21] By constructing an image of a place devoid of human agency and abandoned to the natural vagaries of death and disease, such representations encourage an understanding of poverty as a consequence of local environmental disadvantages, rather than political and economic relationships of power, while legitimizing development interventions by the very same governments and donors that bear significant responsibility for the perpetuation of poverty and inequality.

In Sachs's own description of Ruhiira, 'When we started there was almost nothing. So much disease. So much death. And yet with this great science ... we're seeing a community coming back to life.'[22] The Project reports significant successes in Ruhiira. It claims that maize yields have increased from 1.8 to 3.9 tons per hectare, children receiving free school meals have increased by 69 per cent, malaria prevalence is approaching zero, and the proportion of people using an improved water source has quadrupled. The accuracy of these claims is very difficult to verify. The MVP is extremely secretive about its own data, and extraordinarily controlling in relation to the access it grants to researchers. An MA dissertation on Ruhiira from the Norwegian University of Life Sciences includes details of these controls. The student had to apply to the Earth Institute for access to the Project, which was personally organized by Sachs's wife.[23] His research in Ruhiira was orchestrated by the administrative staff of the Project, who provided his translator and research assistant, as well as a 'facilitator' for focus group discussions, and an engineer for visits to specific project sites.[24] All researchers must sign a 'Data Use Consent Statement', which grants the MVP exclusive access to all research findings for a period 'not usually exceeding one year'.[25] A 'Confidentiality Statement' must also be signed, including the promise: 'I will only discuss the data with which I am working for purposes related to the work I am assigned by the MVP staff and I will not discuss or disclose any information related to this data outside of work or for purposes other than completing my assigned tasks.'[26]

Such paranoid levels of control are unsurprising, given what is at stake in the MVP. After all, this is the project on which Jeffrey Sachs's reputation now rests. In 2012, Sachs was appointed director of the United Nations' Sustainable Development Solutions Network, with the responsibility of formulating and promoting the global development agenda that will replace the Millennium Development Goals (MDGs). His appointment was largely a result of the perceived success of the MVP, and provides him with a platform for presenting the Project as the development model for the rest of the world to follow.[27] Thanks to Sachs's powers of self-promotion, the Project has become the most high-profile development programme in the world. It claims to provide a solution to extreme poverty for the rest of the world to follow, and it has the backing of some of the most powerful institutions, corporations, and individuals on the planet (see Chapter 4).

It is precisely the significance of the Project, however, that makes genuinely independent research essential. The controls that the Project has put in place are extremely problematic in this regard. It is impossible to obtain accurate critical information about a development project from its beneficiaries or employees if known representatives of the project administration are present during interviews and inspections. It is also impossible to assess the accuracy of the claims being made by a development project if the project's own information remains a closely guarded secret. Commenting on these limitations, an editorial in the world-leading scientific journal *Nature* has observed that the Project 'seems to lack a coherent policy on when and how it will make its data available to independent researchers ... Greater transparency is essential to build trust and credibility. The project's approach has potential, but little can be said for sure yet about its true impact.'[28] This is ironic, given that Sachs himself has persistently argued that '[p]eople need to see what aid is achieving ... so that people know what they're putting in and what they're getting out'.[29]

For these reasons, I decided to conduct my research in Ruhiira without seeking the permission of Jeffrey Sachs or the MVP, and without the local administration knowing that I was there. In February and March 2013 I spent some time living in Ruhiira. To avoid detection, I based myself in a village several kilometres from the Ruhiira project office, and over an hour's drive away from Mbarara, the city where the main MVP offices are located. With the help of a Ugandan research assistant, I conducted in-depth interviews with thirty-five households throughout the cluster. Speaking with the implementers of the Project was more difficult, as I was operating without the knowledge of the administration. I interviewed nine employees of the Project and its partners in the Ugandan government, including five health workers, two teachers, a civil engineer, and an agricultural extension officer. I also received emails and notes from other employees of the Project, who were unwilling to speak to me for fear of losing their jobs. After leaving Uganda, I received further written testimonies from two MVP health workers who had recently left the Project. I also came into possession of a dossier of complaints compiled by a group of former administrative staff of the Project, which they had delivered to Millennium Promise in New York. On the basis of contact information included in this dossier, I was able to conduct telephone interviews with four former administrators who had worked in the Project Office in Mbarara, and received a detailed written statement from a fifth. The overall picture that emerged was at odds with the utopian representations of Ruhiira on the MVP website and in the international media. In Ruhiira, the problems of Sachs's development strategy become clear.

RUHIIRA

In my view, the MVP is inaccurate in its depiction of Ruhiira as a god-forsaken place on the boundaries of the civilized world, whose helpless people have been rescued from their miserable plight by the brilliance and magnanimity of Jeffrey Sachs and his wealthy white friends. In my time in Ruhiira, I got to know a different place. Ruhiira is a region with very serious problems of poverty, inequality, and marginalization, in which people are using what resources they have to survive, raise families, and enjoy their lives as best they can. Villages and home-steads are scattered across broad hilltops and steep green valleys, filled with fields of plantain and maize. The villages are connected by a few unpaved roads and a network of paths that weave through the plantain trees. The poorest people live in single-room mud-and-thatch huts, and preferred to speak to me outside their homes. Those a little better-off might have a tin roof, and decorate their walls with the pages of newspapers. The wealthiest have concrete houses with three-piece suites and modern electrical appliances run by privately owned generators. The villages have their own market days, which attract people from across the region, selling fruit and livestock and tools and clothes. Each village typically has a pool table in front of a bar on the main street, which is usually surrounded by young men, while older men sit inside drinking the local banana gin. Women are often left to tend to the fields and the home; many are second or third wives. On Sundays, after church, generators run sound systems blaring pop music from Kampala and the West, and people mingle in the streets, where hawkers sell grilled goat meat and plantain. In the evenings, men often gather to watch European football on satellite TV in one of the local bars, paying 500 shillings (about 20 US cents) to the barman for the right to watch the game. I spent a lot of my evenings with them.

In order to understand the distributional effects of the MVP, it was vital to interview people with a wide range of living standards. My research assistant and I worked with an employee of a local coopera-tive bank, who had an excellent knowledge of the relative standards of living of people in the area, and also sought the advice of local councillors from across the region. Our interviews all included house-hold surveys containing a set of standardized questions designed to determine the living standard of the household. Once the interviews were complete, I divided the thirty-five households into three groups, reflecting 'higher', 'middle' and 'lower' standards of living. There is no single determinant of wealth in a semi-subsistence economy. For example, a landless wage labourer may have a bigger cash income than a subsistence farmer with five acres of land, but the latter is more likely to be able to feed his family. The division that I made was therefore necessarily approximate.

Typically, the adult (and often younger) members of a 'poor' house-hold would be casually employed on other peoples' farms. They would be landless, or have very little land (often less than an acre), and would usually rent land from others. They would have no cattle, and sometimes would have no livestock of any kind. They would not own a motorcycle or a bicycle. Their only income, apart from casual labour, might come from selling a small quantity of their farm produce, or perhaps brewing and selling the local gin. A middle-income household, according to my classification, might not have much more land than a poor household, but would often supplement its farming with a small business – the wife might work as a seamstress, for example, or the husband might have a bicycle taxi. They would not generally work as wage labourers, and might occasionally employ a casual labourer themselves. They might have a few goats and chickens, but no cattle. They might have a bicycle, but would probably not have a motorcycle. The upper-income households would have larger land holdings – sometimes hundreds of acres. They would employ several casual labourers, and most of their agricultural produce would be for sale rather than consumption. Some would run small shops or private schools. Some would have positions in local government. Some would be 'middle men', buying agricultural produce from smaller farmers and selling it on in bulk elsewhere. They would often have large numbers of cattle, as well as other livestock. They would probably own a motorcycle, and maybe a car or truck. According to this classification, nine of the households I interviewed were upper-income, ten were middle-income, and sixteen were lower-income.

All of the households I visited have benefited from the Project in some way. Most households have made use of the improved health facilities provided by the Project, including the upgrading of government clinics and the provision of anti-retroviral drugs, although many complained of inadequate staffing and a frequent lack of basic medicines. The school kitchens and foodstuffs donated by the Project have helped to provide free lunches for primary school children, although the resulting increase in enrolment has not been matched by the employment of more teachers, with the result that education standards are perceived to have declined. The vast majority of households have received free seeds and fertilizer, although some have received them with greater frequency and in greater quantities than others. Water sources have improved for some people, though many identified the continued absence of clean water as among the principle failings of the Project. And everyone has received free bed-nets, although health workers reported their being used to house chickens, or sold in markets outside the Project boundaries. (On an anecdotal level, at least three of my acquaintances in Ruhiira – a man who ate at my hotel, a waitress at the football bar, and my local guide's uncle – contracted malaria during the brief time I was there.)

These limited and qualified achievements should be acknowledged. At best, however, I believe they amount to a disappointing return on the millions of dollars that the MVP has invested every year for several years in this small, impoverished region.[30] And in my view they are a very long way from justifying Sachs's insistence that the MVP is a participatory and sustainable solution to extreme poverty that the rest of the world should follow. As we saw in Chapter 3, Sachs defines the 'extremely poor' as those living on less than US$1 dollar a day. In Ruhiira, the MVP claims that '[a] significant proportion of the community, which is estimated at between 40 [and] 50%, still live in extreme poverty with an estimated annual per capita income of $250'.[31] It is this poorest 40–50 per cent, then, that the Project should be providing with the greatest assistance. In practice, however, my admittedly limited research suggests that the vast majority of the inputs provided by the Project are being appropriated by the better-off, while the poorest are being largely excluded. This is partly due to the Project's misrepresentation of rural Africa as a set of homogenous subsistence 'communities', in which there are no class relations or significant differences in assets and incomes.[32] Like most of rural Africa, Ruhiira does not fit this representation, but is a stratified class society, in which differences in wealth are based on the ownership of land. As I have already mentioned, the poorest farmers I interviewed had less than one acre of land, and in some cases no land at all. They were forced to rent land from wealthier farmers, and to sell their labour to these farmers for as little as 75 US cents a day. The wealthiest farmers I spoke to owned as much as 250 acres of land, and employed twenty or more casual labourers. Differences of wealth and property ownership are also differences of power, in terms of political influence and the control of economic resources. A development project that does not thoroughly take into account such differences is likely to exacerbate them, as the wealthier members of the society will be better positioned to appropriate its benefits. This proved to be the case in Ruhiira.

NOT THE END OF POVERTY

According to Jeffrey Sachs, the MVP's agricultural programme is ending extreme poverty in Ruhiira. On the Tommy Hilfiger Promise Collection website, for example, Sachs claims: 'It's adding up to higher incomes for the farmers and a lot more nutrition and physical health for the children so that they're growing to their full potential.'[33] I believe this overlooks the inequalities of wealth and power that exist in Ruhiira, and the role of the MVP's agricultural inputs in exacerbating these inequalities. In terms of livestock, the MVP has provided cows and goats, but in limited numbers. Individuals could apply to the Project to receive a cow or a goat. Several poorer farmers had applied for a goat, but had been instructed by the Project to construct shelters and plant grass before receiving one. Most did not have sufficient land or resources to do so, leading to their exclusion at the expense of wealthier farmers. This policy had resulted in goats being provided to three of the nine upper-income households I interviewed, compared to one of the ten middle-income households, and one of the sixteen lower-income households. Cows, meanwhile, were perceived to be given only to those with political connections. Only one of the households I interviewed had received a cow. The head of this household was the chairman of the local council, and he already had forty cattle of his own. A poor farmer from a different cluster told a similar story about his local council chairman: 'Those people who receive [things from Millennium]. Do you think they are the same as people who do not? The [local council] chairman received a cow. But you see a cow is such a big thing to come into the village. So you think a poor man would have been chosen to have it?'[34]

Seeds and fertilizers have been more widely distributed than livestock, benefiting almost everyone. The quantity distributed to each farmer, however, depends on the amount of land they own, which again means that the wealthier farmers have benefited disproportionately. Poorer farmers renting land were often unable to benefit from fertilizers, as their landlords would not permit them to use fertilizer, on the assumption that it would impoverish the soil over time. Wealthier farmers also reported receiving seeds and fertilizer more regularly than poorer farmers. Again, many of the poorer farmers perceived this to be a consequence of political connections. One very poor HIV-positive woman, whose husband had recently died, told me:

'For us this end, we don't get anything. For example the third time [the Project brought the seeds and fertilizer], they were received by the leaders [i.e. the local council chairmen and their associates]. But when we came, they told us … you had to buy them.'[35]

The better-off farmers often acknowledged inequities in the distribution of fertilizer and other benefits, but explained this in terms of the supposed laziness and ignorance of the poor. One local council chairman told me that 'those who have not benefited – maybe they don't want to … Some people are just like that. They are just there. They don't want to go and get [what is offered to them].'[36] A major landowner and influential local politician, who was one of the wealthiest people I interviewed, explained the inequalities of the Project in matter-of-fact terms:

Now, there are some people who will benefit [from the Project] according to their status. I'm saying this because you will find that someone will receive fertilizer, but he has nowhere to put it. And then you'll find someone else who has a lot of space and a lot of land benefiting more than the poor … But those who do not have any land are beyond help. How can you help them? What can you do for those who have nothing at all? But they still benefit from … working for other people and getting paid … A poor person who lives around rich people … If he is paid 3,000 [Ugandan shillings, approximately US$1.20 a day], that is something … But some people cannot even look after themselves … Some of them, if you give them money they will go and drink it. If you give them a goat or a pig, they will sell it the very next day.[37]

It is not unusual for those profiting from structures of inequality to perceive them as natural and self-evident. Yet, despite his casual dismissal of local poverty, this man's explanation demonstrates the role of the MVP in the *production* of inequality in Ruhiira: the ownership of land determines access to agricultural inputs,[38] the distribution of which exacerbates existing inequalities, leading to the consolidation of a class division between large land owners and impoverished people with nothing to sell but their labour.

This dynamic has been reinforced by the Project's decision to charge for some of its benefits, which inevitably privileges those with the ability to pay. One aspect of the Project in Ruhiira is energy-efficient cooking stoves. This is an element of the Project's 'business development strategy', the aim being to motivate entrepreneurialism by creating a local market in the stoves.[39] But the price of the stoves – 20,000 shillings (approximately US$8) – is beyond the reach of the poorest households, and none of the sixteen worst-off households I interviewed had been able to afford one. A clean water system has been installed in the centre of Ruhiira, but has introduced a charge for the service of 100–200 shillings (4–8 US cents) for a jerry can. The poorest people told me that they could not afford this small price, and had returned to drinking water from polluted sources, while better-off households were able to benefit from the service. Latrines, water tanks and solar energy connections were all being provided on condition that the recipient contributed to the costs in either materials or cash – US$55 for a solar power connection, for example.[40] Again, only the wealthier households were able to afford this, and none of the poorest households reported receiving any of these benefits. In the case of latrines, four of the nine better-off households I spoke to had received a latrine, compared to only one of the ten middle-income households, and none of the poorest. When I asked one very poor young mother if she had received a latrine from the Project, she laughed and said, 'I have heard about the latrines. They were picking them up from the hospital. They were giving them to the leaders.' After naming three 'leaders' who had received latrines, she added, 'When [Millennium] come they only focus on the rich people. They don't see lower people as important … We would like them to raise the poor up, rather than giving to the rich.'[41]

The distributional inequalities of the MVP can be summarized by comparing the fortunes of two of the householders I interviewed. One is a successful entrepreneur – the vice-president and founder of a local cooperative bank. His father had a high-ranking position in local government, and he speaks good English. He is the proud owner of a beautiful farm. Several buildings are arranged around a large court-yard, surrounded by fields of plantain, beans, maize, and carrots, as well as orange and mango orchards. He employs ten casual labourers. In 2007 he was selected by the MVP to travel to Nairobi for train-ing in commercial agriculture. His visitors' book contains dozens of entries from members of the MVP administration, academics from Columbia University, and visiting dignitaries from around the world. The MVP has provided him with two goats, and is buying the off-spring back from him at above market rates. It has also offered him a cow, and regularly supplies him with a variety of improved seeds and fertilizer. It gave him the trees for his mango orchard, and it has trained him to graft fruit trees. It has also installed a standpipe on the road directly outside his home, providing him with a ready supply of potable water.[42]

Compare this man's fortunes to those of a woman living on the roadside near the MVP office in Ruhiira. She has never been visited by anyone from the Project administration, let alone by any American academics or international dignitaries. She is landless, but rents a small piece of land on which she is not allowed to use fertilizer. She has only received seeds from the Project once, and without the fertilizer they did not grow well. She has not applied for a cow, as she cannot afford to rent enough land to graze it. She did apply for a goat, but was told that she needed to build a shelter and grow grass for it, and she does not have enough land to do so. She cannot afford the charge for the pumped water provided by the Project, and has to use a polluted source instead. The MVP offered to sell her a fuel-efficient cooking stove, but she could not afford it, and she has not received a latrine. None of this is due to laziness or a lack of interest in receiving Project benefits, as is clear from her account of a discussion with Project implementers:

> Even yesterday I was asking them [about the latrines], but they said now they are not going to give anything else – that it's done ... [Then] I was asking about a [mosquito] net for my sons. And they were saying 'OK, maybe we can get that for you. But we don't have any at the moment.' Then I asked again, 'Then why am I seeing the cement and the tops for the latrines [outside the Project office]?' They said 'No, [the administration] have said that they are not going to give away anything.' Then I said 'It's us – the poor people – who were supposed to be given latrines... We are so squeezed, and now you bring the latrine and you give it to the rich person who already has one, and then you give him another one, then we remain just there, without anything.'[43]

IMAGINED COMMUNITY

Despite Sachs's claim to be ending extreme poverty in Ruhiira, my research suggests that the majority of the Project inputs are being appropriated by the better-off members of the 'community', while the 40–50 per cent identified by the Project as 'extremely poor' are being excluded from many of its benefits. This raises further questions concerning Sachs's insistence that 'the villages run everything', and that '[e]verything that is done is led by the community'.[44] The MVP prides itself on its 'community participation', and has set up 'groups' in Ruhiira, through which many of its inputs and activities are organized. But, far from being inclusive and participatory, many of these groups are comprised almost exclusively of the more affluent and influential members of the 'community', and function as a mechanism of exclusion of the poorest. In the case of the comparison that I have just made between the two farmers, for example, the commercial farmer was chairman of his local 'Millennium' agricultural group, while the landless woman was not a member of any of the Millennium groups, and had never been invited to a meeting by the MVP. Eight of the nine better-off households I interviewed were involved in these groups, compared to four of the ten middle-income households, and only two of the sixteen poorest. Many of the poorer people had heard of the groups, but felt unable to join them, either because they could not afford the membership fee, (50,000 shillings – about US$20 – for the 'Kabuyanda Dairy Farmers Corporation', for example) or because they lacked the necessary social status. An agricultural extension officer working for the Project explained this to me as follows:

> You see, to say that 'this is a group', it means someone who has a feeling to join with other people, and shares their view. And in that [sense], those poor farmers may feel that they can't afford to join with the rich people in forming a group. And in failing to join the groups, then we [the MVP] also fail to get them, because we will not know where they are.[45]

This explanation confirms the perception of many of the poorer households that they were being excluded from many of the benefits of the MVP. By operating through these groups, the Project often bypasses the extremely poor completely, as it 'does not know where they are'. This was further explained to me by the daughter of a poor farmer who had received almost nothing from the MVP:

> They [the MVP] choose people to work with. Those people are well-off. But the ordinary people don't get anything. Maybe apart from a mos-

quito net. It's a group. They call themselves to meetings – not everyone. So if they [the MVP] have something to offer, they will organize themselves, and not tell others. [The MVP] should not just meet those people. They should meet everyone. Because not all of us get help. And yet we need it. But not all of us get help.[46]

The lack of inclusive participation casts serious doubt over the sustainability of the MVP after its planned end-date in 2015. By this time, 'take-off' is supposed to have been achieved. Subsistence farmers will have been transformed into small-scale entrepreneurs, and the community will organize to provide the services now supplied by the Project.[47] But many of the poorest people I interviewed were not even aware that the Project was due to end in 2015, and none were involved in collective preparations for driving it forward after this date. The employees of the Project who I spoke to were also unaware of any preparations of this kind, and were unsure of their own role in the process. In the words of one health worker:

Sustainability is becoming a problem, since [the community is] not aware of what is transpiring. Even us on the ground, we are not aware of what is taking place. We don't know if it will just reach [the end of its] time and go, and we are just living in suspense … Three or four years after completion, most of the things will not be existing. Because community people are not owning the Project. It is like top-down. It should be from down, going up. So that people are aware of what is happening and what is taking place, so that if you leave, they will be owning these things.[48]

This perfectly captures one of the central contradictions of the MVP – its claim to generate 'bottom-up' development through the imposition of a top-down blueprint. But sustainability is also being undermined by the Project's failure to adequately acknowledge the politics of inequality. When I conducted my research in 2013, the Project had started to charge for its seeds and fertilizer at a subsidized price, which will move to full market rates once the Project finishes. Even at the subsidized price, none of the poorer farmers were able to afford the fertilizer, and almost none of them could afford the seeds. By contrast, many of the wealthier farmers were buying the inputs, and expected to continue to do so once the subsidies were removed. In general, it was the better-off people who were most optimistic about the future. The poorest households were almost unanimous in their assumption that the benefits that had trickled down to them – school meals, more medicines, free seeds, and fertilizer – would be lost once the Project came to an end.

ON THE BRINK OF COLLAPSE?

Another critical challenge to the MVP in Ruhiira is maintaining its credibility as a project run by a competent, fair administration. In mid-2013, several ex-administrators of the MVP who had worked at the Project Office in Mbarara prepared a dossier containing extensive allegations of corruption within the MVP administration. Entitled 'Ruhiira Millennium Villages Project at the Brink of Collapse,' the twenty-one page dossier opens with the claim that, 'Peasants face hunger, disease & poverty again as the project leadership strays in office battles.'[49] The dossier claims that the management of the MVP has gone downhill since July 2011, when the country coordinator left the Project, and oversight of procurement and recruitment passed from the United Nations Development Programme (UNDP) to the United Nations Office for Project Services (UNOPS). In a telephone interview in September 2013, one of the authors of the dossier, who had been closely involved in the financial affairs of the Project, told me that previously all contracts over US$500 had to be approved by the UNDP but that the Mbarara Office was now in control of contracts for as much as US$15,000.[50] Another ex-administrator explained that from 2011 onwards, money was sent directly from Millennium Promise in New York to the Mbarara Office, with allegedly insufficient oversight by the MDG Centre for East and South Africa.[51] The dossier contains a list of twenty-six workers who were allegedly dismissed or pushed out of the Project through 'forced resignations', in an alleged effort to mask the problems that it describes. To mention but one example of these problems here, the dossier focuses on a contract between the World Food Programme (WFP) and a local agricultural co-operative called the Ruhiira Twijukye Women Association, in which beans grown by the co-operative were sold in bulk to the WFP. According to the dossier and a follow-up interview with an MVP administrator who was working closely with the co-operative, some of the money from the WFP allegedly disappeared.[52]

I have summarized these charges only as allegations that deserve to be rigorously investigated, not as statements of fact – especially given my limited ability to verify their truth. According to its authors, the dossier was emailed to Millennium Promise in New York in August 2013, and Millennium Promise has conducted an internal investigation into the allegations. (As discussed in Chapter 4, Millennium Promise is the philanthropic foundation that Sachs founded in 2005 to finance the MVP. Sachs still sits on the board of Millennium Promise, and holds the position of 'Co-Founder and Chief Strategist'.[53]) As email exchanges[54] and my contacts[55] confirm, the finance director and the associate counsel of Millennium Promise travelled to Uganda shortly after the dossier was sent to New York, and met with three of the dossier authors in Mbarara on September 12, 2013. It is possible that the dossier is the output of disgruntled former employees, or is based on speculation rather than first-hand knowledge – but the seriousness of its charges undoubtedly warrants a searching review by Millennium Promise and the MVP. As of the time this book goes to press in December 2013, the outcome of their investigation remains unclear.

The MVP should also investigate another concern I heard expressed regarding alleged irregularities in the payment of 'top-ups' to government health workers operating in the Project area. These top-ups are intended to incentivize staff and to compensate them for the additional tasks that they perform for the Project. The MVP did not respond to my request for details on the payment of top-ups to medical staff. But according to the reports I received, a senior clinical officer who earned US$350 a month would be promised a top-up of about US$115, while a junior health worker earning US$150 a month would be due a top-up of around US$90 – a significant increase in both cases. However, the five health workers I spoke to, and a sixth who provided me with two written statements, all claimed that the top-up payments were being made irregularly. Two of my interviewees further claimed that they had been personally intimidated into signing documents confirming that they had received the payments even when they had not.[56] Again, I raise these allegations not as factual statements but as areas worthy of serious investigation by the MVP.

WHEN YOU FIND RUHIIRA SHINING

In a video on the website for Tommy Hilfiger's Promise Collection, Jeffrey Sachs celebrates the achievements of the MVP in Ruhiira, claiming that 'the livelihoods of these communities are moving from subsistence to income and expanding businesses. This community will be on its way to long-term economic growth and economic improvement.'[57] My experience of Ruhiira, however, suggests that this is very far from being the case.

The problems that I discovered in Ruhiira, and the evident discontent of many of the implementers and administrators of the Project, make it very difficult to comprehend the basis on which Sachs and the MVP are making their extravagant claims of success. Several people who worked with the Project in Ruhiira had seen these claims on the Millennium Villages website, and were incredulous. One health inspector told me: 'When I see such things, it baffles me, because it's not what is happening.'[58] 'On paperwork it is doing well', another government health worker remarked, 'but down [on the ground] it is not doing what is written on that paper.'[59] And an employee of the MVP made the following assessment of its achievements: 'Some little change has come. But that's really what I can say. *Little* ... So really, what they always put on the internet, that "We have achieved this and this and this", it is not exactly what they are doing. But we have to take what comes ... We are lacking another option. But the situation is not good.'[60]

The celebratory self-representation of the MVP on the internet would appear to be matched by its representation in Ruhiira itself, which may help to explain the rave reviews that Ruhiira has received from journalists, politicians, businessmen, academics, development students and corporate employees who have visited the Project. When comparing these reviews, it becomes clear that everyone who visits Ruhiira through the official channels receives a virtually identical tour of the 'village'. They almost all visit the same clinic, the same school, the same water project, the same IT centre. Many of them even visit the same farmer, whose name appears repeatedly in articles, reports and blogs about Ruhiira. In stark contrast to the impoverished farmers I visited, the MVP has provided this farmer with two cows, several goats, and a variety of grafted fruit trees. It has even given him a state-of-the-art biogas cooking system, which is made to appear as if it is standard issue for every household in Ruhiira, although none of the people I spoke to had received one, or knew of anyone who had.[61] In the words of one MVP health worker, 'No community involvement: They just use certain homes as demos.'[62] Another health worker described the preparations that are made before official visits to Ruhiira:

When we get visits from donor countries – now that is when you find Ruhiira shining! When the visitors are coming. But let them come another time. It is just like that. [When the visitors are coming] of course they have to do some cleaning. They renovate where the situation was going bad … So it is all about pleasing those visitors. Then [the visitors] go back, and they revert to their normal situation… Those farmers they take [the visitors to meet] – before they have of course talked to them and told them that on such and such a day we will be having visitors, so be ready to show them this and this. Meaning that you have to make sure that you have shown them something good, eh? Not to ashame us. That is what happens … In my department, in the time I have been there I just saw them once … They were just donors, whose names I am not sure of. But that's what the office told us, that 'These are the donors, from the US, New York'. That's what they told us.[63]

Visitors to Ruhiira are invariably impressed by these demonstrations of success. A report by a delegation from the University of Notre Dame is similar to many blog-posts and newspaper reports on Ruhiira, and illustrates the care with which the Ruhiira experience is organized by the administration. According to the report, the delegation were greeted by over twenty members of the MVP administration in Mbarara, where they were treated to lunch and presented with the administration's own account of the Project. They were then accompanied by 'the entire Ruhiira Millennium team' for a drive through various project sites, including the office, school, health centre, and a local farmer's home. 'It quickly became apparent that this project had not been imposed on community members without respect for their wisdom and talents,' the report enthuses, 'In fact, the work was led and supported by members of the community.' Before the delegation left the village, a group of women bid them 'farewell with song and dance'. The author of the report considers that he has 'learned a great deal about this country and the Millennium Village project and most importantly, about how the project works collaboratively with community members to seek lasting change,' concluding that 'The Ruhiira village is a wonderful model.'[64]

The perceived success of Ruhiira would thus appear to depend to a significant extent on the way in which it is represented to its visitors. Strangely enough, it would seem that the most spectacular representations of its success are reserved for the visits of Jeffrey Sachs himself.

This is well illustrated by Sachs's visit to Ruhiira in 2010 to celebrate the contract with the World Food Programme discussed above. An American academic working with the Project in Ruhiira posted a blog describing the occasion:

> Everyone at the MVP office was immersed last week in preparations for the visit on Saturday of Jeff Sachs, the Director of the Earth Institute and Josette Sheeran, the head of the World Food Programme. In addition to these two, there were governmental officials, large staffs, armed police, and press people – maybe 50–80 people in a long line of UN white landrovers ... The tour of Ruhiira for the visitors was similar to the one I did last week. However, this time, there were children or community people at every stop lining the entrances, singing and clapping hands.[65]

An official video of the event shows Sachs being escorted through throngs of cheering villagers, from a pristine school to an overflow-ing warehouse and a gleaming water project, in a deluxe version of the standard Ruhiira tour.[66] On this evidence, Sachs's visits to Ruhiira would appear to be carefully engineered occasions, in which every element of his experience is managed to provide him with an image of a flourishing development utopia, which bears very little resemblance to people's everyday reality on the ground. This is not to say that the people who sing and clap are not genuinely grateful to Sachs for the little they have received from the Project. But, in this regard, the MVP is just reproducing the paternalistic relationships characteristic of Uganda's highly personalized power structures. As one Ugandan commentator has explained, 'People from rural areas treat the provi-sion of services as a favour from the government ... Even if shoddy work is done they remain thankful because they never expected it in the first place.'[67] Even so, among the households I spoke to, almost no one had any idea who Sachs was, or had been present at any of his appearances. The only exceptions were three women who were part of a singing group called the 'Millennium Band'. The group was provided with uniforms by the MVP administration and invited to perform on occasions like this, singing songs with lyrics such as: 'Jeffrey Sachs/You have done a lot/God should bless you.'[68]

If this is indicative of Sachs's experience of other Millennium Villages then it is unsurprising that he views the MVP as an unqualified success. Indeed, during his 2010 visit to Ruhiira, Sachs was not a mere spectator, but was an enthusiastic participant in the spectacle being staged for his benefit, apparently unaware of the numerous problems with the Project, which were made so evident to me during the time that I spent there. His performance at the end of this visit is described in rapturous language on the MVP website:

'Welcome visitors, welcome today. We've all been waiting so long!' Coming over the crest of the hill into the Millennium Village of Ruhiira, Uganda, children's singing voices gradually become louder, intermingled with bursts of clapping and laughter. The long-awaited visitor, Jeffrey Sachs, is due to arrive at any moment, and the anticipation is palpable ... For the people of Ruhiira, the visit proved to be about much more than the WFP partnership. It was testament to and a celebration of the fact that today, their story is different. Today, the community was living proof to the world that despite all the scepticism, great stories and dreams can be made a reality as a result of effective synergy between well-targeted aid and community empowerment. 'We haven't done it, you have', proclaimed Sachs, to tumultuous applause and ululation from the crowd of hundreds; babies and grandmothers who had walked from far and wide to catch a glimpse of their hero ... Pledging support to the community until 2015, [Sachs] promised that when that day comes, Ruhiira will be 'a shining example to the entire world ... having shown how this community achieved all the Millennium Development Goals'.[69]

THE DREAM MUST GO ON

Jeffrey Sachs is prone to rejecting criticism of his development strategies by invoking his supposedly unparalleled knowledge of the gritty realities of development, and insisting that 'issues of life and death carry a moral burden to know what you're talking about'.[70] Yet if this visit to Ruhiira is representative of his general experience of the MVP then it is not at all clear that Sachs really knows what he is talking about in this case. In his moralizing promotion of his development agenda, Sachs has insisted that the extent of global poverty is 'unimaginable to anyone that knows or cares to look. The only way we could come to this is if you take the decision never to look, and I'm afraid that's the world we're living in right now'.[71] Could it be that Sachs has taken the decision not to look at the exclusion of the extremely poor from his own development project, and not to hear the accusations of corruption within it? Could it be that the vast resources of the MVP are primarily devoted not to ensuring its effective implementation on the ground, but to projecting an image of its success on the international stage?

My own admittedly limited experience of the MVP is certainly consistent with this possibility. My research suggests that, in Ruhiira at least, the Project is failing to end extreme poverty, or to generate a sustainable and participatory model of rural development. Indeed, by contributing to the legitimation of Museveni's corrupt and authoritarian breed of peripheral dependent capitalism, the MVP could be accused of helping to keep the donor funds flowing, thus unwittingly sustaining the regime in power, and unintentionally contributing to absolving it of any material incentive to become more responsive to the needs of its impoverished population.[72]

In this sense, the MVP can be accused not only of failing to end poverty, but also of helping to ensure its continued reproduction. In contrast to Sachs's wilful vision of the transformation of a subsistence African village into a flourishing market society, the MVP is intensifying the contradictions of rural Ugandan capitalism, characterized by the persistence of extreme poverty, the marginalization and exploitation of the poorest, and the intensification of existing inequalities. In these respects, the outcome of the MVP is little different from that of shock therapy. This is ironic, given the central role of the MVP in Sachs's transformation from Dr Shock into Mr Aid. Indeed, Sachs himself has been at pains to emphasize the gulf that separates the two approaches:

> This is not Poland, this is not Russia, this is not Bolivia … The horror for me, frankly, has been to hear my own words that made some sense in Poland … to hear those same words quoted back to me for years in Africa … And then also people ask me … Did you change? Are you repenting? You know, this is nonsense. Please understand that different places have different problems and the problems in Africa are the most extreme poverty on the planet of people that have nothing and are not successful enough even to stay alive right now.[73]

I would argue that Sachs's representation of Africa here is as problematic as ever, constructing it as a place apart, in which people are reduced to helpless suffering, and where shock therapy is apparently uniquely inappropriate. Yet, despite the obvious differences between shock therapy and the MVP, the two strategies share crucial elements in common. Both attempt to implement a top-down blueprint that is insensitive to local context. Both seek to realize the fantasy of a harmonious commercial society. And both end up reproducing the poverty and inequality of real capitalism. In shock therapy, Sachs sought to liberate the natural order of a market society by dismantling the state. In the MVP, he seeks to produce this supposedly natural order through the agency of a miniature pseudo-state. In both cases, the outcome is an exacerbation of the contradictions of capitalist development that their shared fantasy denies. Indeed, the true 'horror' in this case is that the MVP seems destined to conclude in 2015 with a perverse restaging of shock therapy itself. Having created the incipient structures of a primitive and dysfunctional welfare state, Sachs will suddenly destroy it by bringing the Project to an end. The poorest people will be deprived of the minor supports that the Project has fleetingly provided, while the wealthiest will probably continue to prosper. In this sense, Sachs can be said to be engaged in a monstrous reconstruction of the conditions of his own failure.

Yet while this may be the reality in many of the Millennium Villages, in Ruhiira the MVP has now received a stay of execution. In July 2013 the Ugandan government announced that the Project will be extended beyond 2015, and scaled up to five more districts around Ruhiira, supported by an interest-free loan of US$9.75 million from the Islamic Development Bank. In a press release to mark the occasion, the MVP stated that 'the announcement follows the success of Ruhiira ... which since 2006 has served as a proof of concept of the benefits of an integrated, holistic approach to rural development pioneered by the MVP.'[74] A month later, the Islamic Development Bank announced that its loan to Uganda was only a small part of US$104 million of financing that it is now providing for the scaling up of the Millennium Villages in Uganda, Mali, and Senegal, and the launch of a new project – the Sustainable Villages Project – in Chad, Mozambique, and Sudan, in partnership with the Earth Institute and Millennium Promise. In the words of Jeffrey Sachs, the Sustainable Villages Project will apply 'cutting edge methods to the fight against poverty, hunger, and disease.'[75] As this book goes to press, further projects based on the Millennium Villages model are being rolled out in Benin, Cameroon, Congo, Guinea, Liberia, Niger, Madagascar, Togo, and Zambia.[76] Only one thing really matters: the dream must go on.

6 THE WORLD FALLS APART

If our story had ended here, we might have concluded that Jeffrey Sachs would live happily ever after, cocooned in his imagined identity as Mr Aid, the benevolent saviour of 'Africa'. His fantasy of a harmonious commercial society had been restored by the apparent success of the Millennium Villages Project. His role in Russia was now all but forgotten, and he was internationally celebrated as an economic miracle worker once again. But there can be no escape from the Real. Once a fantasy has been shattered by a traumatic event, its reconstruction can only ever be fragile and contingent, and it remains perpetually vulnerable to a 'return of the repressed'.[1] Ever since the halcyon days of 2005, when Sachs celebrated the 'Year of Africa', his visits to the Millennium Villages have been mere happy islands in a sea of trouble. His journey to the present has been beset by confrontations with the Real of Capital, in the form of the ecological crisis, the Great Recession, and the repeated failure of his own projects. In response, Sachs has been forced into a series of increasingly desperate attempts to hold his world together.

THE STUFF OF NIGHTMARES

Even as Sachs was setting out his extraordinarily ambitious scheme to end extreme poverty in Africa, an even larger and more intractable problem was looming on the horizon of his consciousness, in the form of the ecological crisis. As the first decade of the new millennium progressed, Sachs became increasingly concerned with the question of sustainable development, and his writings began to be plagued by horrifying visions of environmental catastrophe. In a short article for

Project Syndicate in October 2005, for example, Sachs predicted an impending avalanche of ecological chaos, including 'shocking natural disasters ... storms ... rising sea levels ... drought, famine ... fires, mudslides, heat waves ... powerful hurricanes ... AIDS, SARS, avian flu ... dengue fever ... other infectious diseases ... epidemics, climate change, extreme weather events, and earthquakes.'[2] This prophecy of ecological doom was repeated in 2008 in *Common Wealth*, the follow-up to *The End of Poverty*, and another influential bestseller. In *Common Wealth*, Sachs adopts another new persona as a global eco-warrior, warning us that our social and ecological future is 'the stuff of night-mares,'[3] and 'a calamity is inevitable unless we change.'[4]

The world faces very serious ecological challenges, including all the dangers that Sachs identifies, and he is surely right to call attention to the urgent need for action. At the heart of the ecological crisis is capi-talism's insatiable appetite for economic growth, and the exploitation of natural resources on the basis of private profit and market calcula-tions. Sachs's apocalyptic descriptions of our ecological predicament would seem to promise a serious engagement with these fundamental issues, and the very title of *Common Wealth* suggests a radical cri-tique of our current socio-economic order. Instead, *Common Wealth* repeats the formula of *The End of Poverty*. Just as his representation of 'Africa' mobilized a depoliticizing sense of horrified fascination in the readers of that book, so the readers of *Common Wealth* are captivated by his apocalyptic warnings of our collective doom, which serve to coat a set of mainstream policy solutions and technological fixes in a veneer of political radicalism.

Throughout *Common Wealth*, Sachs repeatedly contrasts himself to 'free market ideologues,'[5] and insists that '[m]arket forces alone cannot solve these problems.'[6] Yet, despite these rhetorical challenges to neoliberal orthodoxy, Sachs's policy prescriptions continue to place great faith in market mechanisms. According to Sachs, 'Global market forces can be "reengineered" to channel economic activity in a sustainable manner.'[7]

While he advocates a proactive role for the state in 'creating market incentives,'[8] Sachs continues to eulogize 'the self-organizing forces of the market economy,'[9] and proposes a wide range of market-based solutions to the problems of sustainable development. These include carbon markets for climate change mitigation;[10] trad-able permits for fishing rights;[11] public–private partnerships in the management of water resources;[12] the promotion of 'private ecotourism sites, which ... can harness the profit motive';[13] the guarantee of 'patent-protected profits' for multinational corporations;[14] and even the creation of a market in 'rainfall insurance, or a weather-based derivative'.[15]

None of these proposed solutions are new. In fact, they are all familiar components of a neoliberal regime of environmental governance that has become increasingly dominant over the past two decades, and has been celebrated by the right as 'free market environmentalism'.[16] These market-oriented solutions have been criticized by environmental activists and political ecologists on the grounds that markets are unable to solve environmental problems, and that economic growth and private profit cannot be squared with environmental justice and sustainability. These are not merely ideological objections. The world's first and largest carbon market, the European Trading System, collapsed in 2013, after the economic crisis in the European Union reduced the demand for carbon credits and prices fell so low that companies had no incentive to reduce their levels of pollution.[17] Private ecotourism has been implicated in numerous cases of environmental exploitation and the displacement of indigenous peoples.[18] And tradable fishing permits have led to the destruction of fishing communities and the consolidation of fishing quotas in the hands of international trawling companies with little interest in local sustainability.[19]

Needless to say, Sachs does not engage with any of these criticisms. Instead, the privatization of the ecological commons is to be combined with an extraordinarily ambitious set of technological fixes, on the assumption that '[b]etter technologies can square the circle of economic growth with sustainability'.[20] Increasing energy demands are to be met by innovations in 'wind, hydroelectricity, ocean waves, biofuels ... geothermal energy ... nuclear power and solar energy'.[21] Water shortages are to be addressed by 'harnessing wind, solar, or hydropower for desalination'.[22] Food production is to be boosted by a new Green Revolution, based on 'transgenetic modification ... to engineer crop varieties that ... can thrive in drought-prone areas',[23] along with a 'Blue Revolution', based on 'the domestication and commercialization of marine species'.[24] Faced with dwindling oil reserves, Sachs cheerfully informs us that 'coal can be converted into liquid fuels such as gasoline at low cost. So too can other, nonconventional fossil fuels like oil sands and shale, and potentially the methane hydrates that are abundant on the sea bed'.[25] Meanwhile, climate change is to be counteracted by capturing carbon dioxide 'at its source – the power plants, cement kilns, and steel furnaces – before it is admitted into the atmosphere', and by injecting it 'into underground reservoirs, such as abandoned oil wells; geological formations … areas below the ocean floor … or underground saline aquifers'.[26] Despite admitting that the feasibility of these carbon capture and storage technologies is 'still unproved',[27] Sachs remains emphatically convinced of their efficacy. He even suggests that a 'fascinating alternative … would be to capture CO_2 directly from the air', although he is once again forced to admit that this idea is 'not yet proven in practice'.[28]

The problems with this agenda are too vast and numerous to be discussed here, but a brief consideration of Sachs's proposals on climate change is enough to illustrate the implausibility of his ecological agenda as a whole. The dangers of nuclear energy and shale gas 'fracking' are well established, and the excessive carbon emissions associated with coal and tar sands are well known. Sachs places great faith in carbon sequestration and alternative energy, but even if his proposed array of as-yet-undeveloped technological fantasies were to become operational in the extremely short timeframe required, the environmental consequences of large-scale carbon sequestration are unforeseeable and potentially catastrophic.[29] And even if the necessary treaties, markets, and technologies all fell into place and all functioned perfectly, and Sachs's target of keeping temperature increases below 2°C were met,[30] this would still not be enough to prevent dangerous climate change. The latest climate science suggests that 2°C now represents a threshold not between 'acceptable' and 'dangerous' climate change, but between 'dangerous' and 'extremely dangerous' climate change. This new information has led prominent climate scientists to conclude that avoiding dangerous climate change is 'no longer compatible' with continued economic growth.[31]

BOTH FEET PLANTED IN MIDAIR

We thus return to the unavoidable fact that there is no solution to the ecological crisis within the framework of capitalism, which blindly pursues economic growth regardless of the ecological consequences. Unfortunately, Sachs is incapable of acknowledging this reality. As in *The End of Poverty*, 'capitalism' is almost never discussed in *Common Wealth*. In fact, it often seems that Sachs is desperate to talk about anything else, just to avoid mentioning the word. In the book, Sachs fills the brief intervals between apocalyptic visions and technological fantasies by bombarding his readers with astonishingly elementary factoids, such as the following revelation: 'As water vapour rises and cools, it condenses, until it returns to Earth as precipitation.'[32] He also resorts to the last-ditch right-wing explanation of environmental degradation in terms of Malthus's theory of overpopulation. The subtitle of *Common Wealth* is *Economics for a Crowded Planet*. Invoking what he calls 'the specter of Malthus', Sachs locates the ultimate cause of our environmental predicament not in the exploitation of our common biosphere for private profit, but in the presence of too many poor people who breed too much.[33] Sachs rejects the suggestion that 'sustainable development means ... that the rich have to cut their standards of living sharply to make room for the poor', arguing: 'my own analysis doesn't suggest that the reason that poor people are poor is that rich people are rich. I think rich people are rich because they have developed technology successfully ... and because they were lucky enough not to have some of the ecological barriers that the poor have.'[34] In light of these supposedly natural barriers, Sachs advocates a 'voluntary reduction of fertility rates' among the poor,[35] warning that their failure to heed his words will 'almost surely trigger Malthus's "positive checks" (war, disease, famine).'[36]

The planet cannot sustain a growing population indefinitely, but it seems perverse to place the blame for the over-exploitation of the world's resources on the shoulders of its poorest people, while absolving the wealthiest of any duty to redistribute their wealth or reduce their levels of consumption. In his critique of Malthus, Marx argued that his theory of overpopulation served to obscure the generation of poverty and environmental destruction through the concentration of land and money in the hands of the capitalist class, and was therefore 'in conformity with the interests of the ruling classes, whom Malthus idolized like a true priest.'[37] Sachs's strategy of population control, technological fixes and market-based solutions, and his endorsement of the existing distribution of wealth and power, is equally in conformity with the environmental agenda of today's ruling classes. This is evident from his collaborations with big business at the Earth Institute at Columbia University, New York. As director of the Institute, Sachs has effective control over an annual budget of US$87 million, with over thirty research centres and 850 academic staff.[38] The Institute has a special facility for multinational corporations, called the EI Corporate Circle, which 'allows corporations to take advantage of the latest information, tools, and networks in the field'.[39] In exchange for 'programme investment of at least $100,000 a year', businesses are offered full access to Earth Institute staff and resources, including 'four joint phone conferences per year with Earth Institute Director Jeffrey Sachs'.[40]

Some of the world's most powerful corporations have signed up to the Corporate Circle, including GE, GlaxoSmithKline, HSBC, Merck, Monsanto, Nestlé, Novartis, PepsiCo, and Pfizer.[41] Many of these corporations stand accused of environmental crimes and human rights abuses too numerous to list here – PepsiCo's depletion of underground aquifers in India, GlaxoSmithKline's illegal medical testing on impoverished children in Argentina, and Monsanto's genetically modified seeds that must be repurchased annually by subsistence farmers are just three of the more notorious examples. Their membership of the EI Corporate Circle offers a convenient means for these companies to demonstrate their 'corporate social responsibility' as a counterweight to such damaging scandals. Some have become involved in the Millennium Villages Project (see Chapters 4 and 5), and Sachs has organized a series of high-profile events for his corporate sponsors on a range of environmental issues. In 2007, for example, he hosted the Global Roundtable on Climate Change, which included major carbon emitters such as Wal-Mart, Air France, the World Petroleum Council, and American Electric Power, which emits more carbon dioxide than any other corporation in the United States.[42] It also included other corporations with dubious environmental records, such as Alcoa – the largest aluminium producer in the world and a major polluter – and the chemical company DuPont, which has been involved in the research and development of sulphur dioxide, leaded petrol, CFCs, GM crops, and the atomic bomb.[43] Unsurprisingly, the concluding statement issued by the Roundtable emphasized that any future policy to mitigate climate change must be consistent with 'the global need for energy [and] economic growth',[44] and the event was dismissed by environmentalists as opportunistic 'greenwashing' for multinational corporations intent on continuing with business-as-usual.[45]

Sachs, of course, refuses to engage with such concerns. Instead he behaves as if they do not exist, praising corporate social responsibility[46] and insisting that 'there are no solutions to the problems of poverty, population, and environment without the active engagement of the private sector, and especially the large multinational companies'.[47] This stubborn defence of corporate power suggests that Sachs is less concerned with ecological sustainability than with the sustainability of the status quo. Indeed, it could be argued that his environmental agenda of technological fixes, market-based solutions, and economic growth is not really an ecological project at all, but a strategy for the total mobilization of the Earth's resources towards the monolithic objective of endless capital accumulation in a world of ecological finitude. This contradictory strategy is not peculiar to Sachs, but is at the heart of the project that political ecologists call 'green capitalism':

> To be green means to prioritize the health of the ecosphere, with all that this entails in terms of curbing greenhouse gases and preserving biodiversity. To promote capitalism, by contrast, is to foster growth and accumulation, treating both the workforce and the natural environment as mere inputs. Capital ... must seek to balance perpetual growth with the preservation of the basic conditions for survival. Despite the ultimate incompatibility of these two goals, therefore, capital must to some extent pursue both at once. Although green capitalism is an oxymoron, it is therefore nonetheless a policy objective. Its proponents thus find themselves in an ongoing two-front struggle against, on the one hand, capital's more short-sighted advocates, and on the other, the demand for a far-reaching ecologically grounded conversion of production and consumption.[48]

In *Common Wealth*, Sachs dismisses those who question the feasibility of this fundamentally incoherent agenda as 'pessimists' who fail to appreciate that 'negativism is a state of mind, not a view based on the facts'.[49] Quoting John F. Kennedy, Sachs insists that, faced with the gravity of our shared predicament, we must put aside our differences and acknowledge that '[t]he supreme reality of our time is our indivisibility as children of God and our common vulnerability on this planet'.[50] This is a charming sentiment, but it rings hollow in the context of his insistence that the rich will not have to compromise their living standards, and his willingness to cut deals with corporations while blaming environmental destruction on the 'fertility' of the poor. It also ignores the political realities of power and conflict in the global economy, which Sachs apparently assumes can be overcome by explaining the self-evidence of his agenda to the rest of the world.

Sachs's ecological agenda may appeal to those with a vested interest in propagating the oxymoronic fantasy of 'green capitalism', but it does not convince everyone. In 2007, Sachs was invited to deliver the BBC's prestigious Reith Lectures, which he used to set out his vision for sustainable development. Sachs had anticipated an international radio audience of 150 million people, and had assumed that the world would immediately grasp the simplicity and common-sense of his proposals.[51] Instead, he was met with extreme scepticism. Throughout the lecture series, Sachs was barraged with incredulous questions, which increasingly exposed the implausibility of his proposed solutions to the coming apocalypse.[52] In the final lecture Bernard Crick, the political theorist, democratic socialist, and biographer of George Orwell, responded to Sachs as follows: 'Seems to me that this is sort of H. G. Wells reborn – that scientific wisdom can replace politics. These are surely *political* problems, and you seem to have slipped entirely from a logic of politics into, if you don't mind me saying, starting with both feet firmly planted in midair.'[53]

Sachs attempted to dismiss this criticism, but was immediately caught by another broadside from a professor of philosophy, who pointed out the implicit authoritarianism of Sachs's project, arguing that 'the danger is … a kind of utopianism that may turn itself into either a mass bureaucracy, or a certain kind of global tyranny'.[54] This time, Sachs responded by emphasizing his enduring commitment to 'mechanisms along Smith's market lines'.[55] Far from discounting the totalitarian implications of his project, however, this response only succeeded in further demonstrating the profound compatibility between neoliberalism and authoritarianism that has characterized Sachs's politics since his first shock therapy experiments.

In the final question of his final lecture, Sachs was again asked whether he honestly believed that his plans were realistic. In his response, he sounded tired, almost defeated, and concluded by wearily warning his audience: 'This world has every capacity to go way off the rails. We have every capacity to create incredible damage in the world.'[56] In contrast to the wilful naivety of his gargantuan plan to save the planet, this warning was to prove extremely prescient. As Sachs delivered this lecture, in May 2007, the global economy was still caught up in the ephemeral rush of credit-fuelled growth that preceded the Great

Recession, in which the deepening contradictions of neoliberal capitalism were being held together by vast bubbles of fictitious capital. In this atmosphere of eerie calm, the global policy elite was unconcerned by the possibility of an imminent economic collapse. Yet Jeffrey Sachs was haunted by persistent forebodings of catastrophe, which seemed to be informed by the failure of shock therapy in Russia. As far back as 2004, Sachs had begun to fear the possibility of Russia's crisis recurring in America itself, warning his fellow Americans that they were on an unsustainable course, and that '[i]f we persist in such illusions, we'll eventually follow Russia in going right over the precipice.'[57]

And that is exactly what happened.

INTO THE FURY

In September 2008 the collapse of Lehman Brothers triggered the most severe economic crisis in the United States since the Great Depression. The Real that had confronted Sachs in Russia, and that he had repressed for so long, now surged back into his reality with all the force of its blind destructive power. In Sachs's words, 'the US walked headlong into the fury ... the rest of the world has been carried with it into the fury'.[58] As the heartland of free market capitalism, America had always provided Sachs with a reassuring confirmation of his neoliberal fantasy, and despite his condemnation of the United States for abandoning him in Russia, and for ignoring him in Africa, he had always regarded it as 'a beacon of hope for the world'.[59] Now this stable reference point had been destroyed, and Sachs was gripped by a sudden fear of a resurgent communism. This fear is evident in Sachs's third major book, *The Price of Civilization*, published in 2011, which focuses on America's economic crisis. In the book, Sachs warns his fellow Americans: 'Economic crises open the door to deep political change. The future is up for grabs. Yet the dangers also multiply. There are, after all, many more possible wrong turns than right ones.'[60] For Sachs, the greatest danger remains the threat of communism. He emphasizes that 'Russian chaos was manipulated by Vladimir Lenin to launch the ruinous experiment with Soviet socialism',[61] and suggests that the United States is vulnerable to the same danger, admitting that these 'are morbid thoughts, but they are my darker forebodings prompted by the current political drift in the United States.'[62]

These 'morbid thoughts' and 'dark forebodings' explain the peculiar mixture of Third Way 'social democracy' and demagogic populism that has characterized Sachs's response to the global economic crisis. Despite his unimpeachable record as a free market revolutionary, Sachs now presents himself as an outspoken critic of 'libertarianism' and 'the free market fallacy',[63] and identifies the 'social democracies' of northern Europe – Norway, Sweden, Denmark and the Netherlands – as his models of best practice.[64] This stance has gained him significant media exposure as the mainstream's favoured 'radical' critic of economic orthodoxy – he has appeared on television channels such as the BBC, CNN, and Bloomberg, and has written for periodicals including the *New York Times*, the *Financial Times*, and *Time* magazine. Even such avowedly left-leaning programmes as *Democracy Now!* and *The Rachel Maddow Show* have featured Sachs without mentioning his shock therapy past, and he has written for left-of-centre publications including the *Guardian* and the *New Statesman*. Yet a close reading of his post-crisis policy proposals reveals a depressingly familiar combination of an enduring commitment to neoliberal fundamentals and a chronic inability to confront his own past.

The Price of Civilization is structured around a strident critique of Reaganomics, in which Sachs might as well be attacking himself for his own repressed role in the market revolution. Sachs repeatedly berates Reagan for advocating 'widespread deregulation and privatization of government services',[65] which was precisely the basis of his own shock therapy formula.[66] He also speaks of his 'amazement and consternation' when confronted with 'a huge change in income distribution in the United States' since the early 1980s,[67] in which '[c]apital owners have been the big winners', while workers have suffered 'a grinding squeeze on wages and working conditions'.[68] Yet, as we saw in Chapter 1, Sachs's own work in the late 1970s and early 1980s was explicitly devoted to restoring capital to profitability by reducing wage inflation, weakening unions, and deregulating investment. In contrast to his newfound concern with the 'squeeze on wages', Sachs argued at the time that 'concern ... about real wage behaviour and profitability has been appropriate, in light of the progressive *squeeze on profits*',[69] and celebrated the 'success ... in reducing real wages' that could be achieved through a combination of 'high unemployment ... wage and price controls, and other policy instruments'.[70]

In another bizarre inversion of reality, Sachs now claims to be an admirer of the European social democracies of the 1970s and 1980s, in which strong unions and interventionist states combined to limit the influence and profits of the capitalist class, while ensuring decent working conditions and a high standard of social welfare for the majority of their populations. Challenging the reduction of the role of government in the United States, Sachs accuses Reagan of 'strangling' the state, and complains: 'While Europe decided to boost its tax-to-gross domestic product ratio in the 1970s and 1980s ... Reagan insisted that less government was the key to prosperity and growth.'[71] Yet, in a paper published in 1986, Sachs launched a zealous neoliberal attack on the first years of the Mitterrand administration, which constituted Europe's last great experiment with real social democracy. In the paper, Sachs and his co-author criticize Mitterrand for following 'the general European trend of supply-side mismanagement, with excessive labour costs, a fast growth of the welfare system, and continuously spreading regulation of labour markets.'[72] Against this social-democratic agenda, they assert: *'we share the Reaganomics emphasis on the efficacy of tax reductions.'*[73] They extol 'the virtue of competition in a free market economy',[74] praising the austerity measures that international capital markets had subsequently forced Mitterrand to embrace, and triumphantly concluding: 'The fight against unemployment is no longer at the forefront of the government's objectives. The key words are now: external balance, modernization and rationalization of the economy, greater competitiveness and wage moderation.'[75]

In short, when Sachs attacks Reagan for 'squeezing wages' and 'strangling the welfare state', he is attacking the very policies that he himself promoted at the time. Yet his subsequent embrace of 'Scandinavian social democracy' is not quite as contradictory as it might appear. Sachs is not really praising the Scandinavia of the 1970s, which he has singled out in the past as the worst example of Keynesian largesse. Instead, he is praising the Scandinavia of the present, which has been undergoing its own neoliberal reform process since the 1980s. The contrast between the two models of 'Scandinavian social democracy' can be illustrated by the case of Sweden. In a 1982 paper, Sachs criticized Sweden's social-democratic government for utilizing 'very expansionist policies during 1974–1976 ... A wage boom and severe profit squeeze ensued, which ushered in a number of years of very poor growth. Moreover, the expansionary policies left a legacy of a greatly expanded public sector.'[76] Since then, however, Sweden has been implementing neoliberal reforms in line with Sachs's recommendations in that paper. As a consequence of these reforms, income inequality grew faster in Sweden than in any other industrialized nation between 1985 and 2010.[77] This growing inequality contributed to the circumstances that triggered widespread rioting among the country's marginalized and impoverished immigrant population in 2013. In this context, Sachs's suggestion that 'Nordic ethnic homogeneity has been an important social factor in the success of the social-welfare state'[78] appears particularly unpleasant and ill informed. Nordic countries are not ethnically homogenous, their welfare systems are no longer 'social-democratic', and the equation of 'ethnic homogeneity' with social-welfare 'success' is dangerously misguided at best.

When he identifies himself as a social democrat, Sachs is referring not to the quasi-socialist social democracy of the past, but to the 'Third Way' social democracy of Blair, Clinton, and Schröder, which is the model on which the 'Nordic' economies themselves are increasingly based.[79] The Third Way model accepts the neoliberal fundamentals of free trade, macroeconomic stability, flexible labour markets, and the replacement of the redistribution of wealth with 'equality of opportunity'. Collectivist principles and Keynesian demand-management are replaced with a supply-side-oriented 'enabling' state, predicated on the promotion of global competitiveness, which aims to provide globally mobile capital with a highly qualified workforce, world class infrastructure and an attractive 'business environment'.[80] Borrowing Blair's phrase, Sachs makes the case for a 'radical centrism' of precisely this kind,[81] rejecting both Keynesianism and 'libertarianism', and arguing for the provision of 'critical public goods that are complementary to the private-led economy'.[82] Sachs emphasizes that 'markets need government ... to be deeply engaged in public education, road building, scientific discovery, environmental protection, financial regulation, and many other activities',[83] while defending free trade,[84] advocating 'low corporate tax rates',[85] rejecting Keynesian stimulus,[86] defining equality as 'opportunity for all',[87] promoting 'global competitiveness',[88] and arguing that wages should be determined by 'market forces'.[89]

Sachs's newfound commitment to 'social democracy' is therefore predicated not on the protection of society from market forces, but on the total subordination of social space to the demands of capital accumulation. By representing 'globalization' as a natural and inevitable force, and reducing politics to the pursuit of global competitiveness, Sachs is locking states and workers into a war of all against all, in which there will always be losers, and the winners will be those who most effectively gratify the demands of global capital. By referring to 'social democracy' and 'the northern European economies' as generic terms, without acknowledging the transition towards neoliberalism that has occurred within them, Sachs is able to frame this market-based agenda in terms of 'social justice' and political radicalism. Furthermore, by framing Reaganomics as an attack on government, and casting his own agenda as the radical political alternative, Sachs fundamentally misrepresents the neoliberal project, which has always been about the restructuring of the state, rather than its demolition.[90] Ultimately, it is not 'free market ideologues' who are the guardians of neoliberalism, but the more pragmatic neoliberals like Sachs himself, who are prepared to mobilize all the powers of the state in order to cope with the proliferating contradictions of the neoliberal project, and to block the possibility of genuinely progressive change.

SOMETHING TO HYDE?

The extent to which Sachs remains committed to the neoliberal project is revealed in momentary lapses of judgement and slips of the tongue. It is as if, suddenly gripped by the trauma of the global economic crisis, Sachs is overcome by his old lust for radical austerity, and cannot help committing acts of public indiscretion. One such example is his support for the UK coalition government's austerity agenda, which constitutes the most orthodox neoliberal response to the global crisis of any of the 'advanced' capitalist states. Sachs has been described as a 'friend'[91] and 'personal advisor'[92] of the Conservative MP and chancellor of the exchequer, George Osborne, who is precisely the kind of free market ideologue that Sachs now claims to abhor. Osborne first met Sachs in 2007 on a tour of the Millennium Villages Project in Ruhiira, Uganda. Inspired by Sachs's approach to development, Osborne introduced Sachs 'to the Conservative elite, gave [him] dinner at his home [and] enthused about "One World Conservatism".'[93] In the run-up to the 2010 general election, Sachs and Osborne co-authored an article in the *Financial Times*, entitled 'A Frugal Policy Is the Better Solution', in which they set out the case for rapid cuts in the public sector and the promotion of a private sector–led recovery.[94] Since gaining power, Osborne has implemented this plan with the same zeal with which Sachs once implemented shock therapy. Yet while the plan has pleased financial markets, the 'private sector–led recovery' has not been forthcoming, and the burden of the austerity measures has fallen most heavily on the poorest and most disadvantaged members of British society.

In January 2012, Sachs wrote an article in the *New York Times* in support of the Nigerian government's removal of its fuel subsidy, which had previously functioned as a means of limited redistribution of the country's vast oil wealth to its impoverished population. In another clear echo of his shock therapy discourse, Sachs insisted that the Nigerian population must 'take the tough medicine necessary to build the foundations for long-term growth'.[95] Following the removal of the subsidy, the price of fuel doubled overnight, and the price of basic commodities rapidly increased. People took to the streets, and the army was sent out to control the protests. At least twenty people were killed and hundreds more injured in the resulting clashes.[96] Over the following days, Sachs's Twitter account was flooded with complaints from Nigerians enraged by his endorsement of the government's policy. The situation was summarized by one commentator as follows:

> What's instructive ... is that when dishing out prescriptions to help remedy the situation, Sachs does not suggest that the government reform its own rotten institutions or prevent poaching by the nation's wealthiest families. Instead, we're told that the vast majority of the country's poor – who depend on oil subsidies to make possible everyday things like getting to market and keeping cool – should be forced to shoulder the lion's share of sacrifice as [Nigerian president] Goodluck Jonathan pursues market reform under heavy pressure from the International Monetary Fund. Welcome to Shock Therapy 2.0 ... Sachs' most recent fit of poor judgment will be quickly forgiven – rewarded, even, with future opinion pieces in the world's most influential editorial section. For this very reason, it's worth reminding ourselves of the important lessons to be drawn from this episode: Sachs had no idea what he was talking about, his knee-jerk response to the crisis celebrated policies of austerity and economic shock, and ... neoliberalism, it would seem, is alive and well.[97]

Sachs's continued adherence to neoliberal fundamentals is also betrayed by his vociferous attacks on those advocating 'naive' Keynesian solutions to the economic crisis in the United States, as well as in Ireland, Spain, and Greece. Sachs insists that 'deficit cutting should start now', and emphasizes that the suffering caused by austerity is 'not an anomaly to be fought but an adjustment to be accepted'.[98] This knee-jerk neo-liberal instinct is also evident in *The Price of Civilization*, in which Sachs appears to be afflicted by a kind of neoliberal Tourette's syndrome, through which his 'social-democratic' critique of 'free market ideologues' is repeatedly interrupted by the barking of spasmodic eulogies to Friedrich Hayek and Milton Friedman, who he identifies as providing the 'economic underpinnings' of his own worldview.[99]

A CRIMINAL ENEMY OF THE WORKING CLASS

By September 2011, the worst of the economic crisis seemed to have passed, and Sachs could begin to breathe freely once again. The American economy was showing signs of recovery, and there was no sign of the communist movement he had feared. Then suddenly, as if from nowhere, Occupy Wall Street burst into the centre of American political consciousness. The occupation of Zucotti Park in New York's financial district began on 17 September and rapidly gained in strength, spreading to cities across the United States and around the world. By 27 September, the radical philosopher and democratic socialist Cornell West was telling the restless masses in Zucotti Park: 'We should not be afraid to say "revolution".'[100] This really was the stuff of Sachs's most appalling nightmares: an international and potentially revolutionary left-wing movement, united by the collective assertion of class antagonism – 'We are the 99 per cent' – against corporate power and income inequality, and rooted in the heart of American capitalism. Sachs's response, however, was not to ignore or dismiss Occupy Wall Street. Instead he passionately endorsed it, and sought to position himself as its spokesman, in a determined attempt to twist its political direction away from revolutionary anti-capitalism and towards a populist attack on greedy bankers and corrupt politicians, in defence of capital itself.

In this regard, the publication of *The Price of Civilization* on 4 October could not have been better timed. On CNN, CBC, and Fox News, in the *New York Times*, the *Financial Times*, and the *Huffington Post*, in lecture halls across the country, and in Zucotti Park itself, Sachs promoted *The Price of Civilization* as the political agenda of the Occupy movement, disguising his endorsement of the status quo beneath angry, moralizing sermons on the decadence of America's political and economic elites. Despite having consistently defended economic inequality throughout his work on poverty-alleviation and sustainable development, Sachs now became its most vociferous critic, arguing that 'self-interest can easily turn into unacceptable inequality', due to 'winner-takes-all markets; fraud; and ... the conversion of wealth into power, in order to gain even greater wealth.'[101] Equally, despite his own development projects being sustained by financial speculators and multinational corporations, Sachs could now be found in Zucotti Park ranting that 'The rich have cheated. They cheated and cheated ... They didn't earn their money, they took their money ... And they know how to hide their money. And they know how to game the system.'[102]

In a heated CNN debate on Occupy Wall Street in October 2011, the conservative historian Niall Ferguson told Sachs, 'Having watched what you said at Occupy Wall Street, I have to say I thought you overstepped the mark, and ceased to be an academic, and became a demagogue.'[103] Ignoring Sachs's protestations, Ferguson insisted that his attack on bankers and corporations was 'a demagogic argument. Especially from someone who knows that the principle driver of inequality has actually been globalization, not malpractice on Wall Street.'[104] Ferguson was arguing in defence of the established order, but his characterization of Sachs as demagogic and disingenuous was absolutely correct. Regrettably, however, the political objective of Sachs's bizarre transformation into an anti-capitalist rabble-rouser was not to challenge the capitalist elite, but precisely to neutralize the threat posed to them by the Occupy movement.

In his praise for Occupy Wall Street, Sachs has persistently sought to frame it as 'the new Progressive movement', in reference to the American Progressive movement of the late nineteenth century, which challenged the inequities of the Gilded Age. What Sachs does not mention, however, is that the Progressive movement was primarily concerned with the defence of capitalism against America's increasingly powerful socialist movement, and that its political role was to offer the concessions necessary to quell the threat of revolution.[105] In claiming to speak for Occupy, Sachs has consistently articulated its demands in similarly conciliatory terms. Throughout *The Price of Civilization*, and his subsequent engagements with the Occupy protests, Sachs never advocates collective action or the strengthening of unions as part of his proposed solution to the global economic crisis. He never mentions the working class as a potential agent of progressive change. And he never suggests that any lessons might be drawn from the achievements of organized labour in the past. Indeed, he concludes *The Price of Civilization* with the message: 'No class war is needed or intended.'[106]

For Sachs, the solution to the crisis of global capitalism lies not in radical, systemic transformation from below, but in the voluntary moral renewal of the capitalist class, based on a return to the supposedly traditional bourgeois ethic of temperance, frugality, and responsible investment – Max Weber's 'spirit of capitalism'. In an article for the *Financial Times*, entitled 'Self-Interest, Without Morals, Leads to Capitalism's Destruction', Sachs laments that 'global capitalism has mostly shed its moral constraints. Self-interest is no longer embedded in higher values.'[107] By contrast, 'Europe's original modern capitalists, the Calvinists, pursued profits in the search for proof of salvation. They saved ascetically to accumulate wealth to prove God's grace, not to sate their consumer appetites.'[108] Similarly, in *The Price of Civilization*, Sachs quotes Weber in praising these early capitalists for 'the earning of more and more money, combined with the strict avoidance of all spontaneous enjoyment in life'.[109] Sachs credits this philosophy of joyless avarice with ensuring the stability of capitalism, arguing that 'late-nineteenth-century society tolerated the rich because they lived properly and correctly, by accumulating vast wealth without consuming it'.[110] He then turns to the nineteenth-century philanthropist and murderous strike-breaker Andrew Carnegie, quoting him in glowing terms that illustrate Sachs's own contempt for the working class, and his enduring respect for the capitalist elite:

> America's greatest late-nineteenth-century capitalist, steel man Andrew Carnegie ... distinguished between the worthy calling of making money and the proper use of the money once made. In ... 'The Gospel of Wealth', Carnegie defined what he called the 'duty of the man of wealth ... becoming the mere trustee and agent of his poor brethren, bringing to their service his superior wisdom, experience, and ability to administer, doing for them better than they would or could do for themselves.'[111]

Sachs's loyalty thus continues to lie firmly with the capitalist class, and his abiding concern is for the defence of their privilege, as opposed to the redistribution of their wealth. In *The Price of Civilization*, Sachs hastens to reassure 'the top 1 per cent of wealth holders' that, if his agenda were implemented, their 'net-of-tax income would remain around 10 per cent of GDP, a share of national income two-thirds higher than the 6 per cent of GDP in 1980'.[112] In other words, despite his apparent outrage at the inequities of Reaganomics, Sachs would maintain income inequality at levels significantly higher than they were at the start of the Reagan era.

Sachs's role in relation to Occupy Wall Street was therefore to subtly represent the interests of the 1 per cent, even as he was telling the potentially revolutionary crowd at Zucotti Park: 'We are the 99 per cent! We really are the 99 per cent! And the 1 per cent doesn't get it yet!'[113] Sachs spoke at Zucotti Park on at least three occasions.[114] Beyond the deployment of such apparently radical rhetoric, these performances were consistently directed against the emergence of a revolutionary political consciousness. On one occasion, in which Sachs was holding forth on the evils of the Koch Brothers and Exxon Mobil, an activist interrupted him and asked, 'Are you saying that corporations should not be in private hands?' – to which Sachs forcefully responded: 'No! I'm saying that corporations should do business. They should stop trying to run our country … ' The activist then raised the obvious point: 'How is that possible if they're in private hands? If they're not nationalized? Why would they do what we want them to do for the good of the people?' Sachs again cut in, desperate to shut down this line of thought before it infected the surrounding audience: 'Because *thank God* there are countries that show us that you can have companies and you can still have democracy. Countries like Sweden, countries like Denmark … '[115] Sachs also interspersed his incendiary speeches at Zucotti Park with subtle defences of the status quo. By utilizing Occupy's people's mic. – in which each line of his speech was repeated and amplified by the surrounding audience for the benefit of those standing too far away to hear the speaker – Sachs managed to get the potentially insurrectionary masses to chant some surprisingly neoliberal slogans, such as 'Globalization was good for many poor countries!';[116] 'The purpose of government is to raise productivity!';[117] and 'We're not against markets! We're not even against banks! … We need a market of laws!'[118]

The enthusiastic response of the crowds at Zucotti Park demonstrated the depressing effectiveness of Sachs's counter-revolutionary strategy.[119] Yet this should not lead us to imagine him as a coldly calculating manipulator of public opinion. On the contrary, as I have argued, Sachs was pushed into this role by his paranoid fear of communist insurrection. This fear can only have been exacerbated when he was confronted at Zucotti Park by members of the Trotskyite Internationalist Group, who reported the incident in an blog-post entitled, 'What the Hell Was Economic Hit-Man Jeffrey Sachs Doing at Occupy Wall Street?':

> '*Jeffrey Sachs* is speaking at Occupy Wall Street? That can't be,' a union activist at the City University of New York cried out … Hastening to the square, Internationalist supporters saw Sachs, having finished his presentation, talking to the crowd. A CUNY adjunct who … has written extensively on the struggles of Bolivian miners broke through the atmosphere of adulation to denounce Sachs: 'What about Bolivia? What about the shock treatment you put into effect there? This man is a criminal enemy of the working class. He brought incalculable misery to working people … ' After a brief attempt to disclaim responsibility for the results of his policies, Sachs turned tail and quickly departed … [120]

THE WORLD WILL NEVER SETTLE DOWN …

Occupy Wall Street was closed down by riot police on 15 November 2011, and public support for the movement rapidly receded. This must have come as an immense relief to Sachs, particularly after he had been hounded out of Zucotti Park by revolutionary communists who had publicly accused him of being 'a criminal enemy of the working class'. Yet global capitalism remained in a profound crisis, and Sachs appeared to be losing faith in its recovery. In a lecture in December 2011, Sachs noted, 'The world in many ways has tendencies to fall apart', and wearily admitted, 'The world is never going to settle down, it never has and it never will, to God's kingdom on earth.'[121] But, rather than give up the fight, Sachs insisted on further upping the stakes in his increasingly hopeless struggle to hold his fantasy together. The Earth Institute was no longer adequate to the task, and Sachs decided that he needed an even bigger, more powerful institution, with an even more totalizing global reach. In March 2012, Jeffrey Sachs nominated himself as the next president of the World Bank. Even by Sachs's standards, this was an act of astonishing hubris. The World Bank president was always personally selected by the president of the United States, and no one had ever publicly put themselves forward for the role. But this was 'the leading international organization of global capitalist development',[122] with over 9,000 employees operating in over 100 countries, and it had already lent US$103 billion in the three years since the start of the global crisis.[123] If Sachs was to succeed in his manic mission to save global capitalism, then he desperately needed this job.

Sachs announced his candidacy in an article in the *Washington Post* entitled, 'How I Would Lead the World Bank'.[124] Contrasting himself to previous World Bank presidents, Sachs chose to overlook his long history of cosy relationships with political and financial elites, claiming: 'My track record is to side with the poor and the hungry, not with a corporate balance sheet or a government'.[125] To back up this rather implausible suggestion, Sachs appealed to his work on health, poverty, alleviation, and sustainable development, while neglecting to mention the catastrophic social consequences of shock therapy. For a moment, it looked as if it might actually work. The media jumped on the story, and endorsements were soon pouring in from 'progressive' intellectuals, Democratic congressmen, and presidents and high ranking ministers from developing countries around the world, including President Museveni of Uganda.[126] Yet, before Sachs began his campaign, it had already been compromised by a series of controversies at the heart of the development industry that raised grave concerns regarding the Millennium Villages Project, the Commission on Macroeconomics and Health, and his commitment to sustainable development.

In November 2011, while Sachs was still posing as the anti-corporate firebrand of Occupy Wall Street, investigative journalists at *Sarawak Report* accused him of colluding in the 'greenwashing' of the Malaysia-based multinational corporation Sime Darby – the biggest palm oil corporation in the world.[127] The palm oil industry is notorious for the environmental devastation and population displacements caused by its vast monoculture plantations, and Sime Darby has been accused of destroying large stretches of rainforest in Sarawak and dispossessing indigenous communities in Borneo and Liberia.[128] In 2008 Sachs contributed an article to an advertising supplement funded by the Malaysian government and published in the *International Herald Tribune*, in which he praised Sime Darby for their commitment to environmental sustainability.[129] He then appeared in a documentary shown on the BBC in 2009, and also funded by the Malaysian

government, in which he commended the Malaysian palm oil industry for its support of 'smallholders'.[130] According to *Sarawak Report*,
the explanation for this peculiar behaviour lay in the close relationship
that Sime Darby had cultivated with Sachs and the Earth Institute. In
2008 Sachs allegedly accepted a tour of Malaysia and India in one of
Sime Darby's private jets,[131] and the Earth Institute had invited Sime
Darby to join its Corporate Circle a year later, in exchange for a donation of US$500,000.[132]

Like a cheating spouse caught in the bed of corporate capital, Sachs
angrily rejected any accusation of wrongdoing, insisting: 'Absolutely
nothing is going on here.'[133] The trip had been for research … The
donation had supported important projects … He had no idea that
the documentary was funded by the Malaysian government …[134] At
the very least, however, the incident once again demonstrated Sachs's
wanton submission to the desires of capital, and the wilful naivety of
his harmonious vision of capitalist development. In the words of a
representative of Friends of the Earth, 'The rapid growth in palm oil
plantations is one of the greatest threats to south-east Asian rainfor-
ests and the species that depend on them. Jeffrey Sachs would be wise
to steer clear of the multi-billion-pound greenwash operation of this
highly disreputable industry.'[135]

In December 2011, just after the Sime Darby scandal had broken,
Sachs delivered the keynote speech at an international conference
to mark the tenth anniversary of the publication of the Commission
on Macroeconomics and Health (see Chapter 3). Here, at least, he
would surely be on safe ground, celebrating his success in the warm
embrace of businessmen, political elites, and mainstream academics
from around the world. Imagine his horror, then, when he opened
the conference pack and read page after page of comments criticizing
the Commission for its use of questionable statistics;[136] its reduction of health to a factor of economic productivity;[137] its defence of
the intellectual property rights of pharmaceutical corporations;[138] its
'quasi-religious faith in the market';[139] and its failure to address 'the
causes of poverty and poor health, including the gross inequities of
the global economy and the abysmal failure of decades of neoliberalism'.[140] Rather than engaging with these criticisms in his speech,
however, Sachs simply dismissed them and asserted his own moral
sanctity, announcing: 'I don't accept any of the carping in these
papers … I think it's completely wrongheaded, disingenuous, or just

misunderstood, because we fought a very good battle ten years ago, and we're right.'[141] He then filled the remainder of his speech with anecdotes about his single-handed salvation of the world, ignoring all criticisms, and barely mentioning the Commission itself. Yet this refusal to engage with his detractors did not amount to their refutation, and only reinforced the sense that Sachs was losing faith in his own convictions.

The last remaining bulwark of this faith was the Millennium Villages Project, the success of which, as we have seen, had been critical to the reaffirmation of Sachs's neoliberal fantasy. Yet the Project's dramatic claims to success were now being called into question.[142] Crucially for Sachs's World Bank bid, these criticisms centred around a World Bank working paper that challenged the internal assessment methodology of the MVP.[143] Published in 2010, the paper criticized the failure of the Project to measure its results against external 'control villages', whose own changing development indicators could have been monitored over the same period. Without such control villages, the MVP's claims were essentially meaningless, as it was impossible to verify the extent to which improvements in the Villages were attributable to the Project, as opposed to reflecting general development gains in the region. The paper's findings were widely disseminated, and the MVP was eventually forced to retract some of its claims.

The controversy came to a head in 2012, when the Lancet forced the MVP to officially acknowledge a series of errors contained in a paper published in the journal, and to make a number of corrections to it. The paper had claimed extraordinary successes for the MVP in the reduction of child mortality, but had been challenged by several academics, who demonstrated that the MVP had made a series of erroneous extrapolations from the statistical evidence. The Project was also challenged over claims of success made in another paper, and an editorial in Nature condemned its lack of transparency concerning its data and its finances.[144] In the midst of the scandal, Sachs resorted to a combination of bullying and evasion. In public, he thanked the economists who had drawn attention to the problems with the Lancet article, describing their comments as 'on point and helpful'.[145] In private, however, things were rather different. One of the economists who Sachs publically thanked is Michael Clemens of the Centre for Global Development. I asked Clemens to comment on Sachs's behaviour towards him during the dispute. All he would say was, 'I've had direct confrontations with Sachs on this. It was an awful experience, about which the less said, the better.'[146] An article on the scandal in *Foreign Policy* includes similar reports by economists who had challenged the MVP. Edward Miguel, of the University of California, noted: 'We're all so puzzled by the kind of hysterical attacks on anybody who criticizes Millennium Villages.' He reported that Sachs had sent him a threatening email, which had left him 'really shaken up'. Like many of the people I have spoken to, the economist admitted to being hesitant to talk about Sachs on the record because 'he's a very powerful person'.[147]

When the original study was published in the *Lancet*, Sachs had been eager to take the credit for it, writing a follow-up article for CNN, in which he claimed that the study's 'scientific results' proved that the MVP is 'a hidden revolution ... that can transform the lives of a billion of the poorest people on the planet'.[148] Yet, despite being the director of the MVP, and despite having drawn on the study to make such messianic proclamations of its achievements, Sachs subsequently avoided taking any responsibility for its errors. Instead, the Project's director of monitoring and evaluation, Paul Pronyk, published a personal apology in the *Lancet*, and resigned directly afterwards.[149] But the damage was already done. At a meeting of the Millennium Promise board, Sachs was strongly criticized for the errors in the *Lancet* paper, and the MVP's extravagant claims to success have now been utterly discredited. In the words of an economist at the University of California, 'No one takes the Millennium Villages seriously as a research project – no one in development economics'.[150] Just as shock therapy had eventually destroyed the reputation of Dr Shock, so the Millennium Villages Project was now dismantling the identity of Mr Aid.

Sachs thus began his World Bank bid in the midst of a reputational crisis in which his self-image as an ecological crusader, global health guru, and poverty-alleviation expert was being comprehensively undermined. Commentators interpreted his bid as further confirmation that Sachs was 'clearly not someone who struggles with self-doubt'.[151] Yet it should instead be understood as one last desperate roll of the dice as his social fantasy crumbled under the inexorable weight of the Real of Capital. Needless to say, it didn't work. Indeed, it only served to expose Sachs to an even greater barrage of abuse. Despite receiving widespread support from political and economic elites, Sachs's candidacy was passionately opposed in numerous articles, blogs, and tweets. He was criticized for his belief in top-down social engineering. He was criticized for his faith in technological fixes to political problems. He was criticized for his commitment to market mechanisms, his endorsement of inequality, and his embrace of corporate capital. But most of all, he was criticized for his role in shock therapy.[152] Again and again, development experts and anonymous tweeters emphasized 'the havoc [shock therapy] wreaked on ordinary people' in Bolivia, Poland, and Russia,[153] and insisted: 'Jeffrey Sachs has been one of the world's foremost advocates of … market fundamentalist ideology, and bears substantial personal responsibility for the failed policies that drive growing inequality and environmental destruction around the world.'[154] They also noted, 'Sachs has never, to our knowledge, apologized to those who suffered as a result of his early adherence to austerity measures',[155] and suggested he 'would have more credibility in his claim to be an advocate of the poor if he were to acknowledge that he may at some time in his career have made an error of judgement and accept responsibility for the consequences.'[156]

Far from holding his neoliberal fantasy together, Sachs's bid for the World Bank presidency thus forced him to publically confront the original trauma of shock therapy itself. Unsurprisingly, Sachs did not respond to these challenges by acknowledging his culpability, but plunged further into denial, insisting: 'People who really know me know that I have always believed from the first days of my work as an economist in a middle path, and a moderate course of how economies should work.'[157] On his Twitter account, which was supposed to be a campaign tool for the promotion of his good works, Sachs was obliged to defend himself against an endless onslaught of criticism, resorting to hapless one-liners such as, 'Do you know anything?', 'Why don't you learn something?' 'Give me a break', and 'Why do you blame me?'[158] Finally, having completely reached the end of his tether, Sachs published a twenty-page rant on his website, entitled 'What I Did in Russia', which included everything *apart from* what he did in Russia (see Chapter 2). Once again, Sachs denied all responsibility for any of the negative consequences of shock therapy, insisting: 'I am very proud for [*sic*] what I was able to do, and of my integrity and perseverance in the face of arduous obstacles.'[159]

Ironically, Sachs's denial of his past may have been counter-productive, as it was precisely his impeccable neoliberal record that made him a good candidate for the presidency. This was the World Bank, after all – an institution that had mirrored Sachs's own trajectory in its evolution from the Washington Consensus to the Post-Washington Consensus and beyond. In the end, Obama nominated Jim Kim, a little-known health expert, who inevitably went on to get the job. In a further indication of his utter inability to process criticism or failure, Sachs celebrated this crushing defeat as a personal victory. In an article entitled 'Breakthrough Leadership for the World Bank', Sachs proudly announced: 'Last month, I called for the World Bank to be led by a global development leader ... Now that US President Barack Obama has nominated Jim Kim for the post, the world will get just that: a superb development leader ... Kim's nomination was a win for us all.'[160] More accurately, of course, Kim's nomination was a win for everyone *except Jeffrey Sachs*. In the cold light of day, beyond this febrile celebration of his own failure, global capitalism remained in a profound crisis, and Sachs had failed to gain control of the only institution that might have allowed him to save it.

A HAPPY ENDING

In recent years, as if unable to bear the seemingly endless crisis of global capitalism, Sachs has turned to a question of personal urgency, asking: 'What is the path to happiness?'[161] His spiritual odyssey began in 2010, when Sachs fled from the global economic crisis to the remote Himalayan kingdom of Bhutan. Since the 1980s, Bhutan has pioneered the concept of Gross National Happiness – as an alternative measure of well-being to the standard capitalist metric of Gross National Product. Sachs returned from Bhutan rejuvenated, and wrote an article entitled 'Growth in a Buddhist Economy', in which he praised the country's 'unmatched natural beauty, cultural richness, and inspiring self-reflection'.[162] The experience seems to have had a transformative effect on Sachs. His recent work has been filled with references to Buddha and Aristotle, who 'counselled us wisely about humanity's innate tendency to chase transient illusions'.[163] He even refers to Freud, who he describes as 'the modern discoverer of our unconscious impulses', noting that 'we are a bundle of rational and irrational motives that operate without our conscious knowledge'.[164] Could Sachs have finally grasped the 'illusory transience' of his neoliberal fantasy? Could he at last have realized the extent to which his apocalyptic visions and manic problem-solving were grounded in 'unconscious impulses' operating 'without his conscious knowledge'?

Of course not. Instead of applying these lessons to himself, Sachs has externalized them, casting himself as a kind of self-help guru for the collective American psyche. He speaks of 'the need to plough more deeply into our psyches to get a grip on our behaviour'.[165] He notes: 'People are deeply unhappy, highly anxious ... our health is breaking down, our anxiety is increasing';[166] he asks: 'Have we actually created a world that is programmed to undermine our very balance as individuals?';[167] and he despairingly wonders 'how individuals can maintain their psychological stability in an era of rapid change ... without deranging our own psychological well-being?'[168]

These may be worthwhile questions to ask in the midst of the crisis of American capitalism. Yet Sachs himself appears to have been disoriented by the breakdown of the system, and his 'economics of happiness'[169] veers wildly back and forth between incommensurable positions. In his writings on happiness, Sachs argues that 'not only does gross national product not measure properly what makes us well-off and satisfied, it is leading us now in a very dangerous direction ... If we continue to follow that indicator we'll go right over the cliff'.[170] This argument has genuinely radical implications, to the extent that it challenges economic growth and capital accumulation. But, at the same time, Sachs's work on the economic crisis continues to focus on catalyzing a new round of accumulation, based on the assumption that 'the US (and Europe) needs a new source of long-term growth'.[171] Similarly, Sachs appears genuinely radical in his condemnation of the advertising industry for 'creating wants and longings where none previously existed',[172] and his observation that 'the end result of all this consumption is a society running furiously to stay in place'.[173] Yet he then goes on to offer his readers advice on 'how-to-spend-it', providing us with 'eight specific principles to derive more happiness from income', and promising that the 'anticipation of a future purchase will give us anticipatory joy'.[174]

The contradictions do not end there. For example, Sachs now claims that 'people are, like Aristotle said, social animals. We depend on our sense of participation in communities and if ... people do not co-operate with each other ... then unhappiness soars.'[175] But it is difficult to see how Sachs can reconcile this demand for solidarity with his commitment to 'competitiveness', or how his nostalgia for community can be squared with his enduring faith in the invisible hand of the market. Rather than engage with these apparently irreconcilable contradictions, however, Sachs has cloaked them all in the supposedly profound concept of the 'Mindful Society'. According to Sachs, Americans need 'to achieve a new mindfulness ... to find a more solid path to well-being. Mindfulness, taught Buddha, is one of the eight steps to self-awakening. It means alertness and quiet contemplation of our circumstances ... Through sustained effort, mindfulness leads to insight'.[176]

It is unclear whether Sachs is really addressing Americans here, or is engaged in his own anxious search for happiness and peace of mind. Yet beyond these pseudo-Buddhist musings, the Mindful Society turns out to be just another name for Sachs's Third Way neoliberalism, with the contradictory slogan of 'radical centrism' replaced by the Buddhist concept of the 'Middle Path'.[177] This is evident from the 2012 World Happiness Report, commissioned by the United Nations, published by the Earth Institute, and co-edited and introduced by Sachs. The report reproduces Sachs's Third Way agenda, emphasizing the continued centrality of economic growth, and abandoning his fleeting concern with inequality (which seems to have lasted for the precise duration of the Occupy movement). The report equates happiness with wage labour, claiming that unemployment 'reduces the happiness of those unemployed by as much as bereavement or divorce'.[178] The quality of work is less important than work itself, as '[a] bad job is often better than no job'.[179] But employers should remember that 'happy workers are at least as productive as unhappy ones', and should endeavour to 'develop the intrinsic motivation of their workers'.[180]

Happiness is thus reframed as a further means to labour productivity and capital accumulation. Yet the ideological functionality of the economics of happiness is more complex and disturbing than mere economic reductionism. In April 2012, Sachs and the government of Bhutan hosted a United Nations conference on happiness, with the participation of economists, sociologists, neuroscientists, positive psychologists, and Buddhist monks.[181] In the same year, the UN General Assembly unanimously adopted a resolution entitled 'Happiness: Towards a Holistic Approach to Development'.[182] This consensual vision of a 'holistic', 'mindful' capitalism, in which psychologists and religious figures collaborate with economists in the production of a 'happy' workforce, implies a comprehensive form of social engineering that is eerily reminiscent of Aldous Huxley's *Brave New World*.

The economics of happiness also cleanses capitalism of the brutal contradictions revealed by the global economic crisis, appealing once again to the fantasy of origins that underpins the Millennium Villages Project – that mythical era in which class relations did not exist, and capitalist society was a harmonious community of frugal entrepreneurs. For Sachs, caught in the maelstrom of global economic collapse, Bhutan must have appeared as the last refuge in which this prelapsarian fantasy could be sustained. Despite having implemented a series of market reforms from the 1980s onwards – for which Gross National Happiness has been a very convenient ideology – Bhutan promotes itself as having retained a unique sense of traditional community.[183] Recalling his trip to Bhutan, Sachs wistfully describes 'agricultural communities nestled in deep valleys ... each ... guarded by a dzong (fortress) which includes monasteries and temples', and concludes that Bhutan demonstrates how 'economic modernization [can] be combined with cultural robustness and social well-being'.[184] What Sachs does not mention, however, is that this appearance of organic community has only been achieved through the forced expulsion of thousands of ethnic Nepalese, in the name of an 'authentic' Bhutanese people.[185] This oversight resonates in unpleasant ways with Sachs's identification of the ethnic homogeneity of the 'Scandinavian economies' as a condition of their success, and demonstrates the profoundly conservative tendencies of a politics that attempts to institutionalize capitalist class relations while simultaneously denying their existence.

Like the Millennium Villages Project, Sachs's economics of happiness is thus underpinned by a peculiar combination of modernizing free market zeal and conservative nostalgia for a lost sense of community. This combination is further evident in *The Price of Civilization*, in which Sachs identifies Wilhelm Ropke's *A Humane Economy: The Social Framework of the Free Market* as the chief inspiration for his economics of happiness.[186] Ropke was a German economist, writing in the mid twentieth century. Like Sachs, Ropke criticized free market ideologues and insisted that the market should be subordinated to the higher goals of human happiness and the preservation of traditional community.[187] But Ropke was also a committed neoliberal – indeed, he was a founding member of the Mont Perelin Society, which launched the neoliberal project in the 1940s, replacing Friedrich Hayek as its president in 1961.[188] Like Sachs, Ropke's analysis of the crisis of modern capitalism attacked the crass materialism of consumer society, appealing to the same fantasy of the origins of capitalism – a lost Eden that Ropke called 'bourgeois society', which he opposed to the 'proletarianized society' of mass consumerism.[189] In *The Price of Civilization*, Sachs notes that Ropke 'brilliantly emphasized the need for moral boundaries to protect human values from the overbearing pressures of the marketplace'.[190] Yet Ropke's concern was not with the pressures of the marketplace as such, but rather with their tendency to create a spiritual vacuum within 'proletarianized' society, which he feared would be filled by communism unless the 'bourgeois' values of community and spirituality were urgently revitalized:

> Communism thrives wherever … true community has been removed by proletarianization … it thrives where men … have lost their roots and solidity and have been pried loose from the social fabric of the family, the succession of generations, neighbourliness, and other true communities … The decisive battle between Communism and the free world will therefore have to be fought, not so much on the field of material living conditions … but on the field of spiritual and moral values. Communism prospers more on empty souls than on empty stomachs. The free world will prevail only if it succeeds in filling the emptiness of the soul in its own manner and with its own values.[191]

Like Sachs, Ropke claimed to be a liberal democrat. But his virulent anti-communism and his conservative appeal to organic community are characteristic of the politics of fascism. Sachs's endorsement of Ropke's position as the theoretical basis of his own economics of happiness should therefore give serious pause for thought to anyone tempted to scramble aboard the 'happiness' bandwagon. Žižek argues that we should 'use the term "Fascism" in a very precise way: as the name for the impossible attempt to have "capitalism without capitalism", without the excesses of individualism, social disintegration, relativization of values, and so on'.[192] Understood in this sense, fascism is an ideology in which capitalism is cleansed of its constitutive antagonisms, in which 'everything must change so that everything can remain the same',[193] and in which internal contradictions are displaced and reframed as evil external agents, up to and including the capitalists themselves.[194] This definition of fascism is disturbingly reminiscent of Sachs's later politics. Recall Sachs's 'environmental' commitment to sustaining global capitalism through the technological transformation of the ecological commons (everything must change so that every-thing can remain the same). Consider his populist attacks on greedy bankers in defence of the capitalist system (the displacement of class antagonism into an evil agent). And bear in mind his determined commitment to both free markets and organic community, and his identification of ethnic homogeneity as a means to this end. Jeffrey Sachs is obviously not a fascist. But these tendencies are indicative of the dangers that lurk within neoliberalism, as a political project that refuses to confront the Real of its own internal contradictions, and that pursues an illusory coherence while simultaneously reproducing the very contradictions that make such coherence impossible.

CONCLUSION: THE NEOLIBERAL NEUROSIS

Since the catastrophic failure of shock therapy in Russia, Jeffrey Sachs has taken on an extraordinary number of projects, which have grown exponentially in their scope and ambition. A profile of Sachs in *Vanity Fair* describes how 'day after day, without pausing for air, it seems, Sachs makes one speech after another … meets heads of state, holds press conferences, attends symposiums, lobbies government officials … participates in panel discussions, gives interviews, writes opinion pieces … '[1] According to his wife, Sachs only sleeps for four hours a night, and 'works 90 per cent of the time during his waking hours'.[2] Even while on a family holiday, his wife recalls that Sachs

> often gave two or three speeches a day in addition to meetings starting anytime from 7 a.m. till late at night. He then spent most nights writing technical papers, articles, memos and proposals, while keeping in daily contact with his colleagues, working with them via phone, fax and email. All this, while consuming about a book a day on topics ranging from ecology through tropical diseases.[3]

People who have worked or travelled with Sachs are taken aback by this relentless work-rate. The journalist who wrote the *Vanity Fair* piece found herself wondering 'what kept him going at this frenzied pace'. Another journalist reported, 'I took it all in, and later found myself wondering, Why does he do it?', describing Sachs as 'engaged in a desperate Sisyphean effort'.[4] A development expert who has collaborated with Sachs observed, 'The amount of work he puts in is absolutely mind-blowing. It's complete madness. He is fascinating.

You try to understand what drives him – why suddenly this complete shift from [shock therapy] to poverty reduction? What triggered that?'[5] In an article about the Millennium Villages Project, published in 2008, a journalist suggested, 'he almost seems to be on a quest for some kind of redemption, after his failure in Russia.'[6] Sachs, of course, rejected this suggestion, insisting that there was no substantive difference between his shock therapy programmes and his later projects: 'For me, that part of my career and this one – it's all part of the same person, the same ideas: to help people in need, to help them from the outside ... I am the same person I always was.'[7]

In a sense, Sachs is right. The same ideas have continued to underpin his career from shock therapy to the present. But this continuity has been defined less by a desire to help people in need than by an enduring faith in the neoliberal fantasy – the profound conviction that market society is not a utopia to be constructed, but a natural order already present in the structures of the social world, which will spontaneously flourish if the right conditions are in place. This faith was evident in Sachs's earliest shock therapy experiments, when he argued that the creation of a market society was not about constructing 'a world that had never existed', but was based on the more 'down to earth' strategy of 'cutting away' all other social forms, in order to reveal what was already there.[8] The same faith has continued to infuse his clinical economics, which is predicated not on creating a new reality, but on removing all pathological elements from a diseased capitalism, in order to restore the natural health of the market. This faith also underpins the Millennium Villages Project, which attempts to raise the capital levels of 'African villagers' to the point at which their supposedly innate 'entrepreneurial zeal' will spontaneously generate a functional market system. And the neoliberal fantasy even informs Sachs's populist attack on greedy bankers in the ongoing global crisis, who he accuses of corrupting the austere benevolence of the natural capitalist order.

So Sachs is right to say 'it's all part of the same ideas'. But he's not quite right to say 'it's all part of the same person'. Over the course of his career, Jeffrey Sachs has morphed from Dr Shock into Mr Aid, even as the shadow of his past identity has continued to cloud his 'progressive' and 'ethical' visage. A qualitative change has therefore taken place, which Sachs himself refuses to acknowledge. Yet this change has not been defined by the abandonment of neoliberalism, as both disciples and critics have claimed. Sachs was a neoliberal in the past, and he continues to be a neoliberal in the present. The nature of his transformation is therefore located within the parameters of neoliberalism itself. Ever since the catastrophe of shock therapy in Russia, Sachs has no longer been *just* a neoliberal. He has become a *neurotic* neoliberal. According to psychoanalytic theory, the frenzied activity of the obsessional neurotic is unwittingly devoted to preventing the repetition of a forgotten past event.[9] In a similar way, Sachs's manic schedule, his determined optimism, and his preposterously ambitious schemes all serve to modify and reinforce his neoliberal fantasy against the seething morass of uncontrollable devaluation, violent dispossession, and brutal class relations that confronted him in Russia. In contrast to the swaggering 'market Bolshevism' of the shock therapy era, Sachs's subsequent career has amounted to what Lenin would describe as 'the reactionary attempt of a frightened philistine to hide from stern reality'.[10]

This unfortunate predicament tells us something important about the nature of neoliberalism. If we consider the history of neoliberal ideology, we can see that it has always been driven by an anxious desire to hide the ugly realities of capitalism beneath a fantasy of harmonious order. Adam Smith's original theory of the invisible hand of the market was born in the midst of the violent establishment of capitalism in eighteenth-century Great Britain, providing Smith with a reassuring vision that concealed the harshness of the world around him.[11] The first great experiment with economic liberalism in the nineteenth and early twentieth centuries ended in the Great Depression, the Second World War and the rise of communism.[12] These traumatic events drove the formulation of the neoliberal project by Sachs's intellectual godfathers – Friedman, Hayek, and Ropke.[13] Once neoliberalism had risen to hegemonic status – driven in part by Sachs himself – it became plagued by a return of the repressed, in the form of financial volatility, spiralling inequalities, and innumerable social conflicts. Rather than revealing the harmony of a market society, neoliberalism had generated a series of crises that tore through the fabric of the neoliberal fantasy itself.

In response, neoliberalism has evolved in tandem with Sachs's own trajectory, from the stripped-down fundamentalism of Reaganomics and the Washington Consensus to the more complex interventionist policies of the Post-Washington Consensus and Third Way 'social democracy'. But, as we have seen in Sachs's case, these interventions are aimed not at challenging market society, but at making reality conform to the neoliberal fantasy. The principles of free trade and 'fiscal responsibility' remain sacrosanct, and the invisible hand of the market remains the guiding force of economic activity. There is a role for the state, but only in providing the economic infrastructure and human capital required for markets to operate efficiently. Health and education should be valued, but only to the extent that they improve labour productivity. Poverty should be addressed, but this should be through the voluntary actions of philanthropists and corporations rather than the mandatory redistribution of wealth. And development must be ecologically sustainable, but only as a means of ensuring the sustainability of economic growth and capital accumulation. The neoliberal project has therefore created an ever more elaborate system, in order to cope with the proliferating contradictions of capitalism in such a way that the fantasy of a harmonious market society is preserved. This behaviour resembles that of the 'the obsessional neurotic, who builds up a whole system enabling him to postpone the encounter with the Real *ad infinitum*'.[14]

In other words, although Sachs's neurosis is unique in its personal details, it is also symptomatic of a more generalized condition. This condition is shared by other seemingly 'reformed' neoliberals, such as Joseph Stiglitz. Like Sachs, Stiglitz has made a name for himself as a critic of the neoliberal project, but has remained wedded to its fundamentals, serving as Chief Economist of the World Bank from 1997 to 2000, and masterminding its transition from the Washington Consensus to the Post-Washington Consensus.[15] Other neurotic neoliberals include influential economists such as Dani Rodrik, Nicholas Stern, and Paul Krugman. Despite his current incarnation as a reborn 'Keynesian', Krugman served as an economic advisor in the Reagan administration, and appeared alongside Sachs and Stiglitz in the World Bank conference discussed in Chapter 3, which was so central to the transformation and legitimation of the neoliberal project.[16] Indeed, both Stiglitz and Krugman followed Sachs's lead in rushing to Zuccotti Park during Occupy Wall Street to deliver pseudo-radical speeches that criticized the free market system they had helped to create, while anxiously insisting upon the sanctity of a good and pure capitalism against the supposedly anomalous deviance of the contemporary order.[17]

Not all neoliberals are neurotic. In fact, we could contrast Sachs and others like him to unreconstructed market fundamentalists such as Niall Ferguson and William Easterly, by drawing a distinction between neurotic and *psychotic* neoliberals, to the extent that the latter remain utterly unaware of any dissonance between their fantasy and the Real.[18] But despite the attacks that Sachs endures from orthodox neoliberals like Ferguson and Easterly, and despite his own attacks on them as 'free market ideologues', it is Sachs and his fellow neurotic neoliberals who are the true guardians of the neoliberal project. In their willingness to engage in ever more invasive forms of planning and intervention to sustain the coordinates of their fantasy, the neurotic neoliberals exhibit the peculiar combination of transformability and resilience that has made the neoliberal project so irrationally persistent in the face of its repeated failures. The evolution of the neoliberal project towards increasingly intensive forms of social engineering should therefore be understood not as the meticulous manipulation of social reality by a conspiratorial technocratic elite, nor as the rational unfolding of a comprehensive master-plan, but rather as a series of increasingly desperate attempts to hold reality itself together, against the relentless pressure of the Real of Capital.

Paradoxically, however, the obsessive-compulsive rituals of Sachs and his fellow neurotic neoliberals have only served to intensify the very contradictions they are struggling to contain. The neoliberal project is defined by the drive to liberate capital accumulation from all 'external' constraints, either by removing all impediments to the efficient functioning of the price mechanism (as in the case of shock therapy), or by designing interventions to compensate for 'market failure' (as in the case of the Post-Washington Consensus). But the Real of Capital does not correspond to the neoliberal fantasy of a naturally harmonious market order. No matter what the neurotic neoliberals do, their actions do not result in the smooth tranquility of 'general equilibrium', but only serve to further empower capital itself as an increasingly volatile and destructive force, which is spiralling beyond the bounds of social control and driving inexorably towards economic and ecological collapse. The predicament of the neurotic neoliberal thus recalls that of the sorcerer's apprentice, who, having summoned the forces of the underworld, finds that he is unable to control them, and that his every attempt to do so only serves to strengthen their diabolical powers.[19]

Poor Jeffrey ... Yet before we start to feel too sorry for him, we should remember what Sachs is responsible for, and whose side he is on. Shock therapy caused immense human suffering in Bolivia, Poland, Mongolia, and elsewhere. In Russia, shock therapy resulted not only in the longest and deepest recession in modern history, but also in an unprecedented increase in mortality rates. In other words, *lots of people died.* Sachs was utterly unsympathetic at the time, and scorned 'calls for allegedly more "humane" policies',[20] complacently insisting, 'If you're going to chop off a cat's tail, do it in one stroke.'[21] He has never accepted any responsibility for the appalling social consequences of shock therapy, let alone apologized for them. Indeed, the *New York Times* recently reported that Sachs now blames the Russian diet for the increase in mortality rates that followed shock therapy.[22] The anger that people in the former Soviet Union still feel towards Sachs was reflected in a series of responses on the *New York Times* website, including the following:

> I grew up cold and hungry in the former Soviet Republic of Armenia during the shock therapy years of the 90s. My grandfather was one of the 3 million who died prematurely during those days (incorrect medication and power outages did him in). I would very much like to tie Mr Jeffrey Sachs to a chair and slowly force-feed him every worthless page of every idiotic policy paper he's ever written.[23]

Not content with washing his hands of the social consequences of shock therapy, Sachs now lists his actions in Bolivia and Poland as evidence that '[his] own track record has been consistently on the side of the poor', and claims that he has 'a record of standing for the poorest of the poor for decades'.[24] Anyone still inclined to sympathize with Sachs in this regard should consider his response to events in Bolivia in October 2003, when eighty-one members of 'the poor' were massacred in cold blood by the government of his shock therapy sidekick, Gonzalo 'Goni' Sanchez de Lozada, Bolivia's president. The massacre took place at a demonstration against the government's neo-liberal policies, and resulted in Goni being forced out of office, with the socialist Evo Morales elected two years later.[25] As a man whose 'own track record is consistently on the side of the poor', we would expect Sachs to condemn his old ally in the strongest terms, and to pay tribute to the courage of the working class in the face of the murderous apparatus of the capitalist state. Instead, Sachs celebrated Goni as 'one of Latin America's true heroes' for his role in shock therapy, and lamented his resignation as a 'tragic milestone whose meaning extends far beyond his impoverished country'.[26] Sachs criticized Morales's role in 'the leadership of the insurrection',[27] complaining that 'US interests in Bolivia lie in shambles',[28] and warning that Bolivia would become a centre of 'anti-Americanism, violence, and instability'.[29] The killing of unarmed demonstrators went unmentioned. Instead, Sachs condemned the 'deadly rioting in Bolivia',[30] as if the protesters had massacred themselves.

Looking back across Sachs's career, it is no exaggeration to say that his version of history is a complete inversion of reality, and that his 'track record' has been *consistently on the side of the rich*. Goni, after all, was not only president of Bolivia at this time, but also one of the country's wealthiest capitalists. Sachs's earliest contributions to economics were fixated on returning capital to profitability through tax cuts, productivity increases, and the reduction of real wages. His privatization programmes in Eastern Europe and the former Soviet Union were relentlessly focused on establishing 'real owners' who 'cared about the bottom line'.[31] Sachs has been a staunch defender of private property rights against the interests of the poor, both during his shock therapy era and in his subsequent defence of pharmaceutical companies in his work on health. He maintains close working relationships with billionaire financiers such as George Soros and Ray Chambers, and has gone to great lengths to collaborate with multinational corporations in the Millennium Villages Project and the Earth Institute Corporate Circle. In his popular writings, Sachs has consistently emphasized that inequality is not a problem, and even his recent criticisms of Wall Street are qualified by his eager insistence that he is 'not in the slightest against the accumulation of wealth, even vast wealth', and his firm assertion that he is 'not recommending a "class war". There is no case for equalizing incomes'.[32]

To the extent that Sachs is concerned for the poor, it is only a patronizing concern for the 'extremely poor', understood as passive bundles of human capital to be subjected to his social experiments. In fact, my experience of the Millennium Villages Project in Uganda suggests that Sachs is not even concerned with the poor to this limited extent, as long as his experiments provide him with a stage upon which to perform his imagined identity as Mr Aid, lost in a messianic fantasy of salvation. And Sachs is most certainly *not* on the side of the poor as the collectively organized and potentially revolutionary subjects of the working class. Sachs's early work is marked by a virulent hatred of organized labour, and unions and workers are never mentioned as potential political subjects in his later, more 'progressive' works. In *The End of Poverty*, for example, Sachs provides an extensive list of the great emancipatory struggles of the modern era, including anti-slavery, anti-colonialism, and the civil rights movement, but *excluding* the entire history of working-class struggle, which he replaces with his own philanthro-capitalist agenda for 'ending extreme poverty'.[33] Indeed, it could be argued that Sachs's concern for the poor is primarily motivated by a fear of their revolutionary potential. Recall his promotion of his development model (discussed in Chapter 3) in which he emphasized 'what a deal the poor world is offering the rich world', exclaiming: 'The poorest of the poor are saying "We buy into your system. You can keep your wealth. We don't call for revolution. We just want a little help to stay alive".[34]

Given his consistent defence of economic inequality and the power of capital, we need to ask why Sachs has been so successful in transforming his public persona from shock doctor to 'social democrat'. Sachs is now perceived by many on the left as a champion of their cause – be it poverty alleviation, environmental sustainability, or corporate governance – despite the fact that he has continued to espouse principles that would once have placed him firmly on the right. He was allowed to pose as the voice of Occupy Wall Street even as he continued to praise Friedman and Hayek, while endorsing the sanctity of market mechanisms and the progressive credentials of corporate philanthropy. The attitude of many leftists towards Sachs is typified by the following extract from a 2011 blog-post by Doug Henwood, who was once among Sachs's most vocal left-wing critics:

> Over the last 10 years, Sachs has changed … He has become more and more critical of economic orthodoxy, both in the poorer parts of the world and now increasingly in the US … So what are we to make of this? Some of my friends and colleagues think that Sachs should do penance for his past before we applaud his current work; others think that acting as a high-profile critic of orthodoxy is penance in itself.[35]

The parameters of this little debate exclude the fact that Sachs is not really a 'critic of economic orthodoxy' at all, but a committed member of the economic and political elite, who has consistently defended its interests against threats from the left by adopting pseudo-radical political discourses and advocating limited social programmes in order to legitimize market economics and capitalist class relations. The ease with which this fact is overlooked suggests a wilful blindness. Indeed, it could be argued that the neoliberal neurosis is a condition not only of mainstream economists like Sachs, but also of much of what used to be the radical left. The defeats inflicted by Thatcherism and Reaganomics have been far-reaching and profound, extending to the loss of faith in an alternative future beyond the parameters of global capitalism. Much of the left is now trapped within the neoliberal fantasy, to the extent that it cannot imagine what social life would be like if capital accumulation were no longer the dominant imperative. From such a narrow perspective, Sachs's messianic promises to save Africa, and his populist attacks on greedy bankers, might start to appear progressive. But the alternative they offer is just another version of the same fantasy, in which the capitalist system is fair and inclusive, and everyone participates equally in a harmonious market society. Ignoring Sachs's shock therapy past, denying the continuities between it and his current agenda, and celebrating this agenda as radical and progressive must be comforting for those who would like to forget the right-wing foundations of a system they feel unable to change, and whose contours now appear to structure their reality. In other words, the crisis of the left can be measured by the extent to which Sachs is allowed to pose as its legitimate representative.

A SPECTRE IS HAUNTING JEFFREY SACHS ...

The defeat of communism was central to this closure of political horizons. Sachs played a key role in this historic process, yet he remains gripped by a seemingly irrational fear of a communist resurgence. He reacted to the anti-globalization movement and Occupy Wall Street by seeking to shift them away from anti-capitalism and towards more reformist agendas, and he justifies his recent endorsement of 'social democracy' in terms of its proven capacity 'to deflect the growing mass support for socialism'.[36] Furthermore, Sachs's own policy proposals repeatedly take inspiration from anti-communist strategies in the past, without acknowledging their political content. The Millennium Project is inspired by Rostow's *Stages of Growth*, which was subtitled *An Anti-Communist Manifesto*. Sachs's endorsement of an African Green Revolution draws inspiration from the Green Revolution of the twentieth century, which was conceived as a response to the communist threat.[37] And the Millennium Villages Project echoes the counter-insurgency strategies deployed against communist movements in Vietnam, Guatemala, and colonial Malaya, in which potentially revolutionary populations were relocated into 'model villages', where they were put to work and kept under surveillance.[38]

Sachs's enduring obsession with communism is also evident in his fixation on John F. Kennedy and the Cuban Missile Crisis. Sachs concludes both *Common Wealth* and *The Price of Civilization* by recalling the Cuban Missile Crisis, when 'Americans faced the challenge of defending freedom in its hour of maximum danger.'[39] He quotes JFK's speeches from this period in all five of his Reith Lectures and all three of his bestselling books. Indeed, as I write this, Sachs has recently published his fourth major book, *To Move the World*, which is entirely devoted to JFK's role in ending the Cuban Missile Crisis. This choice of topic seems odd, to say the least. Why would a renowned development economist decide to write a superficial rehash of a well-known moment in history that has nothing to do with development? After all, this is precious time that could be spent in other ways, such as ensuring that his Millennium Villages Project is not failing the people it was supposed to 'save' ... Once again, it seems that Sachs is determined to fill his time with activities that hide him from reality, rather than engaging with anything that might force him to confront it. Sachs's decision to spend an entire book recounting the details of Kennedy's salvation of the world from the Soviet threat makes little sense, unless – to use Sachs's description of Khrushchev's behaviour – it is interpreted as 'a symptom of a deeper anxiety.'[40]

To Move the World can be read as a delusional narration of Sachs's own failure in Russia, according to which the mission was a success, and he was the hero of the hour. Sachs describes the build-up to the Cuban Missile Crisis in terms that might just as easily be a repressed verdict on his own role in shock therapy in Russia, involving 'miscalculations, bravado, and supposedly strategic thinking', and leading Sachs to wonder despairingly if we are 'but flotsam on the turbulent seas of technological and social change, rising and sinking in waters beyond our control?'[41] At this point, however, Sachs introduces JFK as the saviour, praising 'the art of great leadership' in terms that seem designed to invite comparisons with his own approach to 'the end of poverty': 'Define a goal clearly. Explain how it can be achieved in manageable steps. Help others to share the goal – in part through great oratory. Their hopes will move them "irresistibly" towards the goal.'[42] As if describing his own imagined identity, Sachs tells us that JFK 'was both idealist and realist, visionary and arm-twisting politician. The two approaches, one soaring and one with feet firmly on the ground, were necessary for success.' This bizarre attempt to associate himself with JFK's resolution of the Cuban Missile Crisis would even appear to extend to Sachs's photograph on the back cover, in which his hairstyle is eerily reminiscent of Kennedy's on the front of the book.

In *To Move the World*, Sachs celebrates the eventual triumph of 'bourgeois ideals' over the 'cruelty and stupidity' of communism, which he describes as 'profoundly repugnant'.[43] Sachs is right to abhor the atrocities committed by totalitarian regimes in the name of communism, but it seems strange that someone devoted to the alleviation of poverty should be so defensive of 'bourgeois ideals' against a movement that was originally inspired by the collective desire of the exploited and the dispossessed for a more just and equitable world. This brings us to a further paradox at the heart of Sachs's project. In *The End of Poverty*, Sachs repeatedly insists that Africa needs its own version of the Marshall Plan, which was originally designed to prevent post-war Europe from succumbing to communist ideology.[44] The demand for a new Marshall Plan is restated in more general terms in *To Move the World*, in which Sachs emphasizes that the original Marshall Plan was 'a way to forestall Soviet political advances', noting that 'the Bolsheviks came to power in 1917 in the context of Russian economic chaos', and warning us that '[w]e are once again at risk of spiralling out of control'.[45] There is an irony here, of which Sachs remains stubbornly ignorant. In the endless repetition of his futile demand for a new Marshall Plan, Sachs does not pause to reflect that it is precisely the defeat of actually existing communism that has removed the rationale for such a project. It was the appeal of communist ideology to the impoverished majorities of the capitalist world that prompted the Marshall Plan, as well as the Big Push, the Green Revolution, and Rostow's 'anti-communist manifesto'. Without the clear and present danger of communist revolution, global capitalism has no political incentive to engage in the kinds of projects that Sachs is calling for. When Sachs berates the international community for failing to fund his schemes, he should reflect on his own role in destroying the political conditions that made such projects possible.

Given that communism has been so comprehensively destroyed, why does Sachs continue to fear it so deeply? Paradoxically, it appears that Sachs's own attempts to sustain the neoliberal project are pushing him ever closer to the terrible realization that communism – in the sense of the collective management of the social and ecological commons for the common good – might be the only solution to the problems he is seeking to address. Through his futile attempts to resolve the contradictions of capitalism without addressing their source in the capitalist mode of production, Sachs has moved inexorably from an evangelical faith in the spontaneous order of the market towards the increasingly comprehensive planning of social and ecological processes, in order to *produce* the market in its supposedly natural state. But in struggling with the multiple irrationalities of this paradoxical enterprise, Sachs is increasingly confronted with the contingency of the market itself, and with its potential expendability. In his analysis of the ecological crisis in *Common Wealth*, for example, Sachs finds himself arguing that 'running out of natural resources is not the right way to describe the threat ... The problem is that markets might not lead to their wise and sustainable use. There is no economic imperative that will condemn us to deplete our vital resource base, but neither is there an invisible hand that will prevent us from doing so.'[46]

Sachs's faith in the invisible hand of the market is clearly beginning to disintegrate at this point, and his hasty denial of an 'economic imperative' condemning us to environmental destruction suggests that he is all too aware of the monolithic capitalist imperative of economic growth. All that remains is for him to extrapolate from the premises of his own argument, concluding that 'the market' cannot solve our ecological crisis, and that this destructive economic imperative must be overcome. On this occasion, Sachs manages to tear himself away from the communist temptation, and flees back to his comforting fantasies of corporate social responsibility and technological fixes, babbling distractedly about the exciting possibilities of 'climate science, environmental engineering, energy systems, economics, ecology, hydrology, agronomics (plant breeding), infectious disease control, business, and finance'.[47] Yet in the midst of the global economic crisis, the idea of communism has continued to suggest itself with increasing regularity in Sachs's work. In *The Price of Civilization*, for example, Sachs observes: 'We have created a nation of remarkable wealth and productivity, yet one that leaves its impoverished citizens in degraded life conditions and almost completely ignores the suffering of the world's poorest people.'[48] Replace 'nation' with 'economic system' in this passage, and you have a concise expression of the Marxist critique of capitalism. In the introduction to the World Happiness Report, published in 2012, Sachs again expresses a distinctly Marxist sentiment:

> We live in an age of stark contradictions. The world enjoys technologies of unimaginable sophistication; yet has at least one billion people without enough to eat each day. The world is propelled to soaring new heights of productivity through ongoing technological and organizational advance; yet is relentlessly destroying the natural environment in the process.

Compare these words to the following passage from a speech by Marx in 1856:

> On the one hand, there have started into life industrial and scientific forces which no epoch of the former human history had ever suspected. On the other hand, there exist symptoms of decay, far surpassing the horrors recorded in the latter times of the Roman Empire. In our days everything seems pregnant with its contrary.'[49]

It would seem that capitalism has not advanced very far in the 156 years that separate these two statements, in terms of addressing what Marx and Sachs both identify as its fundamental obscenity: widespread poverty and destruction in a sea of plenty. Unlike Marx, however, Sachs stubbornly avoids drawing the political conclusion that leads so clearly from his own argument. Indeed, if anything, such close encounters only fuel his loathing of communism and his defence of the capitalist class. And yet, despite his paranoid demagoguery at Occupy Wall Street, his celebration of anti-communist ideologues in *The Price of Civilization*, and his tireless praise for the moral rectitude of the traditional bourgeoisie, Sachs's speech is increasingly littered with slips of the tongue, in which he accidentally gives voice to distinctly communist sentiments. In recent articles, Sachs has repeatedly interrupted his cloying ethical appeals and dry technological musings by inadvertently blurting out crude leftist slogans concerning the 'class system of catastrophe',[50] the 'avarice of globally mobile capital',[51] and the 'mad pursuit of corporate profits',[52] before composing himself and carrying on as normal. Sometimes, before he is able to stop himself, he finds that he has uttered an entire anti-capitalist sentence – such as, 'The rich will try to use their power to commandeer more land, more water, and more energy for themselves',[53] or, 'Global capitalism presents many direct threats to happiness.'[54] In a particularly embarrassing slip, Sachs begins an article in the *Financial Times* by arguing in impeccably neoliberal fashion that 'self-interest, operating through markets, leads to the common good', only to accidentally conclude it in overtly Marxist terms, by momentarily identifying the 'ultimate paradox: the self-destruction of prosperity at the very moment when technological knowhow enables sustainable prosperity for all.'[55]

According to Freud, a slip of the tongue does not merely give involuntary expression to an unwanted thought. More precisely, it expresses a repressed *desire*. Could it be that Sachs's pathological hatred of communism is a perverted expression of his deepest, most repressed desire? Could this desire be a forbidden, illicit desire for communism itself? Consider Sachs's repeated references to Marx's economic theories and Lenin's political strategies, which seem to betray a hidden admiration. Remember that Sachs was a left-wing activist as a student, and that his father was a staunch defender of workers' rights, who took him on a 'life-changing' trip to Russia as a teenager. Recall that Sachs could not wait to return to the communist world, and chose to spend a summer holiday in East Germany, where he was introduced to Marxism and educated about the injustices of the capitalist system. We may never know what caused Sachs to abandon left-wing politics at this point, and to lose himself in the neoliberal fantasy. Could this fantasy be a defence not only against the realities of capitalism, but also against an unrequited yearning for a different world? Could this world be 'communist' – not in the sense of the totalitarian regimes of the past, but in the sense of a world that is socially collectivist, economically egalitarian, and ecologically sustainable, in contrast to the endless poverty, vertiginous inequality, and environmental catastrophe that are the legacy and destiny of global capitalism? If so, then it only remains for us to remind Jeffrey Sachs of the ultimate imperative of Lacanian psychoanalysis: don't give up on your desire.

ACKNOWLEDGEMENTS

Countless people have informed and improved this book. Unfortunately, many of them cannot be named. These include all those who helped me during my time in Uganda. Thanks first and foremost to my research assistant in Uganda – a true friend. I would also like to thank those employees of the MVP and the Ugandan government who took personal risks to speak or write to me about the MVP, in the hope of improving the conditions of those the Project is supposed to help. And thanks to all the people of Ruhiira who invited me into their homes and shared their experiences with me. I hope that my publication of their testimonies will contribute to a better understanding of the realities of 'development', which are often concealed by powerful individuals and institutions with a vested interest in projecting an image of success on the international stage.

I am very grateful to the academics and members of the development community who agreed to be interviewed, or who otherwise assisted me in my research for this project. Their insights have been indispensable to my analysis. Most wish to remain unnamed. However, Michael Clemens, David Ellermen, and Doug Henwood have all published their own critiques of Sachs's work, so I hope they will not mind me thanking them by name here. Needless to say, the views I express in this book, and any errors it may contain, are entirely my own.

I would like to thank the following people for their extremely helpful comments on a previous draft: Greig Charnock, Susie Cunning, Aggie Hirst, Ilan Kapoor, Andy Merrifield, Stuart Shields, Ioanna Tantanasi, Jane Wilson, and Tony Wood. Many others offered invaluable support and guidance. I would particularly like to thank my editor at Verso,

Audrea Lim, for all the work she put into improving the manuscript. Thanks also to Terrell Carver, Noel Castree, Gary Dymski, Maria Kaika, Fabiola Mieres, Jamie Peck, and especially Erik Swyngedouw for his consistent support and advice.

I am also very grateful to Richard Crompton and his family, who offered me generous assistance at a crucial time.

I would like to thank my parents, my grandparents, and my brothers, Owen and Ben.

And most of all, I would like to thank Ioanna.

NOTES

INTRODUCTION: THE SACHS CONUNDRUM

1   The speech can be viewed at youtube.com, under the titles 'Jeffrey Sachs at Occupy Wall Street' and 'Occupy Wall Street – Economist Jeffrey Sachs 10-15-2011'.

2   For further details of Sachs's achievements and accolades, see jeffsachs. org.

3   Louis Uchitelle, 'Columbia Gets Star Professor from Harvard', *New York Times*, 5 April 2002; Karen W. Arenson, 'For Professor, A Town House Fit for a King', *New York Times*, 20 November 2002. When he was appointed to his current post at Columbia in 2002, Sachs was put on a starting salary of US$300,000, plus benefits, which included the rental 'at normal faculty rates' of an US$8 million Manhattan townhouse. He can also be assumed to receive sizable royalties from his three bestselling books. A recent study calculated that anyone in the United States earning US$343,927 a year or more was a member of the 1 per cent. (Tami Luhby, 'Who are the 1 percent?', *CNN Money*, 29 October 2011.) So unless he hasn't had a raise since 2002, and his royalty deal is very poor, Sachs can be considered part of the 1 per cent, especially given his living arrangements.

4   Jeffrey Sachs, 'Life after Communism', *Wall Street Journal*, 17 November 1999.

5   Jeffrey Sachs, 'Poland's Big Bang after One Year', *Skandinaviska Enskilda Banken Quarterly Review* 1–2 (1991), pp. 3–4.

6   Ibid., pp. 5–6.

7   David Harvey, *A Brief History of Neoliberalism* (Oxford: Oxford University Press, 2005), p. 221; Naomi Klein, *The Shock Doctrine* (London: Penguin, 2007), p. 247.

8   See for example Jeffrey Sachs, 'What I Did in Russia', at jeffsachs.org. This is a particularly forthright expression of Sachs's position, which I address in detail in Chapter 2.

9   Sam Rich, 'Africa's Field of Dreams', *Wilson Quarterly*, Spring 2007; John H. Richardson, 'Society: Jeffrey Sachs', *Esquire*, 3 December 2003; Washington National Cathedral, 'The Prophet of Economic Possibilities for the Poor', at nationalcathedral.org.

10 Throughout this book, I respect the anonymity of my interviewees. It is a mark of the power and influence of Jeffrey Sachs, particularly within the international development community, that many people were unwilling to be interviewed about him, while most who agreed would only do so on the understanding that their comments were non-attributable.

11 Doug Henwood, 'A Critique of Jeffrey D. Sachs's *The End of Poverty*', *International Journal of Health Services* 36: 1 (2006), p. 200.

12 Peter Reddaway and Dmitri Glinski, *The Tragedy of Russia's Reforms: Market Bolshevism against Democracy* (Washington, DC: United States Institute of Peace, 2001), p. 244.

13 John Donnelly, 'The Road to Redemption', *Boston Globe Magazine*, 3 June 2001.

14 Slavoj Žižek, *The Sublime Object of Ideology* (London: Verso, 1989), p. 105. Žižek, of course, is not referring to Sachs here.

15 G.K. Chesterton, 'The Real Stab of the Story' in Robert Louis Stevenson, *Strange Case of Dr. Jekyll and Mr. Hyde: An Authoritative Text*, Katherine Linehan, ed. (New York: Norton, 2003), p. 183.

16 For a more detailed exposition of the theoretical approach informing this book, see Japhy Wilson, 'The Shock of the Real: The Neoliberal Neurosis in the Life and Times of Jeffrey Sachs', *Antipode: A Journal of Radical Geography* 46: 1 (2014).

17 'Ideology is not a dreamlike illusion that we build to escape reality; in its basic dimension it is a fantasy-construction which serves as a support for our reality itself: an "illusion" which structures our effective social relations and thereby masks some insupportable Real … The function of ideology is not to offer us a point of escape from our reality but to offer … social reality itself as an escape from some traumatic, Real kernel' (Žižek, *Sublime Object of Ideology*, p. 45).

18 Slavoj Žižek, *The Plague of Fantasies* (London: Verso, 2008), pp. 222–3; Žižek, *Sublime Object of Ideology*, pp. 169–71.

19 Jeffrey Sachs, *Poland's Jump to a Market Economy* (Cambridge, MA: MIT Press, 1993), pp. 2–3.

20   Sachs, 'What I Did in Russia', p. 1. Note: This essay appears as a Word document on Sachs's website, without page numbers. Here and subsequently I give the page number from the print-out.

1 THE RISE OF DR SHOCK

1   Sylvia Nasar, 'Three Whiz Kid Economists of the 90s, Pragmatists All', *New York Times*, 27 October 1991.
2   John H. Richardson, 'Society: Jeffrey Sachs', *Esquire*, 3 December 2003.
3   Sachs, quoted in ibid.
4   Jeffrey Sachs, cited in Brian Snowdon, 'A Global Compact to End Poverty: Jeffrey Sachs on Stabilisation, Transition, and Weapons of Mass Salvation', *World Economics* 6: 4 (2005), p. 29.
5   Sachs in ibid., p. 29. Sachs claims that this book was '*Historical and Dialectical Materialism* by Karl Marx', but Marx never wrote a book with this title. The fact that Sachs purchased the book in East Germany suggests that it may have been Stalin's introductory pamphlet on Marxism, 'Dialectical and Historical Materialism'. Sachs's confusion would be unsurprising, given the tendency for liberals to conflate Marx and Stalin as a means of discrediting Marx.
6   Snowdon, 'Global Compact', p. 29.
7   Gur Ofer, 'Abram Bergson: The Life of a Comparativist', *Comparative Economic Studies* 47 (2005), pp. 240–58.
8   Jeffrey Sachs, in 'Testimonials to Abram Bergson', *Comparative Economic Studies* 47 (2005), p. 495.
9   Robert E. Norton, 'The American Out to Save Poland', *Fortune*, 29 January 1990.
10 See Jamie Peck, *Constructions of Neoliberal Reason* (Oxford: Oxford University Press, 2010), Chapter 3.
11 Justin Fox, 'What in the World Happened to Economics? Economists Are All Finally Speaking the Same Language, but They Still Can't Answer the Big Questions', *Fortune*, 15 March 1999.
12 Jeffrey Sachs, 'Commanding Heights', p. 31, available at pbs.org. The careers of Foley, Cavallo and Aspe are traced in Jorge I. Domínguez, *Technopols: Freeing Politics and Markets in Latin America in the 1990s* (University Park, PA: Pennsylvania State University Press, 1997).
13 Domingo F. Cavallo, 'Lecture 4: The Mexican Way', lecture delivered at the Department of Economics, Harvard University, spring term 2004.
14 Jeffrey Sachs, *The End of Poverty: How We Can Make It Happen in Our Lifetime* (London: Penguin, 2005), p. 90.

15 Harvey, *Brief History of Neoliberalism*, p. 44.

16 Jeffrey D. Sachs, 'Wages, Profits, and Macroeconomic Adjustment: A Comparative Study', *Brookings Papers on Economic Activity* 2 (1979), p. 269.

17 Ibid., pp. 302, 285. See also Jeffrey Sachs, 'Wages, Flexible Exchange Rates, and Macroeconomic Policy', *Quarterly Journal of Economics*, June 1980.

18 Jeffrey Sachs, 'The Changing Cyclical Behavior of Wages and Prices: 1890–1976', *American Economic Review* 70: 1 (1980), pp. 87–8. The relationship between real wages and economic activity was also the theme of Sachs's doctoral dissertation (Snowdon, 'Global Compact', p. 32).

19 Jeffrey Sachs, 'Comments and Discussion', in Willem H. Buiter and Marcus H. Miller, 'Changing the Rules: Economic Consequences of the Thatcher Regime', *Brookings Papers on Economic Activity* 2 (1983), p. 371. In the paper, Sachs went on to warn Thatcher that further reforms would be needed to change 'union and management attitudes' permanently (p. 372). Thatcher's destruction of the miners' union in her second term suggests that she shared his analysis.

20 Harvey, *Brief History of Neoliberalism*. Sachs's early writings suggest that this was a conscious strategy from the outset.

21 Sachs, *End of Poverty*, p. 91.

22 Ibid.

23 Sachs, cited in Snowdon, 'Global Compact', p. 33. In the same interview Sachs also claims to have been inspired by Thomas Sargent's 1982 essay, 'The Ends of Four Big Inflations', which he took with him to La Paz. Sargent's essay is focused on drawing lessons from hyperinflation for addressing the stagflation of the American and European economies. In terms very similar to those of Sachs's own work on stagflation, Sargent blames inflation on expansionary fiscal policies driving workers' expectations of continually rising wages, insisting that this can only be addressed by permanently changing workers' perceptions through reforms that 'change the rules of the game' (Thomas J. Sargent, 'The Ends of Four Big Inflations', in Robert E. Hall, ed., *Inflation: Causes and Effects* [Chicago: University of Chicago Press, 1982]).

24 Peck, *Constructions of Neoliberal Reason*, p. 108.

25 Sachs, quoted in Norton, 'American Out to Save Poland'.

26 Milton Friedman, quoted in Peck, *Constructions of Neoliberal Reason*, p. 4.

27 Sachs, 'Commanding Heights', pp. 30–1.

28 Jeffrey Sachs, *Understanding 'Shock Therapy'* (London: Social Market Foundation, 1994), p. 15.

29   Jeffrey D. Sachs, 'Crossing the Valley of Tears in East European Reform', *Challenge*, September–October 1991, p. 27.

30   Jeffrey Sachs, 'Life in the Economic Emergency Room', in John Williamson, ed., *The Political Economy of Policy Reform* (Washington, DC: Institute for International Economics, 1994), p. 510.

31   Ibid.

32   Ibid. pp. 509–10.

33   Reddaway and Glinski, *Tragedy of Russia's Reforms*, p. 10. This strategy also echoes Friedman's advice to Reagan that 'a new administration has some six to nine months in which to achieve major changes; if it does not seize the opportunity to act decisively during that period, it will not have another such opportunity' (quoted in Peck, *Constructions of Neoliberal Reason*, p. 115).

34   Jeffrey Sachs, *Shock Therapy in Poland: Perspectives of Five Years*, Tanner Lectures on Human Values, University of Utah, 6–7 April 1994, p. 270.

35   Sachs, 'Commanding Heights', p. 19.

36   Slavoj Žižek, *Violence* (London: Profile, 2008), p. 31.

37   Reddaway and Glinski, *Tragedy of Russia's Reforms*, p. 8.

38   Jeffrey Sachs, 'The Bolivian Hyperinflation and Stabilization', *Washington Quarterly* 24: 3 (1987), p. 279.

39   Harry Sanabria, 'Consolidating States, Restructuring Economies, and Confronting Workers and Peasants: The Antinomies of Bolivian Neo-liberalism', *Comparative Studies in Society and History* 41: 3 (1999), p. 537.

40   Sachs, 'Commanding Heights', p. 4.

41   Ibid., p. 5.

42   Sachs, *End of Poverty*, p. 94.

43   Sachs, 'Bolivian Hyperinflation and Stabilization', p. 281; Klein, *Shock Doctrine*, p. 147.

44   Klein, *Shock Doctrine*, p. 148.

45   Juan Antonio Morales and Jeffrey D. Sachs, 'Bolivia's Economic Crisis', in Jeffrey D. Sachs, ed., *Developing Country Debt and the World Economy* (Chicago: University of Chicago Press, 1989), p. 74.

46   Klein, *Shock Doctrine*, pp. 152–3.

47   Sachs, *End of Poverty*, p. 98.

48   Fernando Romero, former Bolivian minister of planning and coordination, quoted in Leslie Wayne, 'A Doctor for Struggling Economies', *New York Times*, 1 October 1989.

49   Gonzalo ('Goni') Sanchez de Lozada, quoted in Leslie Holstrom, 'Sachs Appeal', *Euromoney*, February 1992, p. 33. Goni was the leader of the

economic change team that worked with Sachs. Though Sachs never mentions it, Goni was also a mining magnate and one of the country's wealthiest capitalists. He went on to become president of Bolivia, before being deposed by a popular uprising in 2003.

50 Gonzalo Sanchez de Lozada, 'Commanding Heights', p. 12, at pbs.org.

51 Gonzalo Sanchez de Lozada, quoted in Holstom, 'Sachs Appeal', p. 32.

52 Klein, *Shock Doctrine*, p. 149; Duncan Green, *Silent Revolution: The Rise and Crisis of Market Economics in Latin America* (New York: Monthly Review Press, 2003), pp. 74–5. Green reports that malnutrition and tuberculosis – another poverty-related disease – also increased during the years following shock therapy.

53 Benjamin Kohl, 'Challenges to Neoliberal Hegemony in Bolivia', *Antipode*, 2006, p. 311.

54 Sanabria, 'Consolidating States', p. 539; Kohl, 'Challenges of Neoliberal Hegemony', p. 311.

55 Holstrom, 'Sachs Appeal', p. 33.

56 Kohl, 'Challenges of Neoliberal Hegemony', p. 311.

57 Sachs, *End of Poverty*, p. 108.

58 Stephen E. Hanson, 'Analyzing Post-Communist Economic Change: A Review Essay', *East European Politics and Societies* 12 (1997), pp. 146–8.

59 Sachs, *End of Poverty*, pp. 109–22. Eastern Europe held personal significance for Sachs, and Poland especially so. His wife and her family had first come to the United States after fleeing from Communist Czechoslovakia (ibid., p. 110), and his own family's roots are in Grodno, Belarus, which in 1989 was part of the Soviet Union, but had previously been part of Poland (Norton, 'American Out to Save Poland'). Furthermore, Sachs's mentor Abe Bergson had invited Sachs to accompany him on a journey to Poland for a conference in 1976, just after Sachs had graduated. The experience was significant in cementing Sachs's disdain for communism: 'As Abe pointed out to me the shoddy socialist maintenance of the conference site, I saw Abe as a true explorer: eyes open, taking in the evidence of socialist Poland' (Sachs, 'Testimonials to Abram Bergson', p. 496).

60 David Lipton and Jeffrey Sachs, 'Summary of the Proposed Economic Program of Solidarity', 18 August 1989, pdf available at earthinstitute. columbia.edu.

61 For a detailed account of this process, see Stuart Shields, 'How the East Was Won: Transnational Social Forces and the Neoliberalisation of Poland's Post-Communist Transition', *Global Society* 22: 4 (2008), pp. 445–68.

62 Sachs, *End of Poverty*, p. 121.

63   Jeffrey Sachs, 'What Is to Be Done?' *Economist*, 13 January 1990, p. 23.

64   Ibid., p. 23.

65   Ibid., p. 24.

66   Simon Clarke, 'Globalization and the Subsumption of the Soviet Mode of Production under Capital', in Said Filho, ed., *Anti-Capitalism: A Marxist Introduction*, p. 188.

67   David Lipton and Jeffrey Sachs, 'Creating a Market Economy in Eastern Europe: The Case of Poland', *Brookings Papers on Economic Activity* 21: 1 (1990), p. 102.

68   Sachs, 'Shock Therapy in Poland', p. 268.

69   Jeffrey Sachs and David Lipton, 'Poland's Economic Reform', *Foreign Affairs* 69: 3 (Summer 1990), p. 63.

70   Lawrence King, 'Postcommunist Divergence: A Comparative Analysis of the Transition to Capitalism in Poland and Russia', *Studies in Comparative International Development* 37: 3 (Fall 2002), pp. 3–5.

71   Sachs, 'What Is to Be Done?', p. 25.

72   Jeffrey Sachs, quoted in Hanson, 'Analyzing Post-Communist Economic Change', p. 148.

73   Jeffrey D. Sachs, 'Accelerating Privatization in Eastern Europe: The Case of Poland', *WIDER Working Papers* 92 (1991), pp. 8–9. Sachs presented this paper at the World Bank Annual Conference on Development Economics in April 1991.

74   Sachs, *End of Poverty*, pp. 112–23.

75   Sachs and Lipton, 'Poland's Economic Reform', p. 59.

76   Sachs, 'Poland's Big Bang', p. 4.

77   Sachs, 'Shock Therapy in Poland', p. 275.

78   Sachs, 'What Is to Be Done?', p. 26.

79   Alice Amsden, Jacek Kochanowicz, and Lance Taylor, *The Market Meets Its Match: Restructuring the Economies of Eastern Europe* (Cambridge, MA: Harvard University Press, 1994), pp. 1–3; Reddaway and Glinski, *Tragedy of Russia's Reforms*, pp. 238–9.

80   Sachs, 'Accelerating Privatization in Eastern Europe', p. 1.

81   David Lipton and Jeffrey Sachs, 'Privatization in Eastern Europe: The Case of Poland', *Brookings Papers on Economic Activity* 2 (1990), p. 304.

82   Ibid., p. 304.

83   Ibid., p. 305.

84   Ibid., p. 307. In another paper on the same theme, also published in 1990, Sachs and Lipton provide an equally absurd alternative formulation of this argument: 'Worker-managed firms … put workers at excessive risk

and cut the firms off from capital markets, because outside investors know that the workers can vote to pay themselves higher wages out of the company's profits' (Lipton and Sachs, 'Creating a Market Economy in Eastern Europe', p. 128). Here Sachs seems to be concerned about workers exploiting capitalists!

85   Lipton and Sachs, 'Privatization in Eastern Europe', p. 308.

86   Ibid. Although there was no capitalist class as such in Poland at this time, there was a class of managers and planners who were well positioned to play this role. (Thanks to Stuart Shields for this point of clarification.)

87   Ibid., p. 298.

88   Ibid., p. 327.

89   David Ellerman, 'Background Notes on Videotape of Polish Interviews about Sachs and on Sachs' Involvement in Slovenia', circa 1993 (document supplied through personal communication).

90   Ibid.

91   Klein, *Shock Doctrine*, pp. 192–3; Amsden et al., *Market Meets Its Match*, pp. 1–16.

92   Sachs, *End of Poverty*, p. 124; John Marangos, 'Was Shock Therapy Really a Shock?', *Journal of Economic Issues* 37: 4 (2003), p. 945.

93   Sachs, 'Poland's Big Bang', pp. 3–4.

94   Ibid., p. 4

95   Sachs, 'What Is to Be Done?', p. 25 (emphasis added).

96   Sachs and Lipton, 'Poland's Economic Reform', p. 60.

97   Wayne, 'A Doctor for Struggling Economies'.

98   Holstrom, 'Sachs Appeal'.

99   Sachs, quoted in ibid.

100 Ellerman, 'Background Notes'.

101 Sachs, *End of Poverty*, pp. 133–4.

102 Jeffrey Sachs, quoted in Richardson, 'Society: Jeffrey Sachs'.

2 RUSSIA

1   Sachs, *End of Poverty*, pp. 132–3.

2   Anders Aslund, *How Russia Became a Market Economy* (Washington, DC: Brookings Institution, 1995), p. 17. The reformer Aslund is referring to here is Aleksandr Shokhin, Russia's minister of labour at the time.

3   Sachs, *End of Poverty*, p. 136.

4   Aslund, *How Russia Became a Market Economy*, p. 19.

5   Quoted in Holstrom, 'Sachs Appeal', p. 35.

6   Sachs has since claimed that Gorbachev had wanted the Soviet Union to

emulate Poland's shock therapy reforms (Jeffrey Sachs, 'Gorbachev and the Struggle for Democracy', at jeffsachs.org). But Gorbachev himself has argued: 'No country can repeat the reforms of another country ... the Polish experience was not directly applicable ... We had several generations that had nothing to do with markets. You cannot just announce markets and then the markets would emerge overnight' ('Commanding Heights: Up for Debate: Shock Therapy: Bolivia, Poland, Russia. Same Policies – Different Results', at pbs.org).

7 Sachs, 'What I Did in Russia', p. 10.

8 Peter Passell, 'Dr Jeffrey Sachs, Shock Therapist', *New York Times*, 27 June 1993.

9 Ibid.

10 David Lipton and Jeffrey Sachs, 'Prospects for Russia's Economic Reforms', *Brookings Papers on Economic Activity* 1992, no. 2, p. 229.

11 Ibid., pp. 229–30. The unemployment scheme that Sachs and Lipton describe in their paper would only provide benefits for a maximum of one year, reducing them incrementally over that period, from 75 per cent of the previous wage in the first three months to 60 per cent in the next four months, and 45 per cent until the end of the twelve-month period, after which payments would be terminated (ibid., p. 230).

12 Sachs, 'Commanding Heights'.

13 See for example Caroline Humphrey, *The Unmaking of Soviet Life: Everyday Economies after Socialism* (Ithaca, NY: Cornell University Press, 2002); Charity Scribner, *Requiem for Communism* (Minneapolis: University of Minnesota Press, 2005).

14 Sachs, 'Crossing the Valley of Tears', p. 30.

15 See Reddaway and Glinksi, *Tragedy of Russia's Reforms*, esp. Chapters 5 and 6. In fact, 'a full 74 per cent of Yeltsin's appointees were members of the nomenklatura' (King, 'Post-Communist Divergence', p. 11).

16 Reddaway and Glinski, *Tragedy of Russia's Reforms*, p. 279.

17 Sachs, *End of Poverty*, p. 136.

18 Peter Murrell, 'What Is Shock Therapy? What Did It Do in Poland and Russia?', *Post-Soviet Affairs* 9: 2 (1993), p. 133.

19 King, 'Post-Communist Divergence', p. 11; Reddaway and Glinski, *Tragedy of Russia's Reforms*, p. 247.

20 For a comprehensive account of the complex practicalities of the mass privatization process in Russia, see Chapter 4 of Andrew Barnes, *Owning Russia: The Struggle over Factories, Farms, and Power* (Ithaca, NY: Cornell University Press, 2006).

21 King, 'Post-Communist Divergence', p. 11.

22 Ibid., p. 12

23 Reddaway and Glinski, *Tragedy of Russia's Reforms*, p. 2.

24 Ibid. pp. 248–50. Reddaway and Glinski have suggested that Sachs deliberately engineered this destruction of personal savings as part of a broader strategy of dismantling the existing regime. They cite the journalist Anne Williamson, who quotes Sachs as saying in 1991: 'We intend to create hyperinflation and wipe out all claims' (p. 675, n. 118). Sachs has denounced the quote as 'phony' (quoted in Henwood, 'Critique of Jeffrey D. Sachs's *The End of Poverty*', p. 201).

25 For Sachs and the reform team, the concentration of wealth through voucher privatization was not a problem. In a 1993 paper entitled 'Privatizing Russia', Andrei Shleifer and other members of Russia's reform team explain that the initial distribution of vouchers to the citizenry was designed primarily to win popular support for privatization and the broader reform process (Maxim Boyko, Andrei Shleifer, and Robert W. Vishny, 'Privatizing Russia', *Brookings Papers on Economic Activity* 1993, no. 2, p. 147). They celebrate the fact that privatization has generally benefited the management at the expense of workers' collectives (p. 169), and marvel at the extraordinarily competitive price that the market was setting for Russian assets (p. 159). They also praise voucher auctions for functioning as a depoliticized method for the construction of a capitalist class, observing that the 'creation of a liquid market for vouchers has enabled the Russian privatization to do what for political reasons it could not accomplish directly: to create core investors for many Russian companies' (p. 170). In his comments, Sachs praises 'Privatizing Russia' as 'an excellent paper' (p. 188).

26 Patrick Hamm, Lawrence King, and David Stuckler, 'Mass Privatization, State Capacity, and Economic Growth in Post-Communist Countries', *American Sociological Review* 77 (2012), p. 302.

27 Lipton and Sachs, 'Prospects for Russia's Economic Reforms', p. 214.

28 Reddaway and Glinkski, *Tragedy of Russia's Reforms*, p. 247.

29 Passell, 'Dr Jeffrey Sachs, Shock Therapist'.

30 Stanley Fischer, in Lipton and Sachs, 'Prospects for Russia's Economic Reforms', p. 278

31 Fischer in ibid., p. 278.

32 Edmund S. Phelps, in ibid., p. 274.

33 Reddaway and Glinski, *Tragedy of Russia's Reforms*, p. 297.

34 Jeffrey Sachs, quoted in Louis Uchitelle, 'Western Experts Feel Russia's

Move to Free Markets Will Continue', *New York Times*, 22 October 1992.

35   Sachs, 'Life in the Economic Emergency Room', p. 504.
36   Ibid., p. 504.
37   Ibid.
38   Ibid., p. 507 (quoting John Maynard Keynes).
39   Ibid., p. 507.
40   Ibid., p. 508.
41   Ibid.
42   Ibid., p. 509.
43   Ibid.
44   Ibid., pp. 509, 520.
45   For a detailed account of these complex events, see Chapter 7 of Reddaway and Glinski, *Tragedy of Russia's Reforms*, on which I base my own account here.
46   Sachs, in Boycko et al., 'Privatizing Russia', pp. 187–8.
47   Sachs, in ibid., p. 185.
48   Sachs, quoted in Klein, *Shock Doctrine*, p. 230.
49   Reddaway and Glinski, *Tragedy of Russia's Reforms*, p. 434.
50   Viktor Chernomyrdin, quoted in Steven Erlanger, '2 Western Economists Quit Russia Posts', *New York Times*, 22 January 1994.
51   Strobe Talbott, quoted in ibid.
52   Sachs and Aslund, quoted in ibid.
53   Chernomyrdin, quoted in ibid.
54   Sachs, *End of Poverty*, p. 143.
55   Clarke, 'Globalization and the Subsumption of the Soviet Mode of Production', p. 187.
56   Reddaway and Glinski, *Tragedy of Russia's Reforms*, p. 2.
57   Ibid., p. 2
58   Klein, *Shock Doctrine*, p. 237.
59   Reddaway and Glinski, *Tragedy of Russia's Reforms*, p. 251.
60   Humphrey, *Unmaking of Soviet Life*, p. 24.
61   Daniel Altman, 'For an Economic Proselytizer, Another Highly Visible Pulpit; Attention, Good and Bad, Follows Jeffrey Sachs', *New York Times*, 29 November 2002.
62   Klein, *Shock Doctrine*, pp. 237–8.
63   Ibid., p. 237.
64   Nancy Holstrom and Richard Smith, 'The Necessity of Gangster Capitalism: Primitive Accumulation in Russia and China', *Monthly Review* 51: 9 (2000), p. 4.

65   David Stuckler, Lawrence King, and Martin McKee, 'Mass Privatisation and the Post-Communist Mortality Crisis: A Cross-National Analysis', *Lancet*, 15 January 2009, p. 1. Unsurprisingly, the claims made in this article have been fiercely contested by defenders of the free market, including Sachs himself. See for example 'Mass Murder and the Market', *Economist*, 22 January 2009; Jeffrey D. Sachs, '"Shock Therapy" Had No Adverse Effect on Life Expectancy in Eastern Europe', letter to the *Financial Times*, 19 January 2009.

66   Stuckler et al., 'Mass Privatization and the Post-Communist Mortality Crisis', p. 6.

67   Michael Burawoy, 'The State and Economic Involution: Russia through a China Lens', *World Development* 24: 6 (June 1996), p. 1,115.

68   Slavoj Žižek, *The Ticklish Subject: The Absent Centre of Political Ontology* (London: Verso, 1999), p. 376.

69   Holstrom and Smith, 'The Necessity of Gangster Capitalism'.

70   Having been one of the most equal countries in the world prior to shock therapy, Russia is now among the most unequal (Tony Wood, 'Collapse as Crucible: The Reforging of Russian Society', *New Left Review* II/74 [2012], p. 21). By 2008, Russia had more billionaires than any other country in the world apart from the United States (Matthew Bishop and Michael Green, *Philanthrocapitalism: How the Rich Can Save the World and Why We Should Let Them* [London: A&C Black, 2008], p. 18).

71   'For Lacan, fantasy is on the side of reality – that is, it sustains the subject's "sense of reality": when the phantasmatic frame disintegrates, the subject undergoes a "loss of reality" and starts to perceive reality as an "unreal" nightmarish universe with no firm ontological foundation; this nightmarish universe is not "pure fantasy" but, on the contrary, *that which remains of reality after reality is deprived of its support in fantasy*' (Žižek, *Ticklish Subject*, p. 57 [emphasis added]).

72   Sachs, quoted in Klein, *Shock Doctrine*, p. 255.

73   Sachs, *End of Poverty*, p. 142.

74   Ibid., p. 130.

75   Sachs, 'What I Did in Russia', p. 15.

76   Sachs, quoted in Klein, *Shock Doctrine*, p. 255.

77   Sachs, quoted in Ed Pilkington, 'How to Save the World', *Guardian*, 5 April 2008.

78   Sachs, 'Commanding Heights', p. 25.

79   Sachs, 'Life in the Economic Emergency Room', p. 503.

80   Ibid., p. 516.

81 An unnamed Russian journalist, quoted in Henwood, 'A Critique of Jeffrey D. Sachs's *The End of Poverty*', p. 200.

82 Ibid. p. 201

83 Donnelly, 'Road to Redemption'.

84 Ibid.

85 Slavoj Žižek, *The Pervert's Guide to Cinema* (DVD), London: P Guide Ltd.

86 Sachs, in Snowdon, 'Global Compact', p. 41.

87 Jeffrey Sachs, 'Why Russia Has Failed to Stabilize', in Anders Aslund, ed., *Russian Economic Reforms at Risk* (London: Pinter, 1995), p. 53.

88 Ibid., p. 54

89 Sachs, *End of Poverty*, p. 141. See also Sachs, 'Why Russia Has Failed to Stabilize', p. 54.

90 See for example Hamm et al., 'Mass Privatization, State Capacity', p. 2; Murrell, 'What is Shock Therapy?', p. 122.

91 Reddaway and Glinski, *Tragedy of Russia's Reforms*, pp. 234–5.

92 As Joseph Stiglitz has observed, 'By 1997 … the country was doing much of what [the IMF] had stressed. It had liberalized, if not completely; it had stabilized, if not completely … and it had privatized' (Joseph Stiglitz, *Globalization and Its Discontents* [London: Penguin, 2003], p. 144).

93 Ibid., p. 234.

94 As Stiglitz has pointed out, 'anyone smart enough to be a winner in the privatization sweep-stakes would be smart enough to put their money in the booming US stock market, or into the safe haven of secretive off-shore bank accounts. It was not even a close call; and not surprisingly, billions poured out of the country' (ibid., p. 144). Indeed, when IMF aid did come, in its US$22.6 billion bailout of the Russian economy following the collapse of the ruble in 1998, the vast majority left the country immediately in the form of capital flight (Janine R. Wedel, 'US Assistance for Market Reforms: Foreign Aid Failures in Russia and the Former Soviet Bloc', *Policy Analysis* 338, [1999], p. 1).

95 The Twitter exchange can be seen in 'The Neoliberal Ways of the World Bank May Be Numbered if Jeffrey Sachs Becomes Its President', at alter-politics.com.

96 Sachs, *End of Poverty*, p. 137.

97 Sachs, 'Life in the Economic Emergency Room', p. 508.

98 Sachs, in Boycko et al., 'Privatizing Russia', pp. 184–5. Note the assumption that market society is a natural order, which will spontaneously flourish unless it is repressed by brute force.

99   Sachs, 'What I Did in Russia', p. 17.

100 Sachs in Boycko et al., 'Privatizing Russia', p. 186. This quote can also be contrasted to a 2005 interview, in which Sachs was asked: 'What do you say to those who took the view that it did not really matter who gets the assets so long as they end up privately owned and in the long run things will work themselves out?' He replied: 'I regard that position as sheer nonsense and could only appeal to people who do not appreciate the fact that societies are held together by ethical standards, by legitimacy, by a sense of fairness and basic political standards' (Sachs, quoted in Snowdon, 'Global Compact', p. 38).

101 Sachs also frequently congratulates himself for ending hyperinflation in Bolivia, while placing rather less emphasis on his role in forcing through subsequent neoliberal reforms (see for example his accounts in *End of Poverty*, Chapter 5 and 'What I Did in Russia', pp. 2–4). In the regard, it is interesting to compare Sachs's account to that of Gonzalo 'Goni' Sanchez de Lozada, the leader of the Bolivian reform team, whose recollection of events is the precise opposite of Sachs's own: 'Although Jeff wasn't really that influential in the initial steps that we took to stop the hyperinflation, he was vital and decisive in permitting us to be able to execute this policy over time … So he was very influential, not in stopping the hyperinflation, but in making sure that it stayed stopped' (Gonzalo Sanchez de Lozada, 'Commanding Heights', p. 12).

102 Sachs, 'Shock Therapy in Poland', p. 275 (see also Sachs, quoted in Snowdon, 'Global Compact', p. 41).

103 For an analysis of the evolution of neoliberalism in Poland, see Stuart Shields, *The International Political Economy of Transition: Neoliberal Hegemony and Eastern Central Europe's Transformation* (London: Routledge, 2012).

104 See for example Murrell, 'What is Shock Therapy?'; and Reddaway and Glinski, *Tragedy of Russia's Reforms*, p. 232. As Stiglitz has argued, 'Poland … did use shock therapy to get inflation down. And some people think, therefore, it is a shock therapy country. But that's not right. In fact … it then took a gradualist policy of restructuring their economy, restructuring their society. And the result of that was the best performance, relative to where they were in the beginning of the transition. So there were alternatives, those who chose the alternatives were more successful than those who chose shock therapy' (Stiglitz, in Commanding Heights, 'Up for Debate: Shock Therapy', p. 15).

105 King, 'Post-Communist Divergence', p. 13; Klein, *Shock Doctrine*, p. 193

106 Sachs, *End of Poverty* p. 114

107 Sachs, 'Accelerating Privatization in Eastern Europe', p. 8.

108 Two comprehensive statistical analyses of privatization in post-communist countries have argued that mass privatization was the key factor in determining the social consequences of the transition process. Both conclude that Poland's success relative to Russia is due primarily to the fact that Poland did not implement mass privatization. See Stuckler et al., 'Mass Privatisation and the Post-Communist Mortality Crisis', p. 7; and Hamm et al., 'Mass Privatization, State Capacity and Economic Growth in Post-Communist Countries', p. 31.

109 Sachs, 'What I Did in Russia', p. 18.

110 Ibid., p. 18

111 Ibid., p. 18. Emphasis added to indicate use of bold type in Sachs's original document.

112 Ibid., p. 19

113 Privatization was a key theme in other countries that Sachs advised on their post-communist transition. Concerning Slovenia, for example, Sachs co-authored a paper in 1992 emphasizing that '[e]ven with relative success in the areas of macroeconomic stabilization and trade liberalization, Slovenia [had] proceeded far too slowly in the area of privatization' (Boris Pleskovic and Jeffrey D. Sachs, 'Political Independence and Economic Reform in Slovenia', in Olivier Jean Blanchard, Kenneth A. Froot and Jeffrey D. Sachs, eds, *The Transition in Eastern Europe* [Chicago: University of Chicago Press, p. 191]). In Mongolia, which Sachs also advised on its transition, mass privatization through a voucher scheme similar to Russia's was implemented far faster and more extensively than other components of the reform package, with social consequences of a severity comparable to those in Russia. See Georges Korsun and Peter Murrell, 'Politics and Economics of Mongolia's Privatization Program', *Asian Survey* 35: 5 (1995), pp. 472–86.

114 Sachs, 'What I Did in Russia', p. 19.

115 See for example Sachs's accounts of his achievements in Bolivia and Poland in *The End of Poverty*, Chapters 5 and 6, and 'What I Did in Russia', pp. 2–7. For a discussion of the political functionality of the Emergency Social Fund in ameliorating the hardships of shock therapy and calming social unrest, see Carol Graham, 'The Politics of Protecting the Poor During Adjustment: Bolivia's Emergency Social Fund', *World Development* 20: 9 (2002), pp. 1,233–51.

116 Milton Friedman's original vision of neoliberalism itself included a role

for the state in alleviating 'acute poverty and distress' (quoted in Peck, *Constructions of Neoliberal Reason*, p. 4).

117   Sachs, 'Crossing the Valley of Tears', p. 28.

118   See for example Jeffrey Sachs, 'Managing the LDC Debt Crisis', *Brookings Papers on Economic Activity* 1986, no. 2, pp. 429–30; Jeffrey Sachs and Harry Huizinga, 'US Commercial Banks and the Developing-Country Debt Crisis', *Brookings Papers on Economic Activity* 1987, no. 2, pp. 494–5.

119   Sachs, 'Poland's Big Bang', p. 7 (emphasis added).

120   Sachs, 'Managing the LDC Debt Crisis', p. 423.

121   John Pilger, *The New Rulers of the World* (London: Verso, 2003), p. 25.

122   See ibid., Chapter 2, for a detailed account of 'shock therapy' in Indonesia. Though the blueprint for shock therapy is generally identified as Pinochet's Chile, Pilger explains that Indonesia was itself an inspiration for the CIA's approach in Chile, and the reform process there was similarly overseen by a group of economists known as the 'Berkeley Boys'. See also Klein, *Shock Doctrine*, pp. 67–70.

123   Sachs, 'Managing the LDC Debt Crisis', p. 423

124   Sachs, quoted in Passell, 'Dr Jeffrey Sachs, Shock Therapist'.

125   Sachs, 'What I Did in Russia', p. 2.

126   Sachs, 'Commanding Heights', p. 27. In the interview, Sachs also praises Keynes for his diagnosis of economic crises, and his promotion of the World Bank and the IMF, before returning to Friedman: 'I also admire tremendously Milton Friedman, who after an onslaught of statism, kept his head very, very much straight on, kept looking forward and understanding that things had swung way too far in the ... direction [of] saying that monetary factors didn't matter, or that government could solve lots of problems that it's simply not equipped to do' (ibid., p. 28).

127   Leszek Balcerowicz and Yegor Gaidar, the leaders of the reform teams in Poland and Russia respectively, were both ardent adherents of Friedman's doctrine at the time of the reforms. Balcerowicz has said that 'Hayek's ideas, and Friedman's ideas ... were right' (Leszek Balcerowicz, 'Commanding Heights', at pbs.org, p. 1), while Gaidar recalls: 'I read Friedman's books with interest, and also Hayek. They were very authoritative for us' (Yegor Gaidar, 'Commanding Heights', p. 5, at pbs.org). Sachs worked closely with both men, and has frequently expressed his great admiration for their commitment to 'reform'.

128   Peck, *Constructions of Neoliberal Reason*, p. 22. Sachs may have even

surpassed Friedman himself in his adherence to the neoliberal fantasy. Reflecting on post-communist Russia in 2002, Friedman acknowledged: 'It turns out that the rule of law is probably more basic than privatization. Privatization is meaningless if you don't have the rule of law' (quoted in Hamm et al., 'Mass Privatization, State Capacity, and Economic Growth', p. 298).

129 Sarah Kay, *Žižek: A Critical Introduction* (Cambridge: Polity, 2003), p. 62.

130 'According to psychoanalytic theory, a human subject can acquire and maintain a distance towards (symbolically mediated) reality only through the process of "primordial repression": what we experience as "reality" constitutes itself through the foreclosure of some traumatic X which remains the impossible-real kernel around which symbolisation turns … "Trauma" is the kernel of the Same which returns again and again, disrupting any symbolic identity' (Žižek, *Plague of Fantasies*, p. 120).

3 THE MAGNIFICENT MR AID

1 Jeffrey D. Sachs, 'Consolidating Capitalism', *Foreign Policy*, Spring 1995, pp. 57, 50.

2 Jeffrey Sachs, 'Beyond Bretton Woods: A New Blueprint', *Economist*, 1 October 1994, p. 29.

3 Marx and Engels, quoted in Sachs, 'Consolidating Capitalism', p. 55. The same passage is quoted in several more of Sachs's publications from this period, including Jeffrey D. Sachs and Andrew Warner, 'Economic Reform and the Process of Global Integration', *Brookings Papers on Economic Activity* 1 (1995), p. 5; Jeffrey D. Sachs, 'Twentieth-Century Political Economy: A Brief History of Global Capitalism', *Oxford Review of Economic Policy* 15: 4 (1999), p. 91; and Jeffrey Sachs, 'Notes on a New Sociology of Economic Development', in Lawrence E. Harrison and Samuel P. Huntingdon, eds, *Culture Matters: How Values Shape Human Progress* (New York: Basic Books, 2000), pp. 35–6.

4 Sachs, 'Notes on a New Sociology of Economic Development', p. 35.

5 Sachs, 'Twentieth-Century Political Economy', p. 91.

6 Sachs, 'Consolidating Capitalism', p. 100.

7 Sachs, 'Twentieth-Century Political Economy', p. 96.

8 Sachs, in Snowdon, 'Global Compact', p. 30.

9 Sachs and Warner, 'Economic Reform and the Process of Global Integration', p. 16.

10 Sachs, quoted in Snowdon, 'Global Compact', pp. 30–1.

11   Sachs and Warner, 'Economic Reform and the Process of Global Integration', p. 4.

12   Klein, *Shock Doctrine*, pp. 234–5; Henwood, 'A Critique of Jeffrey D. Sachs's *The End of Poverty*', p. 200.

13   Sachs continued in his parallel post as director of the Center for International Development, also at Harvard, until moving to Columbia University in 2002. An article in the *New York Times* suggests that Sachs's resignation from the Institute was motivated less by the Shleifer affair than by budgetary mismanagement, though the two were not entirely unrelated: 'In 1999, [Sachs] quit the institute at a time of crisis. Its budget had grown to $40 million, eclipsing spending by Harvard's schools in the fields of dentistry, design, divinity, and education. Part of that money, from the federal government, was to help Russia develop capital markets and new commercial and civil laws. But Washington cut off its support in 1997 after it claimed to have discovered that senior advisers whom Professor Sachs had supervised (and later fired) were speculating in Russian securities even as they were advising the government on economic policy. According to former colleagues, problems with Professor Sachs's management style, rather than these events, led to his departure' (Daniel Altman, 'For an Economic Proselytizer, Another Highly Visible Pulpit; Attention, Good and Bad, Follows Jeffrey Sachs', *New York Times*, 29 November 2002).

14   Marcus Taylor, 'Responding to Neoliberalism in Crisis: Discipline and Empowerment in the World Bank's New Development Agenda', *Research in Political Economy* 21 (2004), p. 26.

15   Sachs, 'Life in the Economic Emergency Room'.

16   Sachs, quoted in Klein, *Shock Doctrine*, p. 191.

17   Sachs, *End of Poverty*, pp. 74–89.

18   Jeffrey D. Sachs, 'Can Extreme Poverty Be Eliminated?', *Scientific American*, September 2005, p. 58.

19   Sachs, *End of Poverty*, p. 76.

20   In Lacanian terms, the development of clinical economics can be interpreted as a shift from repression to disavowal. In repression, the Real is excluded entirely from consciousness, though it remains in the unconscious, from which it continues to exert its destabilizing influences. In the subtler operation of disavowal, the Real is not simply repressed, but is incorporated in the form of 'symptoms' – elements of reality in which the Real appears in a transfigured and unrecognizable form. After his abandonment of Russia, Sachs had initially attempted to repress the Real of

Capital by denying its contradictions. Now he disavowed it, by representing these contradictions as pathologies of a naturally healthy system (see Wilson, 'Shock of the Real').

21 Sachs has made this argument on numerous occasions. A typical example is the following: 'Levels of per capita income, economic growth, and other economic and demographic dimensions are strongly correlated with key geographical and ecological variables, such as climate zone, disease ecology, and distance from the coast' (Jeffrey D. Sachs, 'Institutions Don't Rule: Direct Effects of Geography on Per Capita Income', *NBER Working Paper* 9490, p. 2).

22 See for example Steve Radelet and Jeffrey Sachs, 'Shipping Costs, Manufactured Exports, and Economic Growth', paper presented at the Annual Meeting of the American Economics Association, Chicago, 3–5 January 1998; Sachs, 'Globalization and Patterns of Economic Development', *Weltwirtschaftliches Archiv* 136: 4 (2000), p. 596.

23 Sachs, *End of Poverty*, p. 163. This is just one of several attempts by Sachs to explain China's success relative to Russia by appeal to factors other than the difference between gradualism and shock therapy. For a particularly elaborate example, see Jeffrey Sachs and Wing Thye Woo, 'Structural Factors in the Economic Reforms of China, Eastern Europe, and the Former Soviet Union', *Economic Policy* 9: 18 (1994), pp. 101–45.

24 David Harvey, *Cosmopolitanism and the Geographies of Freedom* (New York: Columbia University Press, 2009), p. 207.

25 Walt Rostow, *The Stages of Growth: A Non-Communist Manifesto* (Cambridge: Cambridge University Press, 1960)

26 Jeffrey Sachs, *Common Wealth: Economics for a Crowded Planet* (London: Penguin, 2008), p. 209.

27 Jeffrey Sachs, 'A Simple Plan to Save the World', *Esquire*, May 2004, p. 128.

28 Sachs, *Common Wealth*, p. 209.

29 Ibid., p. 210; Jeffrey Sachs, 'Helping the World's Poorest', *Economist*, 14 August 1999.

30 Sachs, *Common Wealth*, p. 210; Sachs, 'Globalization and Patterns of Economic Development', p. 591.

31 Sachs, *Common Wealth*, p. 211.

32 Joseph Stiglitz, quoted in Boris Pleskovic and Joseph Stiglitz, 'Introduction', in Boris Pleskovic and Joseph Stiglitz, eds, *Annual World Bank Conference on Development Economics 1998* (Washington, DC: World Bank, 1999), p. 2.

33 James Wolfensohn, quoted in ibid., p. 2.

34   Peck, *Constructions of Neoliberal Reason*, p. 73.

35   Green, *Silent Revolution*, p. 75.

36   Craig R. Janes and Oyuntsetseg Chuluundorj, 'Free Markets and Dead Mothers: the Social Ecology of Maternal Mortality in Post-Socialist Mongolia', *Medical Anthropology Quarterly* 18: 2 (2004), pp. 230–57.

37   Stuckler et al., 'Mass Privatization and the Post-Communist Mortality Crisis', p. 1.

38   Janes and Chuluundorj, 'Free Markets and Dead Mothers', p. 234.

39   Jeffrey D. Sachs, 'The Strategic Significance of Global Inequality', *Washington Quarterly*, Summer 2001, p. 193.

40   Amar A. Hamoudi and Jeffrey D. Sachs, 'Economic Consequences of Health Status: A Review of the Evidence', *CID Working Paper* no. 30 (December 1999), p. 2.

41   Ibid., p. 4. For a similar argument, see Sachs, 'Globalization and Patterns of Economic Development', p. 595.

42   Hamoudui and Sachs, 'Economic Consequences of Health Status', p. 6. Sachs makes a similar argument in an article in *Nature*: 'The economic value of resources invested in infants who do not survive can be significant. Estimates of the number of hours parents spend in child-rearing for every year of a child's life and calculations of the productive time "lost" based on infant and child mortality in high-mortality societies show this to be a substantial cost … If couples are following a child-survivor strategy, at any given time there will be many more young children in the population than are expected to survive into adulthood. This directly lowers GNP per capita (since GNP per capita is produced by adults, whereas GNP per capita is measured by the total population)' (Jeffrey Sachs and Pia Maloney, 'The Economic and Social Burden of Malaria', *Nature* 415 [2002], p. 683).

43   Amir Attaran and Jeffrey Sachs, 'Defining and Refining International Donor Support for Combating the AIDS Pandemic', *Lancet* 357 (2001), p. 57. Against Sachs, Alison Katz has argued: 'The last 20 years of globalization (1980–2000) have shown clear declines in progress as compared with the previous two decades … Progress in life expectancy, and infant and child mortality, was considerably slower during globalization – and these results cannot be explained by the AIDS pandemic' (Alison Katz, 'The Sachs Report: Investing in Health for Economic Development – or Increasing the Size of the Crumbs From the Rich Man's Table? Part I', *International Journal of Health Services* 34: 4 [2004], p. 757).

44   Sachs and Maloney, 'Economic and Social Burden of Malaria', p. 683.

45   John Luke Gallup and Jeffrey D. Sachs, 'The Economic Burden of Malaria', *American Journal of Tropical Medicine and Hygiene* 64: 1–2 (2001), p. 90.

46   Sachs and Maloney, 'Economic and Social Burden of Malaria', p. 681.

47   Ibid., pp. 684–5.

48   Commission on Macroeconomics and Health, *Macroeconomics and Health: Investing in Health for Economic Development* (Geneva: World Health Organization, 2001) pp. 6–7.

49   Ibid., p. 14.

50   Ibid., p. 15.

51   Ibid., p. 16.

52   Andreana Viachou, José Carlos Escuadero and Maria Pilar Garcia-Guadilla, 'Jeffrey Sachs on World Poverty: Three Critiques', *Capitalism Nature Socialism* 11: 2 (2000), p. 122; Katz, 'Sachs Report', p. 175.

53   Sachs, *End of Poverty*, p. 205.

54   Ibid., pp. 188, 194.

55   Ibid., p. 7.

56   Sachs, 'Consolidating Capitalism', p. 59.

57   Sachs, *End of Poverty*, p. 194.

58   Ibid., p. 188.

59   Ibid., p. 210.

60   Jeffrey Sachs, 'The Millennium Villages Project: A New Approach to Ending Poverty', talk delivered at the Center for Global Development, Washington, DC, 14 March 2006.

61   Sachs, 'Beyond Bretton Woods', p. 28.

62   Sachs, *Common Wealth*, p. 227.

63   'The norms of implementation were effective, quick and radical reform, or even "shock". There was often a sense that neoliberal reformers within African states were a vanguard: equivalents of Chile … or … Russia' (Graham Harrison, *Neoliberal Africa: The Impact of Global Social Engineering* [London: Zed, 2010], p. 100).

64   The structural adjustment era produced 'the lowest rates of economic growth ever recorded in Africa' (James Ferguson, *Global Shadows: Africa in the Neoliberal World Order* [Durham: Duke University Press, 2006], p. 11).

65   Harrison, *Neoliberal Africa*, p. 39.

66   Jeffrey Sachs, 'Growth in Africa: It Can Be Done', *Economist*, 29 June 1996.

67   Ibid.

68   Ibid.

69   David E. Bloom and Jeffrey D. Sachs, 'Geography, Demography, and

Economic Growth in Africa', *Brookings Papers on Economic Activity*, 1998, no. 2, p. 269.

70   Jeffrey Sachs, quoted in Allen R. Meyerson, 'In Principle, a Case for More "Sweatshops"', *New York Times*, 22 June 1997.

71   Sachs, *End of Poverty*, pp. 342–3.

72   For a critique of the Heavily Indebted Poor Countries Initiative, see Graham Harrison, 'HIPC and the Architecture of Governance', *Review of African Political Economy* 99 (2004), pp. 125–73.

73   Sachs, *End of Poverty*, p. 353.

74   Sachs, 'Commanding Heights', p. 1.

75   Sachs, *End of Poverty*, p. 354.

76   Sachs, *End of Poverty*, pp. 357–8.

77   Ibid., p. 358.

78   Ibid., p. 289.

79   Sachs, 'Millennium Villages Project', p. 6.

80   Sachs, quoted in Snowdon, 'Global Compact', p. 55.

81   Sachs, *End of Poverty*, pp. 208, 73.

82   Ibid., pp. 217, 70, 180, 195.

83   Jeffrey D. Sachs et al., 'Ending Africa's Poverty Trap', *Brookings Papers on Economic Activity*, 2004, no. 1, p. 139.

84   For a discussion of this process in Uganda, see Chapter 5. Harrison, *Neoliberal Africa*, p. 147.

85   For a critique of the Green Revolution, see Eric Holt-Gimenez, Miguel A. Altieri, and Peter Rosset, 'Food First Policy Brief No. 12: Ten Reasons Why the Rockefeller and the Bill and Melinda Gates Foundations' Alliance of Another Green Revolution Will Not Solve the Problems Of Poverty and Hunger in Sub-Saharan Africa', October 2006, pdf available at foodfirst.org.

86   Sachs, 'Millennium Villages Project', p. 12.

87   Sachs, *End of Poverty*, p. 368.

88   Richardson, 'Society: Jeffrey Sachs'.

89   Sachs, *End of Poverty*, p. 31.

90   Sachs, *Common Wealth*, p. 319. For a lengthy celebration of corporate social responsibility, see *Common Wealth*, pp. 319–24.

91   Sachs, *End of Poverty*, p. 289.

92   Ibid., p. 207

93   For a detailed account of the Global Fund, and Sachs's role within it, see Jon Liden, 'The Grand Decade of Global Health', Chatham House Working Group on Governance Paper 2, April 2013.

94 James Love, quoted in Donnelly, 'Road to Redemption'.

95 Jeffrey Sachs, 'Full Bio', at jeffsachs.org. In 2011, in Africa alone, Sachs was serving as an advisor to the governments of Ethiopia, Ghana, Kenya, Malawi, Mali, Nigeria, Rwanda, Senegal, Tanzania, and Uganda.

96 Nina Munk, 'Jeffrey Sachs's $200 Billion Dream', *Vanity Fair*, July 2007.

97 Jeffrey Sachs, 'Simple Plan'.

98 Sachs, *End of Poverty*, p. 368.

99 Sachs, 'Millennium Villages Project', p. 9.

100 Faith McLellan, 'Jeffrey Sachs', *Lancet* 362: 9,384 (2003), p. 672.

101 Jeffrey Sachs, 'Weapons of Mass Salvation', *Economist*, 26 October 2002, p. 101. Sachs's complex relationship with the United States is explored in greater detail in Chapter 6.

102 Altman, 'For an Economic Proselytizer, Another Highly Visible Pulpit'.

103 Ron Rosenbaum, 'International Man of Misery', *Upstart Business Journal*, 22 April 2009.

104 Washington National Cathedral, 'The Prophet of Economic Possibilities for the Poor'. In the lecture, Sachs referred to the millennium and the jubilee, and claimed that the 'great religious traditions have been behind every great movement for human dignity and justice'.

105 Michael Clemens, quoted in Laura Burke, 'Villages as Laboratories in Debate on Africa Aid', *Huffington Post*, 16 September 2012.

106 See for example Gerry Mooney and Lynn Hancock, 'Poverty Porn and the Broken Society', *Variant* 34/40 (2010), pp. 14–17.

107 Sachs, *End of Poverty*, pp. 8–9.

108 Žižek, *Plague of Fantasies*, p. 24.

109 Sachs, 'Millennium Villages Project'.

110 Jeffrey Sachs, keynote address at 'The Commission on Macroeconomics and Health – Ten Years On', an international conference held at Chatham House, London, on 9 December 2011.

111 Sachs, *Common Wealth*, pp. 327

112 Jeffrey Sachs, 'The Forbes One Billion', *Forbes*, 10 August 2007.

113 Sachs, *Common Wealth*, pp. 327–8.

114 Sachs, 'Simple Plan', p. 146.

115 Sachs, 'Forbes One Billion'.

116 Joe Nocera, 'Can a Vision Save All of Africa?' *New York Times*, 16 June 2007.

117 For a discussion of the ideological operation of philanthropy in the legitimation of contemporary capitalism, see Japhy Wilson, 'The *Jouissance* of Philanthrocapitalism: Enjoyment as a Post-Political Factor', in Japhy

Wilson and Erik Swyngedouw, eds, *The Post-Political and Its Discontents: Spaces of Depoliticization, Spectres of Radical Politics* (Edinburgh: Edinburgh University Press, 2014).

118 Daphne Eviatar, 'Spend $150 Billion Per Year to Cure World Poverty', *New York Times Magazine*, 7 November 2004.

119 Ibid.

120 Within the symbolic universe of Jeffrey Sachs, we can say that Africa has come to function as what Žižek would call a 'sublime object of ideology'. A sublime object is a common material object that acquires a peculiar fascination for the subject due not to some inherent essence, but to its symbolic location as an object that both obscures and embodies the traumatic Real. (Wilson, 'The Shock of the Real'.)

121 The Millennium Project, *Investing in Development: A Practical Plan to Achieve the Millennium Development Goals* (New York: United Nations, 2005).

122 Sachs, *End of Poverty*, p. 299.

123 Graham Harrison, 'The Africanization of Poverty: A Retrospective on "Make Poverty History"', *African Affairs* 109: 436 (2010), pp. 391–408.

124 Sachs, *Common Wealth*, p. 331. The anti-globalization (better described as alter-globalization) movement continued, of course. Indeed, an anti-G8 protest was held at the gates of the resort in Gleneagles where the G8 summit was taking place. Media attention, however, was focused on the spectacles of Live 8 and the Make Poverty History march.

125 Jeffrey Sachs, 'How Africa Lit Up the World', *Sunday Times*, 3 July 2005.

126 Ibid.

4 DEVELOPMENT DREAMLAND

1 Jeffrey Sachs, 'The Facts Behind G8 Aid Promises', *Guardian*, 4 July 2013.

2 The countries participating in the MVP are Ethiopia, Ghana, Kenya, Malawi, Mali, Nigeria, Rwanda, Senegal, Tanzania, and Uganda. Kenya, Malawi, Mali, and Nigeria each had two clusters of Millennium Villages in the first phase of the Project, while the others each had one.

3 The Millennium Villages Project, *The Next Five Years: 2011–2015* (New York: Earth Institute, 2011).

4 Millennium Project, *Investing in Development*, p. 50; see also Japhy Wilson, 'Model Villages in the Neoliberal Era: The Millennium Development Goals and the Colonization of Everyday Life', *Journal of Peasant Studies* 40 (2014).

5   Lidia Cabral, John Farrington and Eva Ludi, 'The Millennium Villages Project – A New Approach to Ending Rural Poverty in Africa?' *Natural Resource Perspectives* 101 (2006), p. 2.

6   Pedro Sanchez, Glenn Denning and Generose Nziguheba, 'The African Green Revolution Moves Forward', *Food Security* 1 (2009), p. 2.

7   Sachs, *End of Poverty*, p. 244.

8   The Millennium Villages Project, *Annual Report: January 1–December 31* (New York: Earth Institute, 2008), pp. 4–6; Overseas Development Institute, *Sustaining and Scaling the Millennium Villages: Moving from Rural Investments to National Development Plans to Reach the MDGs* (London: Overseas Development Institute, 2008), p. 6.

9   Millennium Villages Project, *Next Five Years*.

10 Sanchez, Denning and Nziguheba, 'The African Green Revolution Moves Forward', p. 4.

11 Edmund Sanders, 'Planting a Seed of Self-Sufficiency', *Los Angeles Times*, 05 July 2005.

12 William Easterly, quoted in ibid.

13 Millennium Project, *Investing in Development*, p. 15 (emphasis added).

14 For a critique of Smith's theory of 'original accumulation', see Michael Perelman, *The Invention of Capitalism: Classical Political Economy and the Secret History of Primitive Accumulation* (Durham, NC: Duke University Press, 2000), pp. 171–228.

15 Karl Marx, *A Contribution to the Critique of Political Economy* (London: Lawrence & Wishart, 1970), p. 59.

16 Karl Marx, *Capital, Volume I* (New York: Vintage, 1977), pp. 873–940. According to Žižek, social fantasies tend to be structured around a 'fantasy of origins' of this kind – a fictionalized account of the past that infuses reality with a sense of harmony and order that conceals the traumatic Real. Indeed, Žižek identifies Adam Smith's mythical prehistory of capitalism as the quintessential fantasy of origins (Žižek, *Plague of Fantasies*, p. 11).

17 Sachs also reproduces Smith's narrative in *The End of Poverty*, pp. 51–4.

18 Sachs, 'The Millennium Villages Project', p. 16.

19 Sachs, *End of Poverty*, p. 242.

20 Sachs, 'The Millennium Villages Project', p. 10.

21 Sachs, *End of Poverty*, p. 56.

22 Ibid., p. 232.

23 Mayange visitors' brochure, quoted in Magatte Wade, 'Jeffrey Sachs' Misguided Foreign Aid Efforts', *Huffington Post*, 19 June 2009.

24 Ibid.

25 Ibid.

26 The Millennium Villages Project, *Harvests of Development in Rural Africa: The Millennium Villages After Three Years* (New York: Earth Institute, 2009), p. 7.

27 'Our Partners', at millenniumvillages.org. Full list of partners available from this site as a pdf.

28 Jeffrey Sachs, in World Economic Forum, 'Meeting the Millennium Development Goals', Davos, Switzerland, 29 January 2010, at weforum. org (emphasis added).

29 Celia W. Dugger, 'Philanthropist Gives $50 Million to Help Aid the Poor in Africa', *New York Times*, 13 September 2006; George Soros, 'Scaling Up the Millennium Villages Project', 4 October 2011, at sorosblog.com. Of this second tranche of funding, US$20 million was to be distributed through Soros's Economic Development Fund, and was contingent on local entrepreneurs producing 'investment worthy' business projects.

30 Christian De Cock and Stefan Bohm, 'Liberalist Fantasies: Žižek and the Impossibility of the Open Society', *Organization* 14: 6 (2007), pp. 815–36.

31 Ella Alexander, 'Humble Hilfiger', *Vogue* online, 23 June 2010.

32 Ibid.; Jessica Marati, 'Behind the Label: Tommy Hilfiger's Promise Collection', *Ecosalon*, 20 June 2012, at ecosalon.com.

33 Tommy Hilfiger, cited in Rosanna Greensteet, 'Tommy Hilfiger: I Live in the Plaza in New York and I Love It – All That History, All Those Stories', *Guardian*, 3 December 2011.

34 The Promise Collection, at uk.tommy.com. The collection received widespread media coverage, particularly in the international fashion press.

35 Lisa Ann Richey and Stefano Ponte, *Brand Aid: Shopping Well to Save the World* (Minneapolis, MN: University of Minnesota Press, 2011), p. xiv.

36 Tommy Hilfiger was accused of making racist remarks against blacks and Asians in 1996. He has always denied the accusations, and they remain unsubstantiated, but Hilfiger continues to be seen as a racist by large sections of his potential consumer base (Ruth Manuel-Logan, 'Conspiracy Theories 101: Designer Tommy Hilfiger is a Racist?' *News One*, 14 August 2012, at newsone.com).

37 Jessica Marati, 'Behind the Label: Tommy Hilfiger's Promise Collection'. According to Marati, Tommy Hilfiger is valued at US$4.6 billion, while 'the hourly wage for workers producing Tommy Hilfiger garments ranges from 23 cents to $1.75'.

38 Brian Ross, Matthew Mosk, and Cindy Galli, 'Workers Die at Factories Used by Tommy Hilfiger', 21 March 2012 at abcnews.go.com. The fire occurred in 2010. An investigation found that the deaths were due to hazardous electric wiring, lack of safety equipment, and the fact that the factory gates were locked. When challenged at the event in February 2012, Hilfiger assured ABC News that Philips-Van Hausen, Tommy Hilfiger's parent company, no longer operated in Bangladesh. But shipping records showed that Tommy Hilfiger products continued to ship from two factories in Bangladesh in which deadly incidents had been recorded previously.

39 Sachs, *End of Poverty*, pp. 11–12.

40 Belinda Luscombe, 'Madonna Finds a Cause', *Time*, 6 August 2008; Bishop and Green, *Philanthrocapitalism*, p. 207.

41 The documentary can be seen online at youtube.com.

42 Bernd E. T. Mueller, 'The Agrarian Question in Tanzania: Using New Evidence to Reconcile an Old Debate', *Review of African Political Economy* 38: 127 (2011), pp. 23–42; Carlos Oya, 'Rural Labour Markets in Africa: The Unreported Source of Inequality and Poverty', *Development Viewpoint* 57 (November 2010).

43 Cabral, Farrington and Ludi, 'The Millennium Villages Project,' p. 3; Michael Clemens and Gabriel Demombynes, 'When Does Rigorous Impact Evaluation Make a Difference? The Case of the Millennium Villages', *World Bank Policy Research Working Paper No. 5477* (2010); E. R. Carr, 'The Millennium Village Project and African Development: Problems and Potentials', *Progress in Development Studies* 8: 4 (2008), pp. 333–44.

44 Chris Giles, 'Lunch with the FT: Jeffrey Sachs', *Financial Times*, 6 April 2007.

45 See for example Jeffrey Sachs, 'Tropical Underdevelopment', *NBER Working Paper 8119*, February 2001, p. 23.

46 Chris Giles, 'Lunch with the FT: Jeffrey Sachs'.

47 Rural development practitioner, author interview, 24 November 2011.

5 THE VILLAGE THAT SACHS BUILT

1 Earth Institute, *Infrastructure from the Bottom Up* (New York: Earth Institute, 2009), p. 94.

2 Jeffrey Sachs, quoted in Shai A. Divon and Cassandra E. Bergstrom, 'Unintended consequences of development interventions: a case of diarrhoeal diseases, Ruhiira, Uganda', *Development in Practice* 42: 1 (2012), p. 88, n. 5

3   Millennium Villages Project, *Harvests of Development*, p. 69; Madeleine Bunting, 'Havens of Hope: The Ugandan Villages on Target to Meet the Millennium Development Goals', *Guardian*, 27 May 2009.

4   Munk, 'Jeffrey Sachs's $200 Billion Dream'. See also, for example, Shakilah Bint Sheikh, 'High Level Korean Delegation Witnesses Achievements in Ruhiira', at millenniumvillages.org.

5   Bunting, 'Havens of Hope'.

6   Aili Mari Tripp, *Museveni's Uganda: Paradoxes of Power in a Hybrid Regime* (London: Lynne Rienner, 2010), pp. 183, 186. For a discussion of the neoliberal reform trajectory in Uganda see Sam Hickey, 'The Politics of Staying Poor: Exploring the Political Space for Poverty Reduction in Uganda', *World Development* 33: 6 (June 2005), pp. 995–1,009. In 2012, several donor governments suspended aid to Uganda in response to the increasingly rampant corruption in the country. Sachs has remained silent on the issue (see Liz Ford, 'Uganda Vows to "Defeat These Thieves" in Bid to Reassure Aid Donors', *Guardian*, 20 November 2012).

7   For Museveni's nomination of Sachs for the presidency of the World Bank, see 'Yoweri Museveni, President of Uganda', 22 March 2012, at jeffsachs.org.

8   Badru D. Mulumba, 'Uganda: Museveni, Sachs on Tour to Boost Textile Producers', *Monitor*, 5 March 2003; Munk, 'Jeffrey Sachs's $200 Billion Dream'.

9   'Earth Institute Launches Partnership with Ugandan Stakeholders; President Museveni Welcomes Delegation', at earth.columbia.edu.

10   Sam Hickey, 'Beyond the Poverty Agenda? Insights from the New Politics of Development in Uganda', *World Development* 43 (2013), pp. 194–206.

11   Transparency International, cited in Angelo Inzama, 'Uganda: Oil, Corruption and Entitlement', *Guardian*, 1 October 2012.

12   Tripp, *Museveni's Uganda*, pp. 159–71.

13   UN Security Council Panel of Experts on the Democratic Republic of Congo, *Final Report of the Panel of Experts on the Illegal Exploitation of Natural Resources and Other Forms of Wealth of the Democratic Republic of Congo* (New York: United Nations, 2002). See also Tripp, *Museveni's Uganda*, pp. 172–8.

14   Human Rights Watch, *States of Pain: Torture in Uganda*, March 2004, p. 4.

15   Jeffrey Sachs, 'Doing the Sums in Africa', *Economist*, 20 May 2004.

16   The Millennium Villages Project, 'Ruhiira MVP: Progress to Date', Presentation at Millennium Promise Partners Meeting, 21 September 2009.

17 Earth Institute, *Infrastructure from the Bottom Up*, p. 94.

18 Ibid., p. 94; Millennium Villages Project, 'Ruhiira MVP: Progress to Date', at millenniumvillages.org.

19 Marian Tankink, 'Not Talking about Traumatic Experiences: Harmful or Healing? Coping with War Memories in Southwest Uganda', *Intervention* 2: 1 (2004), pp. 3–17.

20 Ssemujju Ibrahim Nganda, 'Corruption Endemic in Uganda', *Guardian*, 13 March 2009.

21 Anirudh Krishna et al., 'Escaping Poverty and Becoming Poor in 36 villages of Central and Western Uganda', *Journal of Development Studies* 42: 2 (2006), pp. 346–70.

22 Jeffrey Sachs, in the 'Health' video clip on the Tommy Hilfiger Promise Collection website, at eu.tommy.com.

23 Shai A. Divon, 'Externalities Produced by Interplay Between Development Interventions: Impact on Health in the Millennium Villages Project, Ruhiira, Uganda', Master's thesis, Norwegian University of Life Sciences, 2009, p. ix.

24 Ibid., pp. 58, 109, 85.

25 'Millennium Villages Data Use Consent Statement', included in ibid., p. 235.

26 'Millennium Villages Project Confidentiality Statement', included in ibid., p. 236.

27 United Nations Press Release, 'United Nations Secretary General Announces New Sustainable Development Initiative', 9 August 2012, at un.org.

28 Editorial, 'With Transparency Comes Trust', *Nature*, 10 May 2012.

29 Jeffrey Sachs, quoted in Bunting, 'Havens of Hope'.

30 The MVP did not respond to my request for budgetary information, and the lack of transparency in the Project means that financial information is very difficult to access. But if it is investing the US$110 per person that it claims to be spending annually (with the other US$10 provided by 'the community'), then this would amount to an annual expenditure in Ruhiira of US$5.5 million. The Project had been running for just over seven years by the time I arrived there, which would add up to a total expenditure of US$38.5 million.

31 Millennium Promise, 'Ruhiira, Uganda', at mp.convio.net.

32 See for example Bronwen Konecky and Cheryl Palm, eds, *Millennium Villages Handbook: A Practitioner's Guide to the Millennium Villages Approach* (New York: Earth Institute, 2008): see especially Chapter 2,

'Community-Based Approach to Achieving the Millennium Development Goals'.

33   Jeffrey Sachs in the 'Food' video on the Promise Collection website, at eu.tommy.com.

34   Ruhiira household interview #35. Ruhiira, Uganda, 17 February 2013. (Household interviews were predominantly conducted in Runyankole, with interpretation provided by my research assistant. Interviews with implementers were conducted in English.)

35   Ruhiira household interview #19, Kabuyanda, Uganda, 11 February 2013.

36   Ruhiira household interview #16, Kanyawameizi, Uganda, 10 February 2013.

37   Ruhiira household interview #29, Ntungu, Uganda, 16 February 2013.

38   Konecky and Palm, eds, *Millennium Villages Handbook*, p. 35.

39   Jiehua Chen, Macartan Humphreys and Vijay Modi, 'Technology Diffusion and Social Networks: Evidence from a Field Experiment in Uganda', Earth Institute, 2010, at columbia.edu.

40   Earth Institute, *Infrastructure From The Bottom Up*, pp. 95–7, 103.

41   Ruhiira household interview #27, Ntungu, Uganda, 16 February 2013.

42   Ruhiira household interview #9, Kabugu, Uganda, 09 February 2013.

43   Ruhiira household interview # 34, Ruhiira, Uganda, 17 February 2013.

44   Sachs, 'The Millennium Villages Project', pp. 13, 18.

45   Agricultural Extension Worker, Millennium Villages Project, Ruhiira. Interview: Kabuyanda, Uganda, 16 February 2013.

46   Ruhiira household interview #15, Kanyawameizi, Uganda, 10 February 2013 (the daughter spoke English).

47   Konecky and Palm, eds, *Millennium Villages Handbook*. See in particular Chapter 4, 'Agriculture', which includes extraordinarily unrealistic predictions of the Project's success.

48   Clinical Officer for Isingiro District local government, working in Ruhiira. Interview, Mbarara, Uganda, 19 February 2013.

49   'Ruhiira Millennium Villages Project at the brink of collapse', anonymous unpublished document, 2013, p. 1.

50   Telephone interview with one of the authors of 'Ruhiira Millennium Villages Project at the brink of collapse', 11 September 2013.

51   Member of the administrative staff of the Millennium Villages Project 2006–2013. Telephone interview 19 September 2013.

52   'Ruhiira Millennium Villages Project at the brink of collapse', pp. 4, 14; Member of the administrative staff of the Millennium Villages Project 2009–2011. Telephone interview, 18 September 2013.

53 'Millennium Promise Global Board of Directors', available at http://mp.thinkfa.com/millenniumpromise/bod.

54 Associate Counsel of Millennium Promise, 'Re: Complaint regarding Ruhiira MVP' emails sent to an ex-administrator of the Ruhiira MVP, on the 9th, 10th and 12th of September, 2013.

55 Second telephone interview with one of the authors of 'Ruhiira Millennium Villages Project at the brink of collapse', 19 September 2013.

56 Senior Clinical Officer, working in Ruhiira MVP area from September 2012–February 2013, author interview, Mbarara, Uganda, 19 February 2013; Government health officer working in Ruhiira MVP area, author interview, Kabuyanda, Uganda, 13 March 2013.

57 Jeffrey Sachs, in the 'Business and Entrepreneurship' video clip on the Tommy Hilfiger Promise Collection website at eu.tommy.com.

58 Health inspector working for one of the local councils in Ruhiira, author interview, Mbarara, Uganda, 9 March 2013.

59 Senior Clinical Officer, working in Ruhiira MVP area from September 2012-February 2013, author interview, Mbarara, Uganda, 19 February 2013.

60 Millennium Villages Project medical sector worker, author interview, Kabuyanda, Uganda, 12 February 2013.

61 This farmer features repeatedly, for example, in the 'Postcards from Ruhiira' on the Tommy Hilfiger Corporate Foundation website (http://108.166.76.198/2012/06/), and in the press pack for the Promise Collection.

62 Millennium Villages Project health worker – written statement personally delivered to the author in Kabuyanda, Uganda, 11 March 2013.

63 Millennium Villages Project medical sector worker, author interview, Kabuyanda, Uganda, 12 February 2013.

64 Francis L. Shavers, chief of staff and special assistant to the president of the University of Notre Dame, 'Ruhiira Village Visit', at president.nd.edu.

65 Linda Powers, 'Lots of People Visit Ruhiira', at lindapowers.blogspot.co.uk.

66 The video can be seen online at youtube.com.

67 Ssemujju Ibrahim Nganda, 'Corruption Endemic in Uganda', *Guardian*, 13 March 2009.

68 Member of the 'Millennium Band', author interview, Ruhhiira, Uganda, 10 March 2013.

69 Naomi Handa-Williams, 'WFP Director Hails the "Revolution of Hope" in Ruhiira', at millenniumvillages.org.

70 Jeffrey Sachs, keynote address, 'The Commission on Macroeconomics and Health – Ten Years On'.

71 Jeffrey Sachs, in Washington National Cathedral, 'The Prophet of Economic Possibilities for the Poor'.

72 Ben Jones has argued that the Ugandan state is 'extraverted', and that 'project villages' (like Ruhiira) are part of the strategy through which the state sustains revenue streams from Western donors. These aid flows absolve it of the need to expand tax revenues or seek political legitimacy through the development of the countryside. Ben Jones, *Beyond the State in Rural Uganda* (Edinburgh: Edinburgh University Press, 2009).

73 Sachs, 'Millennium Villages Project', pp. 2–4. The slightly garbled delivery of this passage is as it appears in the lecture transcript.

74 Millennium Villages Project, 'Ugandan Government Launches Scale-Up of Millennium Villages Project', press release, 1 July 2013, at millennium-villages.org.

75 Millennium Villages Project, 'Islamic Development Bank and Earth Institute Partner to Meet Millennium Development Goals in Rural Africa', press release, 13 August 2013, at millenniumvillages.org.

76 Millennium Promise, 'Millennium Village Programs Now in More Than 20 Countries', at millenniumvillages.org.

6 THE WORLD FALLS APART

1 The Real is 'the traumatic point which is always missed but none the less always returns, although we try – through a set of different strategies – to neutralize it, to integrate it into the symbolic order' (Žižek, *Sublime Object of Ideology*, p. 69). It is 'the unfathomable X which, although nowhere present, curves/distorts any space of symbolic representation and condemns it to ultimate failure' (Žižek, *Plague of Fantasies*, p. 124).

2 Jeffrey D. Sachs, 'Facing Nature's Fury', *Project Syndicate*, 24 October 2005, at project-syndicate.org.

3 Sachs, *Common Wealth*, p. 43.

4 Jeffrey D. Sachs, 'Need Versus Greed', Aljazeera.net, 4 March 2011.

5 See for example Sachs, *Common Wealth*, pp. 235, 256, 258.

6 Ibid., p. 32.

7 Jeffrey Sachs, 'The New Geopolitics', *Scientific American*, 22 May 2006, p. 33.

8 Sachs, *Common Wealth*, p. 105.

9 Ibid., p. 4.

10 Ibid., p. 149.

11 Ibid., p. 38.

12 Ibid., pp. 131–3.

13   Ibid., p. 148.

14   Ibid., p. 35.

15   Ibid., p. 134.

16   Jonathan H. Adler, 'Free Market Environmentalism', Cato Institute, 2002, at cato.org.

17   *Economist*, 'Carbon Trading: ETS RIP?', 20 April 2013. See also Clive L. Spash, 'The Brave New World of Carbon Trading', *New Political Economy* 15: 2 (2010), pp. 169–95.

18   See for example Paige West, Jim Igoe and Dan Brockington, 'Parks and Peoples: The Social Impact of Protected Areas', *Annual Review of Anthropology* 51 (2006), pp. 251–77.

19   See for example Bonnie J. McKay, 'ITQs and Community: An Essay on Environmental Governance', *Agricultural and Resource Economics Review* 33: 2 (2004), pp. 162–70.

20   Jeffrey Sachs, 'The New Geopolitics', *Scientific American*, 22 May 2006, p. 33.

21   Sachs, *Common Wealth*, p. 102.

22   Ibid., p. 134.

23   Ibid., p. 132.

24   Jeffrey D. Sachs, 'The Promise of the Blue Revolution', *Scientific American* online, 17 June 2007, at scientificamerican.com.

25   Klaus S. Lackner and Jeffrey D. Sachs, 'A Robust Strategy for Sustainable Energy', *Brookings Papers on Economic Activity* 2 (2005), p. 216.

26   Sachs, *Common Wealth*, pp. 100–1.

27   Ibid., p. 100.

28   Ibid., pp. 101–2.

29   Victor Wallis, 'Beyond Green Capitalism', *Monthly Review* 61: 9 (2009), p. 35.

30   Sachs, *Common Wealth*, p. 309.

31   Kevin Anderson and Alice Bows, 'Beyond "Dangerous" Climate Change: Emission Scenarios for a New World', *Philosophical Transactions of the Royal Society* 369 (2011), p. 23.

32   Sachs, *Common Wealth*, p. 118.

33   See for example Jeffrey D. Sachs, 'The Specter of Malthus Returns', *Scientific American*, September 2008, p. 38; *Common Wealth*, pp. 159–202.

34   Sachs, quoted in Amy Barrett, 'The Way We Live Now: Questions for Jeffrey Sachs: Poor Man's Economist', *New York Times*, 15 December 2002.

35   Sachs, *Common Wealth*, p. 185.

36   Ibid., p. 30

37   Marx, *Capital, Volume I*, p. 666, n. 8.

38   Earth Institute, 'Facing the Global Challenge', at earth.columbia.edu; Earth Institute, 'Research: The Foundation of the Earth Institute', at earth.columbia.edu; Richardson, 'Society: Jeffrey Sachs'.

39   Earth Institute, 'Corporate Circle', at earth.columbia.edu.

40   Earth Institute, 'The Earth Institute Corporate Circle', at earth.columbia.edu.

41   Earth Institute, 'The Earth Institute Corporate Circle'; Earth Institute, 'Corporate Circle'.

42   Earth Institute, 'Companies Lay Out Global Framework to Fight Climate Change', press release, 20 February 2007, at earth.columbia.edu; Political Economy Research Institute, 'Greenhouse 100 Polluters Index 2013', at peri.umass.edu.

43   Corporatewatch, 'Corporate Crimes: DuPont', at corporatewatch.org.

44   Earth Institute, 'Companies Lay Out Global Framework to Fight Climate Change'.

45   Thilo Kunzemann, 'Why Some Companies Are Demanding CO2 Reduction', at conocimiento.allianz.com.ar.

46   See in particular Sachs, *Common Wealth*, pp. 319–24.

47   Ibid., p. 52.

48   Wallis, 'Beyond Green Capitalism', p. 2.

49   Ibid., p. 313.

50   Jeffrey Sachs, *The Price of Civilization: Economics and Ethics After the Fall* (London: Bodley Head, 2011), p. 182.

51   Jeffrey Sachs, cited in Giles, 'Lunch with the FT: Jeffrey Sachs'.

52   The one exception to this was the adoring reception that Sachs received in his third lecture, which was held at Columbia University, where Sachs himself is based (Jeffrey Sachs, 'Lecture Three: The Great Convergence', at bbc.co.uk). The other lectures were held in London, Beijing and Edinburgh.

53   Bernard Crick, in Jeffrey Sachs, 'Lecture Five: Global Politics in a Complex Age', at bbc.co.uk.

54   John Holding, professor of philosophy, University of St Andrews, in ibid.

55   Ibid.

56   Ibid.

57   Sachs, 'A Simple Plan', pp. 146–7.

58   Jeffrey D. Sachs, 'Rethinking Macroeconomics', *Capitalism and Society* 4: 3 (2009), p. 1.

59   Jeffrey Sachs, 'A New Map of the World', *Economist*, 24 June 2000, p. 83.

60   Ibid., p. 251.

61   Sachs, *Price of Civilization*, p. 253.

62   Ibid., pp. 253–4.

63   Ibid., pp. 36, 27.

64   See for example ibid., p. xiv; Sachs at Occupy Wall Street, 15 October 2012.

65   Sachs, *Price of Civilization*, p. 64.

66   In the mid 1990s, Sachs attacked 'the debilitating sense of universal enti-
      tlement that helped to bankrupt the old regimes and that still pervades
      the new ones' (Jeffrey Sachs, 'Postcommunist Parties and the Politics of
      Entitlements', *Transition: The Newsletter about Reforming Economies* 6: 3
      [1995], p. 4). He also criticized the 'over-extensive social welfare system' of
      the Soviet Union (Sachs and Woo 'Structural Factors', p. 108). By contrast,
      the Sachs-inspired economic policies of the Yeltsin administration have
      been described as repudiating the state's 'responsibility to promote, or
      at any rate sustain, the welfare of society and to guarantee a subsistence
      income for its disadvantaged members' (Reddaway and Glinski, *Tragedy
      of Russia's Reforms*, p. 630).

67   Sachs, *Price of Civilization*, p. 98.

68   Ibid., pp. 98, 20.

69   Sachs, 'Wages, Profits, and Macroeconomic Adjustment', p. 271 (emphasis
      added).

70   Ibid., p. 312. See also Sachs, 'Changing Cyclical Behavior of Wages
      and Prices', pp. 87–8; Sachs, 'Wages, Flexible Exchange Rates, and
      Macroeconomic Policy', pp. 731–47; Jeffrey Sachs, 'Stabilization Policies
      in the World Economy: Scope and Scepticism', *NBER Working Paper* 862
      (February 1982), pp. 6–7.

71   Jeffrey Sachs, 'Death by Strangling: The Demise of State Spending',
      Financial Times, 16 December 2011.

72   Jeffrey Sachs and Charles Wyplosz, 'The Economic Consequences of
      President Mitterrand', *Economic Policy* 1: 2 (1986), p. 269.

73   Ibid., p. 266 (emphasis added).

74   Ibid., p. 301.

75   Ibid., p. 296.

76   Sachs, 'Stabilization Policies in the World Economy', pp. 9–10

77   Organisation for Economic Cooperation and Development, cited in
      Andrew Higgins, 'Riots Rattle a Normally Placid Sweden', *International
      Herald Tribune*, 27 May 2013.

78   Sachs, *Common Wealth*, p. 265. Sachs repeats this claim on more than

one occasion. See for example *Common Wealth*, pp. 5, 265; 'Reith Lecture 4: Economic Solidarity for a Crowded Planet', London, 2 May 2007, at bbc.co.uk. This belief also informs his calls for the restriction of 'illegal' immigration into the United States (Sachs, *Price of Civilization*, pp. 52, 70–2).

79 See Magnus Ryner, 'Neoliberal Globalization and the Crisis of Swedish Social Democracy', *Economic and Industrial Democracy* 20 (1999), pp. 39–70; Christoffer Green-Pedersen, Kees Van Kersbergen and Anton Hemerijck, 'Neoliberalism, the "Third Way", or What? Recent Social Democratic Welfare Policies in Denmark and the Netherlands', *Journal of European Public Policy* 8: 2 (2001), pp. 307–25.

80 Chantal Mouffe, *On the Political* (London: Routledge, 2005), pp. 44–63; Alan Zuege, 'The Chimera of the Third Way', in Leo Panitch and Colin Leys, eds, *Socialist Register 2000: Necessary and Unnecessary Utopias* (London: Merlin, 2000), pp. 87–114.

81 Sachs, *Price of Civilization*, p. 248.

82 Sachs, 'Rethinking Macroeconomics', p. 5.

83 Sachs, *Price of Civilization*, pp. 32–4.

84 Ibid., p. 95.

85 Jeffrey D. Sachs, 'How to Tame the Budget Deficit', *Time*, 4 February 2010.

86 Sachs, 'Rethinking Macroeconomics', p. 4.

87 Sachs, *Price of Civilization*, p. 38.

88 Ibid., p. 92.

89 Ibid., p. 44.

90 Indeed, as Sachs himself acknowledges, government spending under Reagan did not actually decrease at all. Sachs, *Price of Civilization*, p. 56.

91 Matthew d'Ancona, 'Spending Review: George Osborne's Review is a Bible for the New Generation of Tories', *Daily Telegraph*, 23 October 2010.

92 Jeffrey Sachs, 'Plan B: Agree Financial Transaction Tax', *New Statesman*, 18 October 2011.

93 Matthew d' Ancona, 'George Osborne Has Set Out the Doctrine of a New Realism', *London Evening Standard*, 30 November 2011.

94 George Osborne and Jeffrey Sachs, 'A Frugal Policy is the Better Solution', *Financial Times*, 14 March 2010. A few days later, the *Financial Times* published a response from three prominent economists, accusing Osborne and Sachs of raising unfounded fears of a UK government default, and correctly predicting that Osborne's austerity agenda would lead to falling aggregate demand and rising unemployment (Robert Skidelsky, Marcus

Miller, and Danny Blanchflower, 'Osborne and Sachs are Just Trying to Spook Us', *Financial Times*, 17 March 2010).

95 Jeffrey Sachs, 'Nigeria Hurtles Into a Tense Crossroads', *New York Times*, 10 January 2012.

96 Michael Busch, 'Jeffrey Sachs's Metamorphosis from Neoliberal Shock Trooper to Bleeding Heart Hits a Snag', at fpif.org.

97 Ibid. In response to pressure from Busch and others, Sachs was eventually forced to retract his comments, though he failed to publish this retraction in the *New York Times*.

98 Jeffrey Sachs, 'Time to Plan for Post-Keynesian Era', *Financial Times*, 7 June 2010. See also Jeffrey Sachs, 'How to Have Growth Beyond Stimulus', *Financial Times*, 7 June 2012; and 'Today's Challenges Go Beyond Keynes', *Financial Times*, 17 December 2012.

99 Sachs, *Price of Civilization*, pp. 34, 43, 102, 273.

100 Cornel West, quoted in Jodi Dean, James Martel, and David Panagia, 'Introduction', *Theory and Event* 14: 4 (2011), supplement on Occupy Wall Street, at muse.jhu.edu.

101 Jeffrey Sachs, 'Self-Interest, Without Morals, Leads to Capitalism's Self-Destruction', *Financial Times*, 18 January 2012. Note that Sachs is criticizing 'unacceptable' inequality, as opposed to inequality as such.

102 'Jeffrey Sachs at Occupy Wall Street', 15 October 2011. It is also worth noting at this point that Sachs's philanthropic foundation, Millenium Promise, is incorporated under the laws of the US State of Delaware, which is effectively an 'onshore' tax haven. Sachs therefore also seems to know 'where to hide his money'.

103 'Occupy Wall Street and the State of America', *Fareed Zakaria GPS*, CNN, 31 October 2012, at youtube.com.

104 Ibid.

105 See Howard Zinn, *A People's History of the United States* (New York: Harper Perennial Modern Classics, 2005) pp. 349–54. Sachs emphasizes the role of the Progressive movement and the New Deal in stabilizing capitalist class relations, arguing that Theodore Roosevelt and Franklin Roosevelt were 'really smart, really rich, and really tough … they knew the class they came from and they knew its limits … They said "We're rich, we're powerful, and we're siding with the common people." That's a huge plus' (Sachs in Carnegie Council, 'Ethics Matter').

106 Sachs, *Price of Civilization*, p. 263.

107 Sachs, 'Self-Interest, Without Morals'.

108 Ibid.

109 Sachs, *Price of Civilization*, p. 150. The 'abstinence' theory that Sachs is propounding here is another form of the bourgeois fantasy of origins discussed in Chapter 3, according to which capital is amassed through frugality and thrift, rather than dispossession and exploitation. See Ernest Mandel, 'Introduction' in Marx, *Capital, Volume I*, pp. 61–2.

110 Sachs, *Price of Civilization*, p. 151.

111 Ibid., pp. 151–2.

112 Ibid., p. 231.

113 'Jeffrey Sachs at Occupy Wall Street', 7 October 2012, at youtube.com.

114 There is YouTube footage of Jeffrey Sachs speaking on two separate occasions, on 7 October 2011 and again on 15 October 2011.

115 'Jeffrey Sachs (Columbia University Professor) supports Occupy Wall Street', 7 October 2012, at youtube.com. Sachs's argument here, and in *The Price of Civilization* (pp. 105–31), rests on the neoliberal fantasy of a strict division between economics and politics, according to which 'power' lies exclusively in the political realm of the state, which must be defended from capture by 'special interests' (Razeen Sally, 'Ordoliberalism and the Social Market: Classical Political Economy from Germany', *New Political Economy* 1: 2 ([1996], p. 247).

116 'Jeffrey Sachs at Occupy Wall Street', 7 October 2012.

117 Ibid.

118 'Jeffrey Sachs at Occupy Wall Street', 15 October 2012. As Žižek warned in his own appearance at Occupy, 'Beware not only of enemies, but also of false friends who pretend to support us, but who are working hard to dilute our protest' (Slavoj Žižek, 'Actual Politics', *Theory and Event* 14: 4 [2011], at muse.jhu.edu).

119 The Comments on the YouTube footage of Sachs's speech on 7 October include numerous calls for Sachs to run for US president in the 2012 election. In his speech, Sachs had seemingly encouraged such suggestions, calling for the formation of a 'government of the 99 per cent', setting out a clear policy platform, and concluding coyly with: 'Anything I can do, I'm going to be with you' ('Jeffrey Sachs at Occupy Wall Street', 7 October 2012).

120 'What the Hell Was Economic Hit Man Jeffrey Sachs Doing at Occupy Wall Street?', October 2011, at internationalist.org.

121 Jeffrey Sachs, keynote address, 'Commission on Macroeconomics and Health: Ten Years On', Chatham House, London, 9 December 2011.

122 Taylor, 'Responding to Neoliberalism in Crisis', p. 4.

123 Heather Stewart, 'Celebrity Economist Jeffrey Sachs Bids to Head World Bank', *Observer*, 4 February 2012.

124 Jeffrey Sachs, 'How I Would Lead the World Bank', *Washington Post*, 2 March 2012.

125 Ibid.

126 The thirteen countries were Uganda, Costa Rica, Honduras, Ghana, Chile, Guatemala, Haiti, Bhutan, Namibia, Kenya, Timor-Leste, Jordan, and Malaysia (Bolivia, Poland, and Russia were notable by their absence). Twenty-seven Democratic congressmen signed an open letter to Obama in support of Sachs, and several economists, including Mark Weisbrot and Sachs's protégé Nouriel Roubini, also added their names to the list (Jeffsachs.org, 'Letters of Nomination and Support', at jeffsachs.org).

127 Sarawak Report, 'Top US Economist Jeffrey Sachs Was "Cultivated" and "Influenced" to Become a "Champion" of Sime Darby – Exclusive!', 12 November 2011, at sarawakreport.org.

128 Ibid.

129 Jeffrey Sachs, 'Ecosystems Don't Follow the Rules of Private Property', *International Herald Tribune*, 16 June 2008.

130 Ian Burrell, 'Firm in BBC News-Fixing Row Targeted Poverty Guru', *Independent*, 17 November 2011.

131 Sarawak Report, 'Top US Economist Jeffrey Sachs Was "Cultivated" and "Influenced"'.

132 Damian Carrington, 'Jeffrey Sachs Stung by the Corrosive Mix of Palm Oil and Publicity', *Guardian*, 17 November 2011; Burrell, 'Firm in BBC News-Fixing Row'.

133 Jeffrey Sachs, quoted in Ben Smith, '"Greenwashing" campaign sought Sachs', *Politico*, 14 November 2011.

134 Burrell, 'Firm in BBC News-Fixing Row'; Carrington, 'Jeffrey Sachs Stung'.

135 Kenneth Richter of Friends of the Earth, quoted in Carrington, 'Jeffrey Sachs Stung'.

136 Lincoln Chen, in the *Lancet*, supplementary web appendix to Pamela Das and Udani Samarasekera, 'The Commission on Macroeconomics and Health: 10 Years On', *Lancet* 378 (2011), pp. 1,907–8.

137 Ibid.

138 Dean T. Jamison et al., 'The WHO's Commission on Macroeconomics and Health: Taking Stock after 10 Years', draft document prepared for the event 'Commission on Macroeconomics and Health: Ten Years On', Chatham House, London, 9 December 2011, pp. 12–13.

139 Howard Waitzkin, *Lancet*, supplementary web appendix.

140 Howard Stein, *Lancet*, supplementary web appendix.

141 Sachs, 'Commission on Macroeconomics and Health: Ten Years On'.

142 For an extensive list of these claims, see Millennium Villages Project, *Harvests of Development in Rural Africa*.

143 Michael Clemens and Gabrial Demombynes, 'When Does Rigorous Impact Evaluation Make a Difference? The Case of the Millennium Villages', *World Bank Policy Research Working Paper No. 5477*, 1 November 2010.

144 Retraction Watch, 'Millennium Villages Project Forced to Correct *Lancet* Paper on Foreign Aid as Leader Leaves Team', at retractionwatch. wordpress.com; 'Former Millennium Villages Project Staffer Responds to Critical Nature Editorial', at retractionwatch.wordpress.com.

145 Jeffrey Sachs, quoted in Retraction Watch, 'Millennium Villages Project Forced to Correct *Lancet* Paper'.

146 Michael Clemens, email correspondence, 13 July 2012.

147 Edward Miguel, quoted in Paul Starobin, 'Does It Take a Village?', *Foreign Policy*, 1 July 2013.

148 Jeffrey Sachs, quoted in ibid.

149 Paul Pronyk, 'Errors in a Paper on the Millennium Villages Project', *Lancet* 379 (2012), p. 1,946.

150 Edward Miguel, quoted in Starobin, 'Does It Take a Village?'.

151 Stewart, 'Celebrity Economist Jeffrey Sachs Bids to Head World Bank'.

152 For a broad selection of these views, see the *OpinionNation* discussion, 'Should Jeffrey Sachs Be the Next World Bank President?', 14 March 2012, at thenation.com.

153 Robin Broad and John Cavanagh, 'Why We Are Not Supporting Jeffrey Sachs to be World Bank President', Institute for Policy Studies, 16 March 2012, at ips-dc.org.

154 David Korten, in 'Should Jeffrey Sachs Be the Next World Bank President?'

155 Broad and Cavanagh, 'Why We Are Not Supporting Jeffrey Sachs to Be World Bank President'.

156 Korten, in 'Should Jeffrey Sachs Be the Next World Bank President?'

157 Jeffrey Sachs, quoted in Stewart, 'Celebrity Economist Jeffrey Sachs Bids to Head World Bank'.

158 These quotes are all drawn from a mere thirty-minute period on Sachs's Twitter feed, between 6:59 and 7:24 on 21 March 2012.

159 Sachs, 'What I Did in Russia'. See Chapter 2 for a detailed discussion of this document.

160 Jeffrey Sachs, 'Breakthrough Leadership for the World Bank', *Project Syndicate*, 27 March 2012, at project-syndicate.org.

161 Jeffrey Sachs, 'Introduction', in John Helliwell, Richard Layard, and Jeffrey Sachs, *World Happiness Report* (New York: Earth Institute, 2012), p. 6.

162 Jeffrey D. Sachs, 'Growth in a Buddhist Economy', *Project Syndicate*, 25 August 2010.

163 Sachs, *Price of Civilization*, p. 9.

164 Ibid., pp. 137, 142.

165 Ibid., p. 134.

166 Jeffrey Sachs, quoted in Jo Confino, 'Rio + 20: Jeffrey Sachs on How Business Destroyed Democracy and Virtuous Life', *Guardian*, 22 June 2012.

167 Sachs, *Price of Civilization*, p. 144.

168 Sachs, 'Growth in a Buddhist Economy'.

169 Jeffrey D. Sachs, 'The Economics of Happiness', *Project Syndicate*, 29 August 2011.

170 Jeffrey Sachs, quoted in Confino, 'Rio + 20'.

171 Sachs, 'How to Have Growth Beyond Stimulus'.

172 Sachs, 'Introduction', in Helliwell et al., *World Happiness Report*, p. 4.

173 Sachs, *Price of Civilization*, p. 136.

174 Ibid., p. 168. Sachs's newfound anti-consumerism also clashes with his celebrations of consumerism during his shock therapy era – see for example Sachs, 'The Politics of Entitlements', p. 1; 'Life in the Economic Emergency Room', p. 509.

175 Jeffrey Sachs, quoted in Confino, 'Rio+20'.

176 Sachs, *Price of Civilization*, p. 163.

177 Ibid., p. 162.

178 John Helliwell, Richard Layard and Jeffrey Sachs, 'Some Policy Implications', in Helliwell et al., *World Happiness Report*, p. 91.

179 Ibid., p. 92.

180 Ibid.

181 At the conference Sachs held a workshop, in which 'Richard Davidson, a neuroscientist … explained how happiness is a skill that can be learned; public policy expert Robert Putnam showed us the vital importance of social connections; economist Joseph Stiglitz highlighted the flaws with GDP; Buddhist monk Matthieu Ricard explained the reciprocal benefits of altruism; and Marin Seligman, founder of positive psychology, reminded us that there's much more to a flourishing life than just the

absence of misery' (Mark Williamson, 'The Serious Business of Creating a Happier World', *Guardian*, 11 April 2012).

182 Ibid.

183 Bob Frame, 'Bhutan: A Review of Its Approach to Sustainable Development', *Development in Practice* 15: 2 (2005), pp. 216–21.

184 Sachs, 'Growth in a Buddhist Economy'.

185 Neoliberalization in Bhutan has been accompanied by increasing ethnic tensions, reflecting growing class inequalities. During the 1980s, the Lhotshampa – a Bhutanese minority of Nepali origin – began to be stigmatized by the Bhutanese government as 'illegal immigrants', while modernization was officially pursued in the name of the majority Drukpa culture. As a specialist on Bhutan has explained, 'This led to anti-government demonstrations in 1990, and to a process described by the government as "voluntary migration" … As a result, almost 100,000 ethnic Nepali people from southern Bhutan are living in seven refuges camps administered by the UNHCR in eastern Nepal' (Frame, 'Bhutan', p. 217).

186 Sachs, *Price of Civilization*, p. 273.

187 Patrick M. Boarman, 'Wilhelm Ropke: Apostle of a Humane Economy', *Society*, September–October 2000, pp. 57–65; Sally, 'Ordoliberalism and the Social Market', pp. 245–6.

188 Sally, 'Ordoliberalism and the Social Market', p. 244.

189 Wilhelm Ropke, *A Humane Economy: The Social Framework of the Free Market* (London: Oswald Wolff, 1960), pp. 97–103.

190 Sachs, *Price of Civilization*, p. 273.

191 Ropke, *Humane Economy*, pp. 110–11.

192 Slavoj Žižek, *Welcome to the Desert of the Real* (London: Verso, 2002), p. 133.

193 Žižek, *Ticklish Subject*, pp. 160, 218–19.

194 Žižek, *Plague of Fantasies*, p. 123; Žižek, *Sublime Object of Ideology*, p. 177.

CONCLUSION: THE NEOLIBERAL NEUROSIS

1 Munk, 'Jeffrey Sachs's $200 Billion Dream'.

2 Sonia Elrich Sachs, quoted in Donnelly, 'The Road to Redemption'.

3 Ibid.

4 Rosenbaum, 'International Man of Misery'.

5 Interview provided on condition of anonymity, 2011.

6 Amy Wilentz, 'Jeffrey Sachs's Grand Experiment', *Conde Naste Traveler*, September 2008.

7   Jeffrey Sachs, quoted in ibid.

8   Sachs, *Shock Therapy in Poland*, p. 270; Sachs, 'Commanding Heights', p. 19. See Chapter 1 for the quotes from which these phrases are taken.

9   Žižek, *Sublime Object of Ideology*, pp. 190–3.

10 Vladimir Lenin, *Imperialism, the Highest Stage of Capitalism* (Peking: Foreign Languages Press, 1975), p. 115.

11 Perelman, *Invention of Capitalism*, p. 208.

12 Karl Polanyi, *Origins of Our Time: The Great Transformation* (New York: Farrer & Rinehart, 1944), p. 39.

13 Peck, *Constructions of Neoliberal Reason*, pp. 50, 66.

14 Žižek, *Sublime Object of Ideology*, p. 192.

15 Paul Cammack, 'What the World Bank Means by Poverty Reduction and Why it Matters', *New Political Economy* 9: 2 (2004), pp. 189–211.

16 Japhy Wilson, 'Colonising Space: The New Economic Geography in Theory and Practice', *New Political Economy* 16: 3 (2011), pp. 373–97.

17 Michael D. Yates, 'Occupy Wall Street and the Celebrity Economists', *Monthly Review*, 23 October 2011.

18 Darian Leader, *What Is Madness?* (London: Penguin, 2011), p. 39.

19 This is the predicament noted by Marx and Engels in *The Communist Manifesto*: 'Modern bourgeois society, with its relations of production, of exchange, and of property, a society that has conjured up such gigantic means of production and of exchange, is like the sorcerer who is no longer able to control the powers of the nether world whom he has called up by his spells' (Karl Marx and Friedrich Engels, *The Communist Manifesto* [London: Penguin, 2002], p. 225).

20 Sachs, 'Life in the Economic Emergency Room', p. 508.

21 David Lipton and Jeffrey Sachs, 'Creating a Market Economy in Eastern Europe: The Case of Poland', *Brookings Papers on Economic Activity* 1 (1990), p. 100.

22 R. M. Schneiderman, 'Did Privatization Increase the Russian Death Rate?', *New York Times*, 15 January 2009.

23 Ibid (comment by Arsen Azizyan).

24 Jeffrey Sachs, 'Why I'm the Right Candidate for World Bank President', in 'Should Jeffrey Sachs Be the Next World Bank President?', (emphasis added).

25 Kohl, 'Challenges to Neoliberal Hegemony in Bolivia'. Goni is currently living in exile in the United States. In 2012 the US government refused an extradition request from the Bolivian government for Goni to face charges of crimes against humanity (Glenn Greenwald, 'America's Refusal

to Extradite Bolivia's Ex-President to Face Genocide Charges', *Guardian*, 9 February 2012).

26 Jeffrey Sachs, 'What Bolivia's Chaos Means', *Project Syndicate*, 29 October 2003.

27 Ibid.

28 Ibid.

29 Jeffrey Sachs, 'Call It Our Bolivian Policy of Not-So-Benign-Neglect', *Washington Post*, 26 October 2003.

30 Ibid.

31 Sachs, 'Poland's Big Bang After One Year', pp. 3–4.

32 Sachs, *Price of Civilization*, p. 235.

33 Sachs, *End of Poverty*, pp. 360–4.

34 Sachs, 'The Millennium Villages Project' (see Chapter 3).

35 Doug Henwood, 'Introduction to Jeffrey Sachs', at lbo-news.com.

36 Sachs, *Common Wealth*, p. 255. See also p. 257.

37 Ibid., p. 301

38 Japhy Wilson, 'Notes on the Rural City: Henri Lefebvre and the Transformation of Everyday Life in Chiapas, Mexico', *Environment and Planning D: Society and Space* 29 (2011), pp. 993–1,009.

39 Sachs, *Common Wealth*, p. 339. See also Sachs, *Price of Civilization*, p. 261.

40 Jeffrey D. Sachs, *To Move the World: JFK's Quest for Peace* (London: Bodley Head, 2013), p. 47.

41 Ibid., p. 168.

42 Ibid., p. 78.

43 Sachs, *To Move the World*, p. 153 (quoting John Maynard Keynes and John F. Kennedy).

44 See for example Sachs, *End of Poverty*, pp. 141, 217, 280, 331, 341–2.

45 Sachs, *To Move the World*, pp. 163, 160.

46 Sachs, *Common Wealth*, p. 45.

47 Ibid., p. 51.

48 Sachs, *Price of Civilization*, p. 183.

49 Quoted in Francis Wheen, *Karl Marx* (London: Fourth Estate, 1999), p. 209. Unlike Sachs, Marx concluded with: 'History is the judge – its executioner, the proletarian.'

50 Jeffrey D. Sachs, 'The Class System of Catastrophe', *Time*, 10 January 2005.

51 Jeffrey Sachs, 'A Manifesto for the Fund's New Supremo', *Financial Times*, 31 May 2011.

52   Sachs, 'Economics of Happiness'.
53   Sachs, 'Need Versus Greed'.
54   Sachs, 'Economics of Happiness'.
55   Sachs, 'Self-Interest, Without Morals'.